D1756356

Robert Baden-Powell

Robert Baden-Powell

A Biography

Lorraine Gibson

PEN & SWORD HISTORY

First published in Great Britain in 2022 by
Pen & Sword History
An imprint of
Pen & Sword Books Ltd
Yorkshire – Philadelphia

ISBN 978 1 39900 930 0

A CIP catalogue record for this book is
available from the British Library.

Typeset by Mac Style
Printed and bound in the UK by CPI Group (UK) Ltd,
Croydon, CR0 4YY.

Pen & Sword Books Limited incorporates the imprints of Atlas,
Archaeology, Aviation, Discovery, Family History, Fiction, History,
Maritime, Military, Military Classics, Politics, Select, Transport,
True Crime, Air World, Frontline Publishing, Leo Cooper, Remember
When, Seaforth Publishing, The Praetorian Press, Wharncliffe
Local History, Wharncliffe Transport, Wharncliffe True Crime
and White Owl.

For a complete list of Pen & Sword titles please contact

PEN & SWORD BOOKS LIMITED
47 Church Street, Barnsley, South Yorkshire, S70 2AS, England
E-mail: enquiries@pen-and-sword.co.uk
Website: www.pen-and-sword.co.uk

Or

PEN AND SWORD BOOKS
1950 Lawrence Rd, Havertown, PA 19083, USA
E-mail: Uspen-and-sword@casematepublishers.com
Website: www.penandswordbooks.com

To Steve, Molly and Tilly, you always DYB

Contents

Acknowledgements

Baden-Powell's famous motto 'Do a good turn' runs through the Scouts' DNA today for a good reason – it continues to resonate. I wrote this book through two UK lockdowns, a time of severely restricted movement and communication, so the following people, Scouts or otherwise, went out of their way to do me a good turn.

Chris Albury, auctioneer, for your expert advice and opinion on the surprise appearance of the controversial 'Bloater' telegraph.

David Annand for sculpting the remarkable Baden-Powell statue on Poole Quay that played such a pivotal part in inspiring my book and for letting me in on the secret of its improbable topple-ability.

Karyn Burnham, my editor, for your wisdom, tact and invaluable advice.

Gillian Clay and Robin Clay, for your generosity in sharing insights and stories about your grandfather and your mother, the inimitable Betty. And Adam Baden-Clay and your wife, Nicole, for your kindness, your time and for doing your bit to 'leave the planet a better place than you found it', just as your great-grandfather counselled.

Kate Bohdanowicsz for leading me to Pen & Sword Books.

Dr Phil Cox, senior lecturer in anatomy, for your advice on Brownsea's red squirrel colony.

Bear Grylls, the ultimate Chief Scout, for supporting my story and for your inspirational work with Scouts all over the world.

Katie Heaton at Poole History Centre for sharing your great historical knowledge of the town and its Baden-Powell connections.

Sylvia and Harold (one of the UK's longest-serving Scouts) next door, for lending me your lovely books.

Chris James at Scouts for your help and support, especially with Bear; Caroline Pantling for the wonderful photographs and resources and everyone else I encountered virtually at Scouts HQ.

Tim Jeal, biographer of the superb *Baden-Powell*, for being gracious and generous, for putting me right on Mafeking and for being a peerless source of balance on B-P's life.

Dr Ann Limb, for making history as the first woman to be appointed Chair of the Scouts in 114 years, for your shining example and for the insight into Scouting today.

John Mackenzie for enhancing my battle knowledge through your incredibly helpful website and brilliant maps http://bb.com/

Sue Martin, for your endless encouragement, proofreading of split-infinitive-riddled chapters and for the laughs in between.

Janet Mellors for being so giving of your immense Scouting knowledge, for opening up St Mary's Church for me and for my treasured Brownsea Island badge.

Debbie Moore for helping to transport me not just physically to Brownsea Island, but back in time for a fascinating insight into life in the time of the Van Raalte family and, indeed, your own.

Ed Perkins for alerting me to the report on the Ribbentrop meeting and for 'the Old Woggler', the gift of all B-P nicknames and one of which he would surely have approved.

Jeremy and Hattie Miles for putting me in touch with a rather elusive former Chief Scout.

Clare Rowton of Rose Hill Prep School, B-P's old school, for the fascinating book and Catherine Smith, archivist at Charterhouse School for allowing me access to all sorts of wonders, including B-P's less-than-glowing school reports.

Jack Saunders, Bournemouth Scout leader and District Administrator, for a peek into a life of modern-day Scouting in the town where many of the original 1907 Brownsea Boys came from.

Disclaimer

Some quotes or references in this book are from quotes and texts that were written or spoken in the past.

Consequently, they may use some terms or expressions which were current at the time, regardless of what we may think of them in the twenty-first century.

For reasons of historical accuracy they have been preserved in their original form.

Foreword

In 1907, a new movement was born on Brownsea Island, in Poole Harbour, Dorset – one that would bring skills, adventure and friendships to millions of young people around the world.

It was on that small island that Robert Baden-Powell founded the Scouts, taking a small group of young people from diverse backgrounds, with the goal to learn about the great outdoors, and show that we had more in common than that which divides us.

Since that first camp, Scouting has grown year on year to become today a worldwide family, some 54-million strong, across almost every nation on earth. It is, without doubt, one of the greatest youth movements in history.

The clear purpose back then (and still today) was to unite and inspire young people to learn how to celebrate their differences, to love and protect the outdoor world, to serve communities, and to be empowered with skills for life. And that is the legacy of the Scouts that lives and breathes today.

It is in our nature, as Scouts, to endeavour to be open, respectful, and compassionate to all, and to be leaders of determination and integrity.

That's why those first Scouts, and the ones that followed, made a promise to be kind and helpful. It is the very heart of what we do.

To me, and many Scouts around the world, Brownsea Island is a reminder of that great Scouting vision. It has since helped so many young people gain vital, life-enhancing skills for their own futures.

I truly am so grateful to Baden-Powell for starting the Scouts – a living, breathing, modern movement that has immense power to unite and inspire people. Scouting, to me, is founded on listening to and respecting others, especially communities that are vulnerable or oppressed. Inclusion and acceptance are at the heart of our Scouting values, and we are never afraid to call out language and behaviour that do not match those values.

Baden-Powell may have taken the first step in creating Scouting, but the journey continues today without him. We know where we came from, but we are not going back. We are always looking forward, to a brighter future for our young people.

Bear Grylls OBE
Chief Scout

Chapter 1

The Battle of the Statue

'I have had the rather unique experience of having in my time lived a double life. I don't mean exactly what you would refer from this!'

Robert Baden-Powell
Lessons From the Varsity of Life (1933)

In extraordinary scenes at Poole Quay in June 2020, a group of devotees of the late Lord Robert Baden-Powell, 1st Baron of Gilwell and founder of the Boy Scouts, formed a human shield around his statue to prevent it from being toppled by an angry mob threatening to throw it into the harbour.

From out of nowhere, a gathering of uniformed Scouts of all ages, along with sundry supporters of Baden-Powell, arrived and found themselves embroiled in a heated confrontation with the crowd of activists who were claiming that Baden-Powell was anything but the nice chap that most people perceived him to be.

As fists were shaken or clenched aloft, depending on where loyalties lay, news crews arrived and circled around the commotion like greedy seagulls. Baffled onlookers, a mix of Poole residents and visiting holidaymakers, juggled bags of chips and takeaway coffee cups while attempting to film the melee on their mobile phones.

Not since the 1700s, when local men desperate for work brawled with one another for places on fishing fleets bound for Newfoundland waters to catch cod (which at the time was worth its weight in gold), had such unruly scenes been witnessed on the harbour's edge.

But why on earth were Scouts, famously advocates of peace, preparing for a fight?

And what exactly had the famous old woggler and founder of the Boy Scouts done to enrage the protestors so?

The answers to both of these apparently simple questions are complicated, and in a significant way inspired and formed the foundation of this book. Explaining the situation in a nutshell is impossible therefore, here's a simple outline for now:

The activists' main gripe was that the statue, a life-sized bronze of a seated Baden-Powell in full scouting regalia, was offensive because it was honouring someone they believed to be guilty of all sorts of politically unsound ideals and actions. These included fascism, racism, anti-Semitism, sadism and homophobia so, consequently, they felt that paying homage to him with this ostentatious effigy represented an intentional 'whitewashing' of history, ergo the truth; the statue should, therefore, be 'removed'. Permanently.

As far as the Scouts, backed up by some extremely riled townsfolk (many of whom had contributed towards the statue's £35,000 price tag) were concerned, the antagonists were trouble-making for trouble-making's sake, exaggerating events of the past and degrading their glorious founder. This, in turn, strengthened their resolve to protect the work – which they swore they'd do at all costs.

Reporters homed in as, on one side, the Baden-Powell loyalists expressed – to anyone with a microphone – their undying admiration for the man, as well as their indignation at the protestors' threat to toss him in the drink. To show they meant business, they positioned themselves around the statue and declared they would be prepared to wait for as long as it took to defend not just the statue, but the honour of its subject.

On a positive note, certainly from the Scouts' point of view, the crisis also represented a golden opportunity for them to publicly emulate their idol and do their best, to stand firm and to staunchly uphold what they regarded as important British values.

Contrarily, B-P's vociferous critics, a mostly – but not exclusively – younger crowd, were equally motivated, although by a sense of injustice and anger at what they insisted was the glossing-over of the misdemeanours of a man who had much to be maligned for.

It reached stalemate, with both groups utterly convinced they were in the right and both believing that they were acting for the greater good. Nevertheless, they had one thing in common; they were all too busy fighting their corners to realise that the entire scenario was a perfect metaphor for the deeply conflicted character of the very person over whom they were so passionately arguing.

The stark conflict of their ideals and viewpoints were the very essence of Baden-Powell himself, for if ever there were one word that perfectly sums up the Chief Scout of the World, it is 'contradictory'.

Robert Baden-Powell was arguably the most famous and influential Englishman of the twentieth century, but for two very different reasons: Mafeking and Scouts.

In May 1900, the dawn of a new century, he was worshipped, both at home and internationally, as a triumphant war hero. A magnificent military strategist who had, against all odds, ended the long-running South African Siege of Mafeking where, despite being greatly outnumbered by Boer fighters, he had defended the town and preserved valuable land-tracts, rich with mineral reserves, for his beloved Empire and his sovereign, Queen Victoria.

Hailed a fearless warrior, he was welcomed home from his victory by huge crowds who blocked the streets of London and declared him the Hero of Mafeking.

By 1907, he'd laid down his gun and changed uniforms, by forming the Boy Scouts; a movement for peace and wellbeing, designed to help boys of all backgrounds become friends, stalwarts and adventurers; equally importantly, it would allow him to release his inner-child.

For, throughout his army career, all he had really wanted was to be a boy again. Had he discovered the elixir of eternal youth, he wouldn't have needed to invent the Boy Scouts at all.

Today, Baden-Powell is still held in the highest esteem by millions of people around the world, hardly surprising as the number of Scouts (at the time of writing) currently stands at 54 million and counting. Many members are utterly devoted to him and his legacy.

Although not read out at every meeting any more, Scout Law is followed almost to the nth degree, and followers speak wistfully of their charming, chirpy, go-getting late boss, whose entire raison d'être was to encourage global harmony and create a world of happy, healthy and fulfilled children.

To many others, however, Baden-Powell was a deeply-flawed and, at times, sadistic individual. A predictable by-product of his privileged, often unstable, upper middle-class Victorian upbringing, he's also regarded an imperialist, an entitled snob, a social-climber, a fantasist and egotist. The list goes on, with accusations that he was opportunistic, controlling, self-aggrandising and a phony.

His approbation of aspects of the Nazi party's ideology (he once described *Mein Kampf* as a 'wonderful book') and revelations of allegations of a war crime associated with the contentious execution of Matabeleland's Chief Uwini in 1896, only served to deepen the criticism that led to the dramatic flashpoint at Poole Quay.

Poole Scouts expert and local historian Janet Mellors, who lives near Brownsea Island, home of the first ever Scouts' camp, has a deep knowledge of the movement and of Baden-Powell himself. She comes from an old-school Scouting dynasty and as the guide to all things Scouting and Guiding on Brownsea, she and her family have met many of Baden-Powell's family and descendants. Janet meets thousands of young, contemporary Scouts from all over the world, so she has insight into feelings across the spectrum:

> Local people and many in Scouting and Guiding today think the whole business of B-P being a friend with Hitler and racially prejudiced is not true. I think someone read the book about him written by Jim Jeal [*Baden-Powell* 1989] and got on the bandwagon.
>
> We need to remember how society has changed since B-P was born in 1857 and as local people said on TV, think of all the good he did.

While she agrees that some remarks and phrases concerning race which would be considered offensive in today's society were used by Baden-Powell in personal letters and memoirs, she also points out that it was the norm so long ago. She doesn't aim to justify them, nor make their use acceptable, just cites them as factual reasons.

To his die-hard fans, B-P, as they fondly call him, is akin to a superstar, a broker of peace, who to this day is the person responsible for giving many young people a sense of purpose, confidence, and a raft of practical skills that help ease them through life.

To others, he was an oddball, a 'man boy' (a description he coined for himself), overly fond of killing (both humans and animals) and a little too fixated on the boys he entranced; a Pied Piper in shorts and a Stetson.

So, not only did the statue debacle highlight gaping differences in public opinion, it also served as a revealing snapshot of the mood of the nation at a time when it was careering blindly through the worst crisis it had experienced since the Second World War – for the younger generation, the worst crisis *ever*.

For at precisely the moment Robert Baden-Powell's reputation was hanging in the balance in this bizarre sculpture-based tug-of-war, the United Kingdom, along with the rest of the planet, was in the vice-like grip of the first wave of the COVID-19 pandemic. Virtually unheard of at the close of 2019, the deadly virus stole into the country early in 2020, took root, like a grotesque weed, and proceeded to wreak havoc; from the spring onwards, thousands of people became physically and mentally-ill, devastated and isolated. Thousands more died – at an alarming rate with no foreseeable cure or vaccine.

Thousands were infected worldwide and, in a bid to slow down the infection rate, in March the UK entered its first lockdown. Movements and activities were severely curtailed throughout the summer and people were afraid, confused, and feeling desperate about the increasing death count.

These feelings were exacerbated by confusing reports and ever-changing advice, and while people understood the need for isolating and restriction of movement, they were also sick and tired of sanctions and restrictions being imposed on their day-to-day lives.

Adults were mainly working from home, furloughed from their jobs or made redundant. Children stayed away from school and parents became teachers and the NHS was constantly overwhelmed. Weddings, proms and celebrations were cancelled; holidays were banned and sport was kicked into touch. To the majority, it felt as though life itself had been cancelled.

Added to this, although the British weather was unusually hot, beaches and beauty spots were out of bounds. Even so, some people – including some senior government officials – were seen to be flagrantly breaking the rules, and there developed a perfect storm of high emotions and short tempers.

Embers of this suppressed anger were then fanned by a shocking event in the USA on 25 May which was filmed live by witnesses on their mobile phones and subsequently broadcast around the globe. The world was left reeling at footage of the killing of a 46-year-old man named George Floyd in a Minneapolis street, by a police officer who pinned his knee on the victim's neck and kept it there for nearly nine minutes.

Mr Floyd, an unarmed black American, had been apprehended on suspicion of a minor misdemeanour, attempting to pass a counterfeit $20 banknote in a shop. The highly incendiary incident in which Mr Floyd could be heard gasping: 'I can't breathe,' triggered riots in pockets of the United States. In response, President Donald Trump appeared to offer little or no condemnation of the act and Mr Floyd's sympathisers began describing his death as a murder, a public execution and a lynching.

The outrageous injustice based purely on a victim's skin colour was the catalyst for the release of much pent-up rage and resentment. On-going racial tensions, and myriad COVID-19-related problems that saw the US suffering the highest death rates in the world, were the last straw.

The knock-on effect was a build-up of resolve in black and other ethnic-minority communities and the political movement Black Lives Matter (BLM), moved to highlight the plight of marginalised and persecuted groups by staging demonstrations designed to get the message across that they were no longer prepared to accept oppression and police brutality.

People were rising up against those accused of systemic racism and inequality in all its various guises. They were being called to arms, but rather than a loaded gun, their weapon was direct action.

Many sportsmen, dignitaries and celebrities demonstrated their solidarity by publicly 'taking the knee', a kneeling gesture that shows support for subjugated parties, and when social media platforms embraced the message, it became a global phenomenon.

More drastic than taking the knee, however, was the symbolic and visually emotive gesture of defacing – or even tearing down – statues and monuments erected in honour of historic figures who may have been magnanimous and philanthropic, but also had provable dark episodes during their lives, meaning their main legacies were not those of munificence, but of greed, self-interest and injustice. From the perspective of BLM and their supporters, these figures had been complicit in slave transportation and trading, along with other associated, racially-motivated wrongdoings. It seemed that, regardless of status and whatever benevolences these sanctified and feted individuals may or (depending on one's opinion) may not have bequeathed upon the public, none of them were too important to be placed under the microscope of intense scrutiny, where it generally transpired that for every good deed taken into consideration – a school built here, a town hall gifted there – there was an equal, if not greater, number of controversial acts. Humanitarian skeletons in the shape of slavery, infringements of human rights and callous profiteering, rattled in firmly-closed closets.

It worked. People sat up and took notice.

This toppling of figureheads as a form of protest is nothing new, it's been going on since time began. Take the famous statue of the Pharaoh Hatshepsut, whose face was chipped to a pulp in order to prevent anyone having to suffer the awful memory of having a female for a king. Then there's the ancient Romans. They just chopped the heads off the statues of defeated emperors and carried them off in triumph.

The practice remains the go-to visual method of dissent, disgust and occasionally, delight, as was seen in the joyful dismantling of Saddam Hussein's towering likeness in Firdos Square in April 2003, as it symbolised both the end of his power and the end of the Battle of Baghdad.

And so, for those historical characters found wanting in the long, hot summer of 2020, the statue-toppling began again in earnest. There is even a dedicated website bluntly named 'Topple the Racists', which features maps marked with the UK locations of many of the offending effigies, including – you guessed it – Baden-Powell's.

Before you could say: 'Be prepared', the spotlight fell, not just on obvious memorials to the likes of the prominent seventeenth-century Bristolian slave trader, Edward Colston, whose generosity to Bristol was funded by the fortune he amassed from the enslavement and human misery of thousands of Africans, but on the previously-unremarkable, bush-hatted sculpture of the internationally adored, Sir Robert Baden-Powell, who, even now, many people still only know as 'that bloke who started the Boy Scouts'.

The loyal B-Pers, outraged at the unexpected and, in their opinion, unjustified, attack on the man responsible for founding an international institution as cherished, decent and wholesome as the Scouts, considered the whole affair 'political correctness gone mad'; others, who were aware *only* of his scouting legacy, were simply baffled as to why anyone would find such a nice fellow so offensive.

In a nutshell, around the world, in a deepening pandemic crisis that no one could see an end to any time soon, different generations were being forced to find a middle-ground between the honouring of historic figures for their indisputable achievements, services to society and general altruism, and holding them to account for their far less palatable and, by today's standards, wholly-unacceptable beliefs and deeds.

As previously mentioned, this global divide was mainly a generational thing, but not entirely, particularly when considering the Baden-Powell brouhaha at Poole Quay. There were the older traditionalists, advocates (or at least uncritical) of statues, landmarks and memorials to their heroes. These were regarded by the younger generation as folk who viewed the past through rose-tinted glasses, who revelled in the glories of bloody military victories and colonialism while being wilfully blind to the often obvious resultant humanitarian failings, war atrocities slavery, fascism, sexism, exploitation, forced-labour or all of the above.

Then there was the younger, historically enlightened generation, with its heightened global awareness, cultural empathy and damnation of historical injustices. The resultant criticism, resentment and feelings of anger they held compelled them to express their disapproval. These campaigners tended to be roundly dismissed by the 'other side' as being too 'liberal', 'namby-pamby', constantly looking for the bad in things and generally being too 'sensitive.'

'Snowflake warriors', if you will. Another derogatory term.

Interestingly, in the warring factions of 2020's Battle of the Statue of Poole Quay, these lines were blurred.

Scouts, you see, come in all shapes, sizes and, of course, ages; so while the opposing opinions *did* fit the model of the general, global divide, the actual age groups bucked the trend with young supporters joining the old brigade to, often literally, wave the flag for their beloved B-P.

Even the Anti-Stats (statues) movement, while mainly younger, still didn't quite fit the bill, as older activists and supporters, opposed to this glorification of villains and for myriad other reasons, joined them in a bid to add a few more decibels to their voices of dissent.

It was all pretty peaceful in the end, though one local retired Scout, Len Banister, unphased by the protesters, told the news channels that he was indebted to the Chief Scout of the World for everything he'd done for him and his family. 'I was a Scout, my son's a Scout leader and my grandchildren are Scouts,' he said proudly.

So incensed was Len at the attempt to remove, or worse – deface or even destroy, the iconic statue of his benefactor, he swore to protect it with something more than mere words. 'I'll give a bunch of fivers [*sic*] to anybody that touches it,' he warned, clenching his fists and pumping them up and down for the benefit of the delighted press lining the waterfront.

Baden-Powell, always the maverick, forever the showman, while appalled at the accusations, would be more likely to be chuckling with delight than spinning in his grave at the momentous turn of events and ensuing mayhem, for there was nothing he liked more than being the centre of attention, of being on stage – especially the world stage.

The statue, a jaunty and quite uncanny likeness by Scottish sculptor David Annand, himself a Scout as a boy, has B-P dressed in his trademark scouting uniform with knees bare, and a woggled kerchief draped over his shoulders. His small piercing eyes, gaze from under the brim of his bush hat, or 'lemon squeezer', across the water – and the years – towards Brownsea Island, location of his first Boy Scout camp experiment more than a hundred years earlier.

Unveiled in August 2008, it took Annand ten months to complete and weighs a hefty 200kg, so dislodging it, let alone dragging it all the way from its base next to the bright-yellow Brownsea Island boat's ticket kiosk to the edge of the harbour wall and lobbing it into the depths, as was the fate of Colston, would have been quite the feat.

As news of the proposed fate of his statue unfolded, David Annand, ironically a supporter of BLM, remained pretty sanguine about it:

> I installed Baden-Powell in Poole so I knew that they couldn't throw it in the harbour because the anchors are so strong they would have had to take the stones with them.
>
> The council tried to remove it but the old Scouts stopped them. They probably knew it couldn't be moved as well.

On the subject of the animosity towards his, well, subject, Annand said:

> B-P *was* a racist and took part in all sorts of nasty stuff when in the army. But he did go on to found one of the world's best organisations, to create a massive brotherhood of boys and girls from every country.
>
> The Scout law used to say that a Scout is a friend to every other Scout no matter what country class, or creed. When I was in the Scouts we were allocated a group of Japanese Scouts to host at the Jamboree in Blair Athol [in Scotland].
>
> This experience wiped the racism out of our narrow little minds in the '60s. We had a brilliant time with them, learning their skills and culture.

When erecting the statue at the Quay he chatted with lots of Scout and B-P fans, including a memorably enjoyable encounter with a family who were on holiday in Poole.

> I was mobbed by a family from Zimbabwe. They were so surprised to see him, they took turns to pose with the statue. And me! ... I think they should leave the statues and add the details of their [subjects'] involvements in slavery. For the record, I firmly support Black Lives Matter.

Lacking Annand's confidence of the statue's ability to resist a watery end, to protect it (and to protect the protestors from Len Banister's fists, or a night in the local police station), the council encased it where it sits, in a vast, box-like crate, and fenced it off with mumblings about possibly moving it to the local museum or somewhere well out of harm's way until things died down.

Scouts, being Scouts, rallied and promptly covered the barricade with hastily-penned, hand-made cardboard signs, including one that commanded in bold, uppercase letters:

'PEOPLE OF DORSET DO NOT LET BADEN POWELL FALL!'

To say that times have changed since Baden-Powell first took twenty hand-selected boys to Poole's Brownsea Island at the beginning of the last century for his now-famous prototype Scouts' encampment project, is a huge understatement.

Obviously, many of the social mores, opinions and actions that we find unacceptable today were regarded as acceptable in the Victorian era. Therefore, although we cannot condone any of Baden-Powell's darker deeds, which will be further examined as we follow his journey from childhood to final days, I feel we should, perhaps, consider the context of the age in which he lived when examining how he is perceived and judged in the present day.

Were some, if not all, of his activities and opinions down to his being a typical example of the colonialist attitudes of almost every member of his class and generation?

Did his privileged background mean that he was more-or-less pre-destined to have the entrenched senses of entitlement and superiority that he clearly, but perhaps unknowingly, demonstrated on so many occasions?

Are his dubious moments so plentiful and so terrible that they will conspire to overshadow all of his admirable ones? Or could his legacy now forever be accepted as a complicated blend of both, as it shifts and evolves under levels of scrutiny far fiercer in death than he'd ever experienced in life? It's possible.

As we've seen, he remains deeply respected, in fact loved, for creating the astonishingly successful Scout movement, and for his undeniable services to boy-kind, including the enabling of working-class lads to escape – for a while at least – the grim reality of their harsh, often brutal, lives; and for his advocacy of peace, albeit coming after what was undeniably a prolonged period of decidedly enthusiastic blood-thirstiness.

Millions of children and adults around the world, regardless of colour, creed or, eventually even gender, still merrily unite to march to Lord Baden-Powell's tune of kindness, preparedness and happiness.

In stark contrast, he's also widely pilloried for having been a xenophobe, a snob, a fascist with a lofty disregard for human rights. As for accusations of homophobia, that is a prime example of the ambiguous nature of his make-up, considering that throughout his life Baden-Powell is believed to have struggled to repress his own homosexual feelings, and was constantly wracked with guilt about them.

Today's Chief Scout, Bear Grylls, TV presenter and all-round action man, could match Lord Baden-Powell in daring and a sense of adventure; he could also give him a run for his money when it comes to ingenuity and survival.

However, he's far from in tune with his famous predecessor regarding the failings, real and perceived, thrown into the spotlight by the statue struggle.

Writing in the *Telegraph* at the time, he made it clear that while the movement should acknowledge its founder's history and credit him with creating the foundations of Scouting, the Scouts have moved on, continuing in the knowledge of where they came from, but clear that they will not be 'going back.'

Grylls, who in 2009 became the youngest ever chief scout at the age of 34, praised Baden-Powell for uniting young people and enabling them 'to learn how to celebrate their differences, to love and protect the outdoor world, to serve communities, and to be empowered with skills for life,' but he also asserted that the Scouts must evolve.

On the statue conflict, he wrote:

This last week, people have expressed much confusion and anger at the possible removal of a statue of Lord Baden-Powell in Poole.

To me, and many Scouts, Brownsea Island is a reminder of that great Scouting vision that has since helped so many young people gain vital, life-enhancing skills.

He went on to say that it was the right thing to do to take time to listen and:

to educate ourselves and reflect on our movement's history. We need the humility to recognise there are times when the views and actions from our Scouting's past do not always match the values we live by today. We must learn, adapt and improve.

To gain this better understanding of the complex character of Baden-Powell the man, one has to consider Baden-Powell the boy. Few would argue that one's childhood plays a fundamental role in defining one's adulthood to varying degrees, and for him this was most certainly the case.

Robert Stephenson Smyth Baden-Powell was born at home at 6 Stanhope Street, Paddington, near London's Hyde Park, on 22 February 1857, somewhat prophetically the year of the Indian rebellion against British colonial rule.

He was the eighth of ten children of the Reverend Professor Baden Powell and his third wife, Henrietta Grace Smyth, almost thirty years his junior. He was named after their friend, Robert Stephenson, the pioneering railway and civil engineer, and most notably, the creator of the famous 'Stephenson's Rocket' locomotive; Stephenson also became his godfather.

The safe arrival of their sixth son was less than joyful, coming as it did in the wake of a tragic and traumatic period (that we will visit later) for the family, but especially for his mother.

Almost immediately, the family began referring to baby Robert as 'Stephenson', before finally settling on the nickname 'Stephe' (pronounced Stevie); it continued to be used right into his adulthood. The Robert in his Christian name was used later in school and throughout his military career, but to those close to him, he was always Stephe.

His father, Baden, was a Church of England priest, an academic and a professor of mathematics at Oxford University, where he held the prestigious post of Savilian Chair of Geometry, a position founded in 1619.

One of Professor Powell's most noteworthy students was the 'Alice in Wonderland' author, Lewis Carroll (Charles Dodgson), who particularly enjoyed attending his 'enlightening' geometry lectures.

The professor was also a prominent, liberal theologian who promoted what many of his peers at the time considered controversial ideas regarding Darwinism and evolution. Unwavering in his views, it was a brave stance to take in an establishment drenched in conformity and entrenched thinking; he unflinchingly (many felt unwisely) called into question the prevailing wisdom of the day, displaying a maverick side that he most certainly passed on to Stephe, as shall be seen anon.

Although staunch and imposing in the halls of academia, Baden was a gentle and very indulgent father who loved his children deeply. He enjoyed their company, encouraged their questions and spent a great deal of time with them on walks to the park, teaching them at home, playing games and reading them stories. It's here where we see the kernel of another trait, that of a doting, playful father, that the young Stephe would turn out to also have inherited in (considerably) later life.

Henrietta was the daughter of the Reverend Powell's friend, Captain William Henry Smyth, an admired naval man who was also a gold medallist of the Royal Astronomical Society, a vice-president of the Royal Society and the author of a guide to the movement of the stars. Stephe's proclivity for mapping the lie of the land, more of which later, was clearly in the family genes.

Henrietta vaguely knew Baden from her teens when he would visit her father but was reintroduced to him by her parents in her early twenties. Unlike her scholarly elder brothers, but like so many girls of the Victorian era, her education had been somewhat haphazard and as a result, she was of the view that success, for herself at least, was something that would be best achieved through *who* she knew rather than *what* she knew.

Fond of the finer things in life, she was forever on the look-out for opportunities for upward mobility, so enthusiastically and, it appears, quite strategically, wooed Baden, now a widower for the second time, with a heady blend of openly admiring his intellect and wholeheartedly agreeing with his ideas and opinions.

Given that Baden had plenty of fellow academics and theologians with whom he could discuss the finer details of his studies, it is more likely that his marriage proposal was inspired by Henrietta's constant talk of her enjoyment in looking after the young children at the Sunday school which she ran. After all, while there's little doubt that Baden would have been attracted to the youthful, affable, redhead, he was also a widower and entirely responsible for the care and wellbeing of four young children; Henrietta telling him how she 'so gained the affection and confidence of the children that they opened their little hearts most unreservedly to me and this enabled me to give, I hope, really suitable advice', must have been a strong aphrodisiac.

With her parents' blessing, they married in March 1846 at New St Luke's Church in Chelsea. Henrietta was 21 to Baden's 48. Unfortunately, despite her prenuptial fervour for childcare, she quickly decided that she didn't like her four stepchildren. The three elder siblings, all girls, were farmed out to a handy aunt in Tunbridge Wells with only the youngest, a 4-year-old boy named Baden Henry, remaining at Stanhope Street.

Henrietta's first child, a son named Warington after one of her brothers, was born after 'indescribable agonies', not quite a year after her wedding, in February 1847; he was followed a mere ten months later by another boy, George. In 1849, Augustus came along and then Francis (Frank) a year later. In the gaps between her pregnancies, Henrietta was far from idle. She liked nothing better than to underpin her social status as the Reverend Professor's wife by entertaining a variety of distinguished visitors.

The guests at one of her social 'dos' in the year Warington was born were members of the prestigious British Science Association who were attending a meeting at Oxford, and so she happily found herself playing hostess to some of the country's most eminent scientific minds.

The glittering and no doubt meticulously curated attendees included William Fox Talbot, Sir John Herschel, Sir George Airey and Sir Henry De la Beche.

At another of her popular soirees, the son of an eccentric Oxford professor pitched up toting a bag full of snakes and a bear kitted out in its own graduation cap and gown. She would have revelled in the quirkiness of this and been acutely aware of how every detail of the amusing incident would have spread like wildfire through her social circle.

Her fecundity continued apace with the birth of Robert, the sixth son of her ten children, three of whom had sadly died in infancy prior to his arrival.

Tragically, the three who died had all done so within a very short time of one another. Little Henrietta, her first, longed-for daughter died at the age of 2 in March 1854, followed by her brother, John, who died in the December of the following year, aged 3; in a further cruel blow, baby sister Jessie, another longed-for girl, died at just 8 months old the following July.

Diphtheria is believed to have been the cause of two of the deaths with pneumonia being the cause of a third. Diseases like these were rampant in the mid-1800s, largely due to insanitary conditions and contaminated water supplies, and with no effective vaccines in sight, high infant mortality rates were an unfortunate fact of life and not just among the poor, as death notoriously has no regard for wealth or status.

According to the Medical Officer of Health for the City of London in 1849, twelve years after Queen Victoria's reign began, the death rate for children under 5 years of age stood at about 33 per cent in some areas of the city. In Kensington alone, Henrietta and Baden's neighbourhood and a relatively wealthy district of London, over the course of that year there was a combined total of 1,022 deaths among infants and children.

Fact of life or not, the death of a child was always agonising and this series of events would have been an unbearable loss for the family, particularly Henrietta, who at the time of Jessie's death was already expecting Robert.

Inadequate medical expertise and vague advice exacerbated her anguish and for a time she was so traumatised that she found it impossible to process the fact that her babies had died. Confused and devastated, she tried positioning each of their corpses close to the fire in a bid to prevent them from growing cold.

So, while history has revealed her to have been a feisty, capable and sometimes cold woman, the reality is that Henrietta would have been left utterly bereft by this terrible episode in her life. Unfortunately for Robert, his birth in early 1857, not even a year after Jessie's death, appears to have been more of an excruciating reminder of all that Henrietta had lost rather than a cause for joy and celebration. Disappointment hung weightily in the air, a disappointment that would cling to him and keep his mother distant from him throughout his childhood and beyond.

As if matters couldn't get any worse, in 1860, when Robert was just 3 and now with a new sister and brother, Agnes and Baden Jnr to play with, Baden the doting father and dutiful husband, also died of pneumonia. This left the still-young Henrietta to bring up her seven remaining children, as well as manage her unrelenting grief, alone.

Once more this indomitable woman, with her intense drive and burning ambition, needed all the strength she could muster, this time to cope with her husband's death, which would have been shattering for her, coming so soon after the loss of their three children.

Yet remarkably, Henrietta somehow did manage to pull herself together and as time went on, even flourished.

Her sheer tenacity and willpower kept her going and eventually even galvanised her into action. She began in earnest what she then considered to be her life's work: to ensure that every one of her children attained dizzying heights of excellence and became the very best they could possibly be. This she did with relentless gusto. Unfortunately for Stephe.

Her ambition for her children to succeed intensified. Almost all of her decisions sprung from a desire to climb as high as possible on the social ladder, and she did everything in her power to achieve this.

Aware of the importance of superb lineage, of being from 'good stock', one of the first things she did was to give the family name a reboot. Not for Henrietta and her brood the simple 'Powell' appendage. Why stick with a single surname, when one could go by the infinitely more imposing, double-barrelled moniker of Baden-Powell?

Non-cynical souls at the time would have seen this as a good and fitting way for Henrietta to honour her late, lamented husband. Others could, and did, regard it as a clever ploy to up the family's status by making them sound far nobler and more important than they actually were; there was also the added bonus of clearly identifying her natural children as separate (not to mention superior) to her stepchildren.

She even somehow managed to get the family's coat of arms officially changed, after much hoop-jumping and wheedling, to incorporate a link to a highly distinguished, but completely unrelated, Baden family in order to appear more well-connected.

Under her guidance – make that 'fist of iron' – her children did do extremely well, apart, that is, from Stephe; much to her chagrin, and despite her getting him a place at the prestigious Charterhouse school, he was anything but a star pupil. He was, she decided, destined always to be the black sheep of the Baden-Powell dynasty.

Far more interested in being an artist and an adventurer than an academic all-rounder, he preferred creative pastimes and outdoor pursuits to books and learning. He did have talents, with a flair for piano and drama, and was artistic, as is evident in the quality of the illustrations he created for many of his future books, cards and letters. In later years, he would, completely by accident, also discover that he was a good sculptor, too.

But perhaps his greatest skill at that time was that of eluding his exasperated Charterhouse masters by slipping off into the nearby woods, where he'd imagine himself as a romantic back-woodsman. Henrietta, as one can imagine, was not at all impressed with these fanciful antics and made it quite clear at every opportunity how disappointed she was in his academic shortcomings.

Stephe was painfully aware of her feelings towards him but even so, little could he have imagined then that one of the hardest challenges he'd face throughout his life would be trying to win his mother's approval.

Chapter 2

The Disappearing Schoolboy

'The child is the father of the man.'

William Wordsworth

Over the years, Stephe's constant devotion to his mother, especially apparent in his numerous personal letters to her, has often been misinterpreted as evidence that he was Henrietta Grace's favourite child.

In reality, nothing could be further from the truth. His affectionate words and unselfconscious public musings on her wonderful attributes disguised a flawed relationship that was, as with most aspects of his life, complicated and conflicted.

While Stephe wore his heart on his sleeve, his adoration was largely unrequited and as for him being her favourite child, there was no question that his big brother George (with his younger brother Baden a close second) already held that particular title.

What was behind Henrietta's aloofness in the face of her son's admiration and gratitude? Why the distance and, on occasion, the downright callousness?

For the answers, we must start at the beginning, for this one-sided mother-son bond seems to stem from Stephe's unfortunately timed birth in February 1857, just months after Henrietta had buried her third child (the longed-for daughter, Jessie) in three years. In the face of such profound grief, she would have been in a tumultuous emotional state and would have found it hard, impossible even, to treat her new baby boy as a priority at what was a crucial bonding time for them.

Sadly, Stephe continued to wallow at the bottom of the family pecking order and apart from during a pre-school learning phase and then later in 1863, a year marred by further family tragedy, he was granted very limited time on his own with his mother.

This must have affected him deeply at an age when it would have been difficult to comprehend the reasons why. How could he have understood that she was in despair and very likely to be suffering from grief, post-natal and general depression?

Competing for parental attention and affection is standard procedure in large families, but Stephe does appear to have borne much of the brunt of (or in view of the bleak situation, the blame for) Henrietta's emotional fatigue.

Compared with his siblings, especially George and 'baby' Baden, born three years after Stephe and whom he jokingly (though clearly with shades of jealously) mocked by repeating his mother's nicknames for him, a favourite being 'the precious babe', he didn't get much of a look in. Even his little sister Agnes got more time with her.

Unsurprisingly, his feelings of abandonment increased around the time of Baden junior's arrival in 1860, when his sister Agnes was barely a year old, however, any possible anxiety brought on by this event was completely eclipsed three weeks later by the death of their father from pneumonia, after desperate weeks of nursing by an utterly wrung-out Henrietta.

Worse was to come. To allow his overwhelmed mother to cope, he was exiled to the countryside to live with his grandparents for two months. To Stephe, this represented a sudden loss of not just one adored parent, but two and, predictably, he missed his mother terribly.

When he did finally return home, there was no time for the comfort of his mother's longed-for lap as, since drained and exhausted from giving birth and looking after her husband, Henrietta then left home to stay with cousins in Kent in a bid to improve her own wellness, taking only baby Baden with her.

Again, Stephe was beside himself.

This happened several times during his formative years and whenever she left, he'd be intensely miserable and prone to bouts of inconsolable sobbing. In a contemplative moment, having been absent for yet another prolonged period, Henrietta confessed in a letter to her mother that she was feeling guilty 'about poor little Stephe', and explained, 'I do not feel as if I was doing my duty to him while so long away – though he is so well taken care of.'

The word 'duty' is potent – he was 4 years old when she wrote this.

From then and through the following year at least, he had regular outbursts of weeping and tantrums, which Henrietta referred to as his 'strange fits of passion'. Sadly, she never seemed to associate these episodes with the fact he all he wanted was love and attention.

As uncomfortable as it is to imagine this lack of maternal warmth or empathy towards a clearly unhappy small boy, it is equally so to read the words of a depressed, much-bereaved woman describing feelings of guilt for failing to juggle her children on her own while wracked with heartache.

That Stephe's mother was ever detached or unfeeling towards him comes as a shock to many people due to his seeming – outwardly, at least – worship of her. However, reading between the lines, throughout his life there is a sense of his desperate willingness to please her, to win her approval and of his regret at having somehow been a disappointment to her.

This feeling of having let her down, even late into adulthood when he had become an internationally acclaimed war hero and had founded the Boy Scouts, never left him and, upon her death in 1914, this was his telling, slightly brittle, eulogy to her:

> There is only one pain greater than losing your mother, and that is for your mother to lose you – I do not mean by death but by your own misdeeds. Has it ever struck you what it means to your mother if you turn out a wrong 'un or a waster? She who bore you as a baby, and brought you up and was glad when you showed that you could do things.
>
> As she saw you getting bigger and stronger and growing clever she had hoped in her heart of hearts that you were going to make a successful career and to make a good name for yourself – something to be proud of. But if you begin to loaf about and do not show grit and keenness, if you become a slacker, her heart grows cold with disappointment and sorrow – all her loving work and expectation have been thrown away, and the pain she suffers through seeing you slide off onto the wrong road is worse than if she had lost you in death … Make your career a success, whatever line you take up, and you will rejoice her heart. Try not to disappoint her but to make her happy in any way you can; you owe it to her … *The Scouts Newspaper*, October 1914)

A typical Victorian matriarch, domineering and controlling her brood with a steely determination, so much so, that she ran the Baden-Powell family like a business, Henrietta Grace is frequently cast as a pantomime villain, often with good cause. However, as always, there are deep-seated explanations for some of her less appealing character traits.

Further in her defence, or simply for the sake of balance, when it came to the education of her children, she was encouraging, indulgent and considerate of their needs.

Of course, one could argue that this stemmed from her burning ambition that all of her offspring, like their father and her own brothers, should excel in every undertaking in order to raise the family's status and, on a statelier plain, be of service to the Empire; that's probably true, but during their nursery-school days she was uncharacteristically tender towards them, especially to the three youngest, Stephe, Agnes and Baden Jnr.

Whether this was an episode of heightened awareness and sensitivity to the children's emotions for Henrietta or yet another manipulative move towards world domination, it still stands that in what would have been a time of vast personal loss, she summoned the strength to step into the late Baden's shoes and guide them in their learning.

All lessons took place at home and were taught by both Henrietta and by their governess, Fraulein Groffel. It was, by all accounts, a happy, enlightening and positive experience for them. The two women organised group lessons for the little trio to allow them to work together, thus ensuring constant companionship as well as shared learning goals. Henrietta also insisted on two school rules (for the Governess, not for the children); one, they should be reprimanded 'lovingly' and two, that their good behaviour should reflect 'firm but gentle guidance'.

Although Henrietta wasn't educated to the high level of her brothers, who became important public figures – Warington, Mineral Inspector to the Crown (literally looking for gold); Fiazzi, Scotland's Astronomer Royal; and Henry, Governor and Commander in Chief, Malta, she was a very clever woman. She was good at languages and maths, a notable artist and was interested in science and nature.

So, along with de rigueur reading, numeracy and writing lessons, she also encouraged them in art and factored singing, dance and exercise into their itineraries, which Stephe, being a creative child, would have adored. With little more than a year between them age-wise, he and Agnes, now the only girl in the family, grew extremely close; they played with dolls and he would help her make little outfits for them.

It was a typically no-nonsense Victorian practice for very young children, regardless of gender, to be dressed in tunics to facilitate easy nappy changing and toilet training. Agnes taught Stephe how to use his tunic to 'skirt dance' as she did, which basically involved holding the hem and ruffling it about while twirling. A far more elaborate version of this skirt dancing, using women's frocks in place of the tunic, was deployed to great effect later on in many of his theatrical performances.

Henrietta, understandably paranoid about her family's wellbeing, was aware that health benefits could be gained by being outdoors (that pre-marriage Sunday school experience was valuable after all) and so she incorporated this into their daily timetables.

Her 'pupils' were taught outside whenever possible and she emulated her husband by taking them on long country walks where she would teach them all about wildlife and nature, which they relished. She also encouraged them to read books from their father's library, in particular, his wonderful natural history collection, built on his love of nature and the sights and sounds of country life. This was a hugely important period in Stephe's early years, in fact, in his life; for it was then, in those open-air classes and happy treks through woods and fields that the foundation of his love of the great outdoors and of the natural world was laid, by none other than his mother.

It also represents the time when he was closest to Henrietta and therefore was at his happiest as a boy. This explains why, throughout his life, he was always at his calmest and most contented while at one with nature and sleeping under the stars.

The only other prolonged length of time Stephe spent with his mother as a child was brought about by a tragedy. In 1862 his older brother Augustus, with whom he had grown very close in spite of a six-year age gap, became ill. He had contracted tuberculosis, so it was decided that he should live with his aunts in the country where he would have peace and quiet and endless fresh air.

Stephe was beside himself, this time because his brother was now going to disappear. Augustus helped by writing home regularly; Henrietta always read his letters aloud to the children and he had often included little messages for him: 'Thank dear Stephenson for his nice picture and tell him that it was very well drawn indeed.'

Despite the country air, Augustus' health deteriorated and Henrietta, fearing that the end might be near for her 'darling boy', decided that they should *all* go and live with him for a month.

Given the circumstances it was a happy time; Augustus adored having them with him and he took great delight in sitting at the window, watching little Stephe ride his aunt's pony. At the age of 6 Stephe was already a competent rider, and was in his element being in the saddle and entertaining his brother at the same time. Not only did he have Augustus back, he got to spend more time with his mother, too.

After this pleasant interlude Augustus rallied a little, though it was unfortunately short-lived; as his condition worsened, Henrietta found herself facing the death of a child once more. She wrote: 'I have explained to him, as nearly as I can his exact state, and it makes him quite happy to know that all must now be left to God's will, whether he may live or die.'

Augustus died on 3 April 1863 at the age of 13, having bequeathed his treasured telescope, stamps, scrapbook and compass to his dear Stephenson.

These relentless episodes of unexpected, crushing loss and maternal abandonments during his boyhood formed the basis of Stephe's intense need to please his mother. After all, if he could keep her happy, it would at least prevent her from leaving him, too.

Life continued, including Stephe's first dose of formal education at a dame school in Kensington Square, near their home on Stanhope Street. Dame schools were small, private schools and were extremely popular in the British Isles and the colonies at the time. They ran on a model that had proven successful since the 1600s and tended to be located at the end of a road, or at least within the parish boundaries. The name comes from the 'school dame', who would be an educated woman who managed the establishment and provided lessons in reading, writing and arithmetic for a small fee.

This was an astute choice of Henrietta's, not just because of the school's proximity to the house, but also, crucially for a perpetually cash-strapped widow, the cost was low.

Stephe walked there and back each day. His London was a safe one of smart streets, lined with imposing houses attended by uniformed gatekeepers and of pedestrians who were either fragrant and corseted or sporting top hats. Interestingly though, in years to come he said that the people who really struck him on his school walks were not the well-heeled residents but the poor boys, most of them not much older than he was, who were employed as crossing-sweepers, clearing the streets of mud and horse droppings all day, every day, whatever the weather, in order to prevent the affluent locals from soiling their gowns or shoes.

His social conscience was clearly pricked for it was around this time that he wrote his *Laws For When I Am Old*. In true Stephe style, it's a little haphazard but charmingly earnest. Henrietta may have had a hand in it since she had strong links with Christian socialists and encouraged the children to share her beliefs; or perhaps he was influenced by big brother George, who had similar leanings to his mother. Regardless, with hindsight, the sentiment would have been his own:

Laws For When I Am Old
I will have the poor people to be as rich as we are, and they ought by
rights to be happy as we are, and all who go across the crossings shall
give the poor crossing-sweeper some money and you ought to thank
God for what he has given us and he made the poor people to be poor
and the rich people to be rich and I can tell you how to be good. Now I
will tell you. You must pray to God whenever you can but you cannot be
good with only praying but you must try very hard to be good.
     By R.S.S. Powell, Feb 26th 1865

At the age of 11 he left his dame school and moved to Rose Hill, the
Tunbridge Wells prep-school that his father had attended before him and
where, according to his masters, he behaved beautifully, meeting not just the
school's but his mother's very high standards.

The wife of the typically strict, disciplinarian headmaster, Thomas Allfree,
complimented Stephe on his 'painstaking and industrious conduct', and even
told Henrietta that when he left for Charterhouse that 'his influence on the
moral tone of the school was so great' that she would have gladly kept him
on without fees.

Being at Rose Hill was another significant milestone in Stephe's childhood,
for he later credited his time there – not the learning, but his escapes into the
woods to engage with nature – with contributing to his creating the Scouts.

Just as the school left its mark on him, he in turn left his on the school.
Fast-forward to today and Rose Hill, one of the UK's oldest preparatory
schools, remains proud of its Baden-Powell connection, with staff and pupils
celebrating his birthday every year and having one of its houses named after
him. The thing that would delight their famous old boy most of all, though,
is that it runs thriving Cubs, Brownies and Rainbow clubs.

So, it was a case of 'so far, so good' on the education front, but as soon as
the time came for Stephe to go to 'big school', it was also time for Henrietta
to get down to the serious business of finding an establishment that would
provide a suitable route to a successful career for the son who preferred
playing and acting to reading and writing.

As with most matters, her decision was influenced by the kudos the
right sort of school would offer and, of course, the cost. She set her eye on
Charterhouse public school, but while she'd managed to secure places in
excellent schools for her other sons, through connections and their natural
academic prowess, Stephe was different. Undeterred, she wrote, 'Computed

what was best for us. Charterhouse seems the best.' What made it 'best' from her point of view was the possibility of Stephe somehow winning a place as a 'gown-boy', the name given to pupils who gained one of the school's scholarships, which were as rare as hen's teeth.

This became a vital undertaking, for not only would it maintain the illusion that the Baden-Powells were a robustly eminent family, as opposed to a precarious, fiscally unsteady upper-middle-class one but the fees, should one have had to actually pay them, were eye-wateringly expensive.

An added bonus as far as she, although possibly not Stephe, was concerned, was that 'the precious babe' Baden, was already a Charterhouse gown-boy and could therefore teach him the ropes. All she had to do was don her string-pulling gloves and set about securing his place.

When Henrietta Grace set her heart on something, she invariably got it and she was determined that this would be no exception. She embarked on a major offensive of advanced networking, entertaining and downright pestering. Her excellent contacts and dogged determination paid off. She convinced her friend the Duke of Marlborough to nominate Stephe who, to her relief, won the prized scholarship, and at the age of 13 joined Baden at Charterhouse in November 1870. Winning these places for her sons through exhausting and relentless machinations was a considerable feather in her cap and further proof of her immense tenacity.

Now her two youngest boys would be schooled in the manner they deserved and would hopefully follow in their father's and older brothers' footsteps to Oxford.

That was the theory, at least.

Sporting not just his new uniform but also the new-and-improved Baden-Powell surname which his mother had engineered for them the year before, Stephe arrived at Charterhouse unaware that he was entering another significant phase in his life, for it was there that his boyhood dreams of being an adventurer would, to some degree, come true.

The Baden-Powell brothers were not, as one might expect, ridiculed or looked down upon due to their free-place status, quite the opposite. Gown-boys (derived from the distinctive robes scholarship boys traditionally wore over their school uniforms), of which there were only sixty in total spread throughout all the year groups, were regarded as an elite bunch since they'd won their places on their own merit (or in some cases their mother's), rather than merely through family wealth.

Unexpectedly, from Stephe's point of view, Charterhouse, like Rose Hill, turned out to be an excellent choice.

As well as being one of the country's preeminent schools, it was also one of its most beautiful, occupying the ancient medieval cloistered buildings of a former monastery close to Smithfield butchers' market in London. Awash with history and tradition, it had been home to a closed order of Carthusian monks and enjoyed the dubious distinction of being one of the first Catholic churches to fall victim to Henry's VIII's punitive dissolution of the monasteries campaign. John Houghton, prior at the time, was afraid of the Tudor king's ruthless intentions and in desperation visited Thomas Cromwell, seeking an 'oath of supremacy', in the hope that it would save him from a grisly end. It didn't work. He was taken to the Tower of London, charged with treason and carted off to Tyburn, the capital's go-to execution arena, and brutally hanged, drawn and quartered in classic medieval style.

After its dissolution, the monastery eventually became home to Thomas Howard, the Duke of Norfolk who, to shield himself from London's characteristically inclement weather while walking to his tennis court, commissioned a covered walkway to be built. He also boarded up the rooms where monks would previously have spent hours transcribing their manuscripts and added arched windows along the hallway making it a garden gallery. From then on it was referred to as the 'Norfolk Cloister'.

Charterhouse and its land were eventually bought by a wealthy businessman called Thomas Sutton who, on his death in 1611, bequeathed the entire grounds and enough money to fund a hospital, an alms house and a school. The site became wholly dedicated to boys' education, with a focus on team games and good sportsmanship. This tradition of focusing on active pursuits endured which, along with the school's inherent laissez faire approach to learning, suited Stephe down to the ground. At Charterhouse, any display of overtly scholarly ambitions was deemed gauche, even distasteful, while larking about and being 'one of the boys' were qualities considered thoroughly admirable.

Once he discovered this, he could work around his general aversion to academia and make a name for himself in other far jollier ways.

All sixty gown-boys, all of varying ages, belonged to and lived in the same house, Girdlestone (the house master's name), where they would congregate in a large, ornately ceilinged common room they called the 'Writing School'.

Hogwarts it wasn't, and under the guardianship of the 26-year-old Frederic Girdlestone, whose idea of discipline involved leaving it entirely to the older boys, or 'uppers', who were still permitted to dole out corporal punishment, Stephe and his cohorts were subjected to regular 'swishings' or floggings.

Swishings were the punishment of choice for anyone unfortunate enough to have three 'offences', no matter how petty, recorded in the 'Black Book' and were administered on what was referred to as the 'flog block', a gnarled wooden kneeler, repurposed for leaning on in order to facilitate the infliction of pain. The 'Girdlestonites' were a like-minded, stoical bunch and most of them endured the swishings and various other forms of bullying with a grudging resignation, while no doubt consoling themselves and one another that they were character building.

Predictably, many boys went on to repeat these bullying and abusive behaviours when they became uppers, but in Stephe's case, it was quite the opposite.

'... in his attitude to the younger boys,' said his headmaster, Dr Haig-Brown, 'he was generous, kind and encouraging, and in those early days gave no slight indication of the qualities which have since gained for him the confidence, respect, and love of all the soldiers who have been under his command.'

As a 'hop' or new boy, Stephe was expected to 'fag', in other words, be at the beck-and-call of an 'upper' boy. The 'fagging' system should have been long gone by that time, however, it was still prevalent throughout English public schools and younger boys were still forced to do their seniors' bidding at all hours of the day and night. Tasks could include cooking their breakfast, polishing their shoes, or, as Roald Dahl found out at Repton School, warming the toilet seat for them.

Unsurprisingly, the system was open to all sorts of physical, mental and sexual abuse, although this became less so in later years. Still, it didn't entirely fizzle out until as late as the 1990s and many boys would hide in the shadows to avoid being selected for 'duty'.

Stephe, on the other hand, didn't mind fagging at all. It helped that his designated upper, Edward H. Parry, one of the school's top sportsmen and a particularly brilliant footballer, was also his hero.

He and Parry formed a tight bond with Stephe going out of his way to please him (a mother substitute, perhaps). He later credited Parry with inspiring his own love of football. Their friendship endured beyond their schooldays but it was unusual in that they appear never to have met nor corresponded at all after Charterhouse, only acknowledging one another years later through separate, personal memoirs in which neither revealed the other's name. Post Charterhouse, Parry played – and scored for – the Old Carthusians team that won 1881 FA Cup Final before playing for England.

Stephe wrote in his old age of the 'honour of holding his overcoat while he played' and of 'cleaning his boots', while never mentioning his name.

They would, of course, have recognised themselves through specific anecdotes and descriptions found within their respective memoirs, but both were clearly torn by a compunction to acknowledge the closeness they'd shared while feeling the need to keep it private. This could have been a case of what goes on in Charterhouse, stays in Charterhouse, but it could just as easily have been that they didn't wish to embarrass themselves with anything that hinted at 'unmanliness' at a time when some public schools were under scrutiny for sexual misconduct. Consider also that in public schools at that time, most of the boys would be away from their families for about eight months of the year and so would rarely mix with other people, let alone with girls. School friends and masters were their surrogate families and there was little choice but to seek the company and comfort of one another to compensate. And if they went on to have military careers, the situation continued well into their adult lives too, for they would often go straight from school into their regiments, ending up stationed in unfamiliar places, often abroad and living among indigenous peoples, with only their fellow soldiers as company. This is the reason why so many middle- to upper-class men of those eras married late in life. Stephe, a classic example, was in his 50s when he finally said 'I do'.

So, he survived school, often by the seat of his pants as his school reports clearly confirm, but survive he did. With his peers, in fact most of the school, functioning under this controlled propensity for not being too enthusiastically scholarly, he won friends (and not just boys but masters, too) by cultivating an exaggerated version of his already quirky personality that his fellow pupils found great fun and which his tutors, on the whole, found only mildly irritating and therefore tolerable.

In his middle-school years, Stephe joined The Druids, a 'secret' society in which each member had an amusing, mildly-cryptic nickname. His surname being Baden-Powell, he was given the prophetic soubriquet of 'Lord Bathing-Towel', while Parry became 'Captain Perrywinkle'. As one of the school's most talented artists, sometimes drawing skilfully with both hands just for entertainment, it fell to Stephe to create an impressive title page for the society's minutes book. Examining the artistic result closely, one can see that each of the detailed letters spelling out the word 'DRUIDS' carries coded sketches representing the members' nicknames. The 'S' at the end depicts a bathing towel in serpentine form and nestling underneath it, a tiny periwinkle shell. Baden-Powell and Parry immortalised forever in ink.

Even with so many admiring friends, the opposing sides of Stephe's character could cause confusion, even trouble now and then. Normally, he'd always have a ready smile and a new joke, but he could suddenly turn serious and reserved, or hive off into the woods to be on his own for hours on end. One minute he'd be up to his usual antics, sliding on his belly all the way down the dining table, skirt dancing (learned from Agnes in his pre-school days), or playing the clown, the next he'd be silent and withdrawn. This dual personality made him unpredictable and, on some occasions, his ribbing would backfire and he'd unsettle newer boys who, unused to his acerbic, quick-fire wit, believed him to be making fun of them.

This was rarely the case but his sense of humour *was* an acquired taste, being a bit too close to the bone at times. In essence though, his manner was one of harmless eccentricity and was rather endearing – most of the time. Edward Parry summed this up when he wrote that Stephe, who was a redhead with freckles and 'twinkling eyes' was 'gifted with an admirable species of madness'.

He was lively for sure and a bit of a showboat, yet he was conversely self-deprecating, too. Naturally he was mad keen on acting, but according to biographer, Marguerite de Beaumont, one of the group of ground-breaking girls demanding to be scouts at the Crystal Palace Boy Scout rally of 1909, while he was excellent on stage, 'he was never conceited about what he did, and looked upon most of it as tremendous fun.'

She adds:

He had many friends, and was always popular because he was not afraid to get into a scrape and own up afterwards. This was one of the reasons why he made friends with the schoolmasters as well as the boys.

It was not unnatural that when he grew up his old schoolmasters still continued to be his friends.

The Wolf That Never Sleeps November 1944,
London, The Girl Guides Association

It is true that Stephe and his Headmaster, Dr William Haig-Brown, seem to have had a mutual admiration for one another. Haig-Brown was impressed by his respectful manner, for while he could josh and prank as well as the next one among his peers, he always showed courtesy to his elders. Haig-Brown found his honesty disarming and referred to it many times. He also noticed, when others close to Stephe (including Henrietta Grace) did not, leadership qualities in him that indicated the sort of man he might become. A man who would see the streets of London lined with throngs of cheering people, proclaiming him a war hero and who would also one day conceive a movement for peace and good that would touch the lives of millions of children – and adults – across the world.

Clearly, the headteacher knew him well. He once wrote of him:

> though it is not always easy to found on observation of early life a prophecy of the future career, it is not so difficult when characteristics have found a field for display, to trace in the memories of youth the qualities that have formed a great man, and that the boyish life of Baden-Powell furnishes an illustration in point.

He reiterated these thoughts frequently and once, more succinctly, by quoting the words of William Wordsworth: 'The child is the father of the man.'

Essentially, what Haig-Brown was getting at – and obviously felt proud of – was that many of the traits people saw in the famous grown-up, were ones he'd recognised in him, 'his love of fun and of sport, ... his self-respect', and his 'great truthfulness', when he was but a schoolboy. For all his wordiness, perhaps the most affectionate compliment Haig-Brown paid him was in the simple phrase: 'He was a boy whose word you could not doubt.' *William Haig Brown of Charterhouse*, Brown, H.E. Haig, (Macmillan & Co., London, 1908)

Years later, confirming the importance he placed on this mutual respect, Stephe, grown-up and now with the title Lord Baden-Powell wrote:

> Nowadays you often hear boys and girls running down their teachers. They have rude and stupid nicknames for them and do everything they can to give them a bad time.
>
> This is a great pity, because no great adventure is complete unless we can make friends with people who can teach us things, and people who have spent their lives learning in order that they may pass on knowledge to other people deserve a good deal of respect and gratitude from the young beggars they are trying to teach.
>
> *Lessons From the 'Varsity of Life*,
> Pearson, London, 1933

So, with the headmaster as an ally, a fervent zeal for the Victorian public-school ethos for getting stuck in to sports and being an all-round good egg,

Stephe's six years of Charterhouse schooling were a success, despite his academic performance being almost entirely woeful. It may not have had a profound effect on his scholastic learning but it did on his character, fine-tuning him into the energetic, team-spirited, audacious adult Haig-Brown already sensed he'd become.

During his second year at Charterhouse, the school moved from its cramped, noisy, malodourous site next to the meat market to new premises near Godalming in leafy Surrey. (Knowing the relocation plans in advance was another reason Henrietta had chosen the school.) While it had been smelly and distractingly raucous, Smithfield *had* given the Charterhouse boys another form of sport and one that was unlikely to be played in other public schools, that is the game of fighting butchers' boys. Pitched battles had been going on between the pupils and the market lads for at least a couple of hundred years and Stephe got in on the action not long after he arrived. Happily watching a football game on the school grounds, he suddenly saw a hail of missiles flying over from behind some hoardings. It was the butchers' boys who, he reported, 'attacked with shower of stones and brickbats. This was responded to by our side ... in like manner, with occasional sorties by strong bodies over the wall.'

As he looked on, Haig-Brown said: 'I think if you boys went through that door in the side wall, you might take them in the flank.' When a boy pointed out to the headmaster that said door was locked, he fetched something from his pocket and announced: 'That is so, but here is the key.' According to Stephe, 'he sent us on our way rejoicing, and our attack was a complete success.'

By then team-sport wasn't just a hobby at Charterhouse, it was a religion and even today, the school's rich sporting heritage remains at the core of its character. It is widely acknowledged as having invented a medieval sport, a 'mob' game with a ball, played indoors in the school's cloister, by anyone who was about and regardless of numbers, that then became a two-sided affair that subsequently became Association Football.

The original indoor version eventually got a set of rules, mainly to make it a little less riotous. Players divided into two teams which, in opposing mass scrums, would compete to push a single ball towards the doors (ergo, goals) situated at either end of the cloister's long, stone-floored corridor. It was always a harshly played event and regularly resulted in injuries to many of its participants. Later on, an outdoor form of the game which the players called 'Runabout' was created, where skilfully dribbling the ball with one's feet was very much the done thing.

Even the word 'soccer' – widely believed to be an Americanism – is reputed to have its origins at Charterhouse when it became the nickname used for football in the late 1800s by English footballer and Old Carthusian, Charles Wreford-Brown. Debate, however, still rages on about whether 'soccer' stemmed from the saying 'sock it to them' (as in, 'let them have it'), or was a typical public-school abbreviation of Association (Football), as in 'assocer' in much the same way 'rugger' is short for the game of rugby.

One thing is certain, the rules, officially drawn up by a group gathered in the Freemasons' Tavern at Great Queen's Street, West London, must have come from somewhere and the unique layout of the Norfolk Cloister certainly lends itself well to supporting the assertion that the first throw-in, executed from outside and lobbing the ball back into the cloister via the open windows, and the off-side rule originated there to make the games less chaotic.

Early Charterhouse football is universally recognised as having a major influence on the development of today's 'beautiful game', and research seems to confirm that there's little reason to dispute the validity of its claim to football fame.

The new Godalming Charterhouse, with its flat and open grassy spaces, saw the cloister game come to its natural end, making way for Runabout, which then really took off. While Stephe did play other games, notably cricket and racquets, thanks to Parry, football was his first passion, and goalkeeping was his favoured position. He would later use the sport as an analogy for a basic code for Scouts saying: 'The whole secret of success in life is to play the game of life in the same spirit as that played on the football field.'

The school's *Football Annual*, 1876, states that 'R. S. S. B.-P. is a good goalkeeper, keeping cool, and always to be depended upon.' Haig-Brown may well have noted this as another precursor of things to come.

Athletic exercises and sporting discipline featured large throughout his schooldays, much of which transferred into his adult life, and his friend Marguerite from the Crystal Palace days, believed that his various military campaigns were strengthened by his fondness of football: 'The two qualities (coolness and resourcefulness) were there before, of course, but the goalkeeping added a new fibre or two of strength to them.' One memorable habit he had as goalie was when the football action moved down the pitch, he'd delight the boys crowding round the quiet goal by cracking jokes, which only stopped when he'd suddenly spring forward to defend an attack.

As well as football, Stephe's other love – and for which he had considerable talent – was acting; in the school's theatrical presentations he became such a star that simply walking on to the stage would elicit whoops and cheers from his audience.

He was always manically busy, though not with anything as dull as studying. He wrote for the school magazine, and helped illustrate it; he sang in the choir, and convinced the powers that be to start a school orchestra. Naturally musical, he played a variety of instruments and was skilled at the violin. He was once found playing the piano with his toes and, as mentioned previously, being ambidextrous, could play and sketch with both hands to everyone's amazement.

He was pivotal in forming the school rifle corps and wound up competing as one of the Charterhouse VIII in the Wimbledon Public Schoolboys Rifle Shooting Competition three years running.

As if he knew that his future did not lie in anything he would find in textbooks, Stephe did as little as was required in lessons, resulting in dreadful school reports, full of comments that describe him as 'paying not the slightest attention' in science, or having 'to all intents given up the study of maths', and even sleeping in French class. What would have been a truly damning report to his mother, would at least have been an absolutely superb one to his peers.

He had, however, a natural intelligence for useful, practical skills so, when faced with matters cerebral, he would, wherever possible, use his wiles to escape the confines of the school, plunging deep into the surrounding woods, which was utterly forbidden and, therefore, all the more alluring to the young won't-be-told, to make maps, study wildlife at close-quarters and to hunt:

When I was a small boy at Charterhouse, outside the school walls was 'The Copse', a long stretch of woodland on a steep hillside extending for a mile or so ...

It was here I used to imagine myself a backwoodsman, trapper and scout. I used to creep about warily looking for 'sign' and getting 'close up' observation of rabbits, squirrels, rats and birds.

As a trapper I set my snares, and when I caught a rabbit or a hare I learned by painful experiment how to skin, clean and cook him. But knowing that the Redskins were about, in the shape of masters looking for boys out of bounds, I used a very small, non-smoky fire for fear of giving away my whereabouts.

Lessons From the Varsity of Life

These sojourns into the wild in a small way replaced the adventurous boating trips he'd enjoyed during the holidays with his older brothers, where they'd sail around the south coast, eat on the hoof and camp under the stars.

And it was in The Copse where his scouting began in earnest. He became so highly skilled in bush-craft that he really could cook an entire rabbit over a fire so miniscule, that its smoke never once betrayed his hiding place. It is worth mentioning here that while Stephe had indubitably inherited his parents' appreciation and understanding of nature and his maternal grandfather Admiral Smyth's talents for navigating, mapping and 'reading' the night skies, there was another ancestor whose DNA featured strongly in his genes.

Henrietta is believed to have been related to Captain John Smyth, the seventeenth-century adventurer, explorer, and soldier who captured French ships and fought off Ottoman enemies in America, defeating three of their main warriors in a single fight. Later, Smyth was taken prisoner by a Native American tribe and was only saved from certain death (or so the story goes, some say he merely mistook being rescued for being part of a 'rebirth' ceremony) by the intercession of 'La Belle Sauvage' or, the beautiful Pocahontas, and the rest, as they say, is history, as retold Walt Disney-style in their animated film, *Pocahontas*. Smyth, who went on to be one of the founders of Virginia, was another of Stephe's heroes.

Even so, while mathematics may not have been his strongest subject, even he could work out that all this messing about in the undergrowth equated to diabolical marks and further disappointment for mother. While the inner adventurer and consummate show-off in him yearned for a thespian life or perhaps that of a pioneering missionary – both professions that would place him centre-stage, performing to adoring crowds who'd hang on his every word, just as they did in school – in reality he was facing the future bursting with character and verve, but with very few career options.

Naturally, Henrietta was ahead of the game and ready to take things in hand. She had the Baden-Powells' hard-won reputation to uphold, after all and, equally pressing, a stringently managed household budget that, if they were to keep up appearances, would soon be requiring an injection of cash from any salary Stephe would end up earning. Under her formidable leadership, the family finances were managed like a business and there was even a special pot placed in the centre of the table into which funds were placed by all earning siblings to be spent with infinite care and frugality on whatever mother saw fit. There were meetings about who should get what and when, and special cost-cutting measures were devised, including decamping the entire family to the south coast every summer so that their impressive London residence could be rented out, discreetly of course, for profit.

Stephe's older siblings were incredibly money conscious, thanks to Henrietta Grace's constant lectures and demands. They loyally donated most, often all, of their salaries to the mother-fund to help with the family's general expenditure, so little brother would be expected to do the same.

Chapter 3

The Reluctant Recruit

'It is a well-established fact that very many of the greatest men in the world have acknowledged that they owe much of their success to the influence of their mother.'

Robert Baden-Powell

It is almost comically ironic that the young Robert Stephenson Smyth Baden-Powell, destined to become one of the twentieth century's most celebrated war heroes, was an exceptionally reluctant recruit. At 17 and fresh from the familiar cocoon of Charterhouse's sixth-form, Stephe's head was filled with romantic notions of following his dreams to become an actor, an artist or an intrepid explorer.

Since his mother had other ideas, he was put through an intense period of private tuition in an attempt to secure a place at Oxford; it didn't work and he failed to get into Balliol College and even Henrietta Grace's second choice, Christ Church.

She was incensed. In fact she was so embarrassed about his inability to get a place at the family's traditional seat of learning that for years afterwards, she and by default, Stephe under her direction, went to extraordinary lengths to conceal the fact that, even after the tutoring and the family being on excellent terms with many of Oxford's influential professors, there was simply nothing that could be done to shoehorn him in.

Suspecting it might happen, Henrietta Grace had already set about planning escape routes for him via the military and even consulted her brother, Henry, a commandant at the Royal Military Academy at Woolwich, about viable options. Woolwich it transpired would not be one of them, as men had to be at least 18 years old to be accepted.

Undeterred, she entertained a variety of individuals whom she felt might be useful to her cause, and it can't have hurt that she was friends with the wife of Lieutenant-Colonel John Miller, Colonel of the 13th Hussars. This, interestingly enough, happens to be the regiment that Stephe would eventually join.

Stephe's Oxford disaster and the subsequent collusions over it were never referred to and simply became part of his mother's master plan, a carefully crafted deception that implied that he *had* got an 'unattached member' place (fictional, by all accounts) at Oxford but then on a whim, had decided to sit the army entrance exams at the eleventh-hour and having achieved such spectacular results (out of more than 700 people who took the entrance exams, Stephe did spectacularly well, coming second in cavalry and fourth in infantry) he had no choice but to forgo his Oxford place and follow his destiny along a military path.

Stephe carried both the weight of Henrietta Grace's dissatisfaction and this elaborate fabrication of facts around with him for most of his life. It wasn't until after she died that he felt free to reveal a version of events closer to the truth that would finally put to rest the ghosts that had caused him considerable stress, leading to his lifelong disdain for the importance of academia.

Although there are various examples of Stephe's complicity in Henrietta Grace's fairy tale, again one should consider his almost blind obsequiousness to her and the anxiety he would have felt at disappointing her yet again. This passage from the compendium book, *Playing the Game* is perhaps one of the most telling:

I had for the time to take up my position as an 'unattached member'. Within a few days of joining I went up for the Army examination to test my possibilities in that line, but without any special hope of passing in my first attempt.

A few weeks after the examination, I was on board the *Gertrude*, a yacht belonging to Professor Acland, Regius Professor of Medicine at Oxford, an old friend of my father's.

One of the guests on board was the Dean of Christ Church, who accosted me … with the news that, according to the newspaper, a namesake of mine had passed his exam for the Army. And there, in black in white, was my own name!

To my astonishment I found that I had passed, and not only passed but that I was very near the top of the list.

This would have been an abrupt wake-up call for Stephe, for while he was happily surprised to have done something that would finally please his dear mama, all he wanted was to stay a boy and to carry on having lots of fun and adventures.

In essence, he wasn't keen on the idea of growing up and this aversion to being an adult remained with him throughout his life, so much so that he often referred to himself as a 'boy-man', and has been labelled as having a 'Peter Pan complex'. Even his quite startling achievement in the army entrance exams did nothing to diminish these boyish dreams and he stubbornly displayed not the slightest interest in becoming a soldier.

Naturally, Henrietta Grace disregarded all of his wishes and demanded that he sign-up immediately; as it was ingrained in him, and so many boys of that era, to do whatever his mother told him to, there was no way out. Unwilling, or possibly afraid, to defy this overbearing matriarch who had loomed so large over almost every aspect of his childhood, he bent to her will and resigned himself to the fact that she would now be in control of his adult life, too.

Henrietta Grace had always been opinionated and strong-willed, but by this stage she had evolved into the sort of formidable character only the very brave would dare to stand up to.

He was accustomed to watching her control every aspect of the family's life, even to the extent of poisoning her older sons' minds to the idea of marriage in order to keep them at home, therefore safeguarding their finances by continuing to insist that they donate most of their earnings to the Bank of Baden-Powell. By this time, the older sons were all in their late twenties.

She had no intention of sacrificing her increasingly lavish lifestyle on the wedding altar of love by allowing hard-earned cash reserves to be frittered away on any high-maintenance, flibbertigibbet of a wife. Even as adults, as Stephe was now rapidly finding out, her main objective for her children was that, in her own words, 'They should be pleased to do my will.'

In an insightful summing-up of her character in Channel 4's 1995 documentary *Secret Lives*, her great grandson, Robert Baden-Powell, 3rd Baron of Gilwell, said:

She was a martinet. She was a very commanding woman. If one sees pictures of her, she is red-haired, she's big, she's buxom and she was determined that her children would be very great within the British Empire.

Financially, she managed them as any businessman would manage the business. And at the start of their careers, they actually used to sit around the dining-room table and virtually put money into a central kitty … and she would extract hers and then dole out the pocket money.

As extreme as this seems, Stephe's own quote on the importance of mothers (read as Henrietta) at the beginning of this chapter is remarkably astute, for there is no doubt that without her insistence that he join the army, despite his deep and obvious reluctance, he'd unlikely have become the renowned figure he is today. Without her bulldozing him into a life militant, he would almost certainly not have gone to India where he met the best friend he would ever have, nor subsequently to Africa and, therefore, to Matabele (now Rhodesia) and Mafeking, with all the glory and controversy those places bestowed upon him.

It was, after all, his ability to hold the Boers at bay during the siege of Mafeking while vastly outnumbered and with a largely inexperienced army, that made Stephe an international hero (current opinions notwithstanding) at the dawn of the 1900s and the peak of imperialistic fervour.

Additionally, it could be argued that without the sheer depth of experience he gained in active army service around the colonies, he couldn't have acquired the depths of skill and expertise, the expedient connections, the opportunities and the sheer chutzpah to invent the Scouting movement, let alone turn it into one of the most successful outdoor philosophies the world has ever known. So, an army life it was and in 1876, with an obedient but heavy heart, he obeyed his mother's wishes and joined the Household Cavalry as a Sub Lieutenant in the 13th Hussars Regiment.

Throughout his teenage Charterhouse years, Stephe became so used to downplaying his natural intelligence and snoozing through his learning that he continued to do so into adulthood. The truth is, while he clearly lacked much enthusiasm for studying, he had a natural, irrepressible cleverness and in his pre-indolent years he actually won first prize in French and did consistently well in classical studies. Nevertheless, he frequently insisted that much of his success was down to good luck (at times in the form of mother, one suspects) and being in the right place at the right time.

Proof of this 'luck', above and beyond his bagging the gown-boy scholarship and those military tests results, was when, by dint of being at the top end of the test tables, he completely bypassed the customary two years of training and instruction required at Sandhurst and went straight to being an officer. He was just 19 years of age:

> by some strange luck the first six [candidates] were excused … and were at once gazetted to regiments. I had my commission in September and was in India, a full-blown officer of the 13th Hussars, in November.

With orders from Henrietta Grace to write home every week and to include sketches, Stephe sailed to India aboard HMS *Serapis*, one of a fleet of troopships that transported thousands of men to the subcontinent, where among the chief enemies they'd face were typhoid and cholera, making it one of the Empire's most hazardous places in which to be stationed.

His first posting was at Lucknow and when he disembarked at Bombay (now Mumbai), he immediately disliked everything about India. The oppressive heat and cacophony of noise would have been a complete culture shock to the pale, freckled, redhead; he found it intolerably stifling and the clearly evident levels of disease alarming. From the start he was unhappy and thoroughly homesick, although in *Indian Memories*, clearly wishing to live up to his hero status and come across as having been more adaptable to the situation than he really was at the time, he wrote:

> I can remember to this day the smell of India which assailed our nostrils before we had set foot ashore at the Apollo Bunder [Mumbai's former pier at the five-star Taj Hotel where the Gateway to India now stands].
>
> I can well remember the bother which my companion and I had in getting our baggage safely ashore, loaded on to a bullock-wagon and conveyed from the docks to the hotel.
>
> We had donned our best uniforms and were not a little proud of ourselves in the early parts of the day; but as hour followed hour in that soggy heat we seemed to melt into the thick tight-bound cloth.
>
> On reaching Lucknow he thought it even worse than Mumbai, describing it to his mother as having 'no regular town, except when you come on a bazaar, and that is an arrangement of mud hovels.'

It is in these letters home where the first evidence of Stephe's casually-racist language appears and, since racism is one of the accusations being levelled at him now and was part of the narrative around the Poole Quay statue incident, this aspect of his character must be considered as we continue on this journey, using facts and context where possible.

If one takes his remarks (which would have been in common use by the majority of his fellow officers at the time) at face value, such as when he is derogatory towards Indian people and uses the word 'nigger', then yes, they are unquestionably racist. While this language is abhorrent today, it wasn't the case then; among white officers of the Raj, at least.

Neither era nor generational 'norms' are an excuse; they are, however, a fact. British author L.P. Hartley's novel, *The Go-Between* opens with the thought-provoking line: 'The past is a foreign country; they do things differently there.'

It is impossible for the current generation to comprehend some of the machinations of previous ones. Therefore, although these attitudes are inexcusable and to be condemned, they remain an unpalatable reality. This was the 1870s, when racial respect and equality were rarely considered.

British imperialism was raging over entire continents, acquiring and controlling whatever it could lay its hands on, before the likes of Russia could, in the name of the greater good of queen and country, and the upper-class, colonial mindset of superiority and privilege, especially within the hierarchy of the military, was at an all-time high. At the start of his tour of duty, apart from his initial dismay at being in such a strange and inhospitable land, Stephe was of the idealistic opinion that all India really needed was a phase of modernisation to bring about great improvements in the quality of its infrastructure and the lives of its people. This forward-looking, pioneering zeal quickly sank under the entrenched views of most of his hardened fellow officers that the country was probably best left alone, based on the knowledge that the survival of the British Raj was wholly dependent on them regarding themselves as, or being regarded to be, superior, if it were to have any hope of enduring.

Stephe may have been in India (and later Afghanistan and Africa) and suffering a variety of genuine hardships, including being bullied by older officers, loneliness, and a string of illnesses resulting in constant diarrhoea and fevers that laid him low for long stretches at a time, but in truth, for much of the time, he existed in a bubble of blind entitlement.

As a self-absorbed now 20-year-old, keen to fit in, he wouldn't have considered for a moment that what he was saying was either malicious or offensive. It was the sort of language used by everyone around him and which had become firmly embedded long before he arrived on the scene.

Considering his later life choices, one wonders whether Stephe would have had a different outlook had he been born in a later era, or into a different class. Or avoided a military career altogether.

I ask Gillian Clay, Baden-Powell's granddaughter, who at 84 years of age is still an ambassador for international Scouting, for her take on Baden-Powell's prejudices.

It is easy to look back and find fault with previous generations, and ourselves. And no doubt this generation will be criticised in the future.

We can't really judge previous generations against ours. Human beings go on learning, sometimes for worse, but mostly for better. So, with exceptions, I think that, thank goodness, we now live in a much kinder and more caring society than in my youth, let alone my Grandfather's!

He did change his point of view, or at least attempt to make amends, but it wasn't until he grew older and presumably wiser. When first publicly introducing the Scouts, he declared it 'a new movement for global peace and friendship'. It was to be an organisation that would promote 'health, happiness and helpfulness', and welcome all young people of the world, irrespective of colour, creed or class.

He then proceeded to practice what he preached with gusto throughout his remaining days.

Well, almost. Accusations of anti-Semitism also cast dark clouds over his legacy and we will look at this later.

For now, regarding the Indian and black African peoples whom he had scorned, he appears to have experienced an awakening where he not only came to realise how much he loved their vibrant, messy and diverse countries (so much so, that he lived out his last days in Africa and referred to it as 'home'), but finally came to respect and admire their indigenous people and their unique, informed cultures.

The revelation came late because it came not in his first life, but in his second. He explained: 'I have had the rather unique experience of having in my time lived a double life.'

If there's one thing Stephe always acknowledged and had an uncharacteristically singular opinion on, it was the double-sidedness of every aspect of his life. Referring to what he called 'Life One' in his book, *Lessons from the Varsity of Life 1933*, he said:

There was … the romance of seeing strange lands at my country's expense, [all hail, Henrietta Grace, another major saving for the family kitty] through serving successively in India, Afghanistan, South Africa, West Africa and Egypt.

There was the campaigning, the sport, the comradeships; there were hardships and sickness and partings, the shadows of which enabled one the better to appreciate the sunshine.

Then I started my life Number Two, beginning an altogether new life, one on an entirely different plain, but like Number One, it includes Scouting.

I married her who was to be my right hand in bringing up, not only our own children, but the vast family of Boy Scouts and Girl Guides which then came into being.

We have enjoyed the extraordinary experience of seeing this movement grow from the tiny acorn of twenty boys encamped on Brownsea Island [in Poole Harbour, now watched over by his controversial bronze statue] into a Brotherhood and Sisterhood which embraces almost every country of the world.

Returning to the late nineteenth century and his inflammatory correspondence, we also find him complaining to Henrietta in the aforementioned dismissive manner of one who is clearly a stranger to racial, religious or ethnic empathy, let alone has any appreciation of them, about how the servitude of the 'locals' discomforts him: 'every native, as he passes, gives a salute. If he has an umbrella up, he takes it down, if he is riding a horse, he gets off.'

Too self-absorbed or naïve, or both, he didn't grasp that this servility was based on intelligence and experience and was a means to an end, that of survival, because being employed by monied Europeans when food was in very short supply, meant the difference between being able to feed one's family or not. Conversely, he also cheerily informed his mother: 'I like my native servants.'

It's during this early, initially gloomy phase in his military career that the complexity and deeply conflicting aspects of his character come most glaringly to the fore. The fondness for his servants clashing with his dismissiveness towards others. His deep affinity with horses and love of dogs, alongside the lust for hunting down almost anything else with a pulse.

Then there was his relationship with his regiment. On paper his adventurous spirit, his self-sufficiency, his superb fitness and his scouting talents alone should have made him an excellent fit for army life on the subcontinent. Add to this his tolerance of strict discipline, his riding and shooting expertise and his enthusiasm for all things outdoors and he would seem to have had all the attributes of a natural soldier.

However, these qualities only reflected one half of his dual personality; his alter-ego, the impulsive art-lover, the actor, the snobbish aesthete and possessor of a not inconsiderable maverick streak, meant that he was constantly at odds with his feelings.

Being in a cavalry regiment, he could indulge in his equine obsession, regularly riding and playing polo. He enjoyed the more machismo elements such as the weaponry, the sport and the male camaraderie (his preference for male companionship was by then a given) however, he found the repetitive drilling, endless rules and general day-to-day routines of army life so humdrum they jarred with the more whimsical and exuberant parts of his nature. The latter, which once witnessed, was impossible to forget.

Now feeling acutely melancholic and also unwell much of the time, the letters home to his mother, which he obediently accompanied with the requested sketches, reflected this and were littered with more and more complaints and pleas to return home. There wasn't a chance of that happening though, so with no alternative but to maintain a stiff upper lip, he needed to find ways of making his unbearable soldier's life work. Being conscientious of course, he continued to take his role seriously and excelled at most undertakings, impressing his leaders with the depth of his practical expertise and by generally just being rather brilliant at everything. He passed the Garrison Course for Lieutenant, 1st Class, with, unsurprisingly, an 'extra' certificate for reconnaissance.

No doubt tapping into his early Charterhouse experience, he decided the best course of action, if he were ever to 'belong', would be to work out who the real movers and shakers were and which chaps were the most fun to be around and then simply charm them into liking him. He even found channels for two of his main interests. The prolific and accomplished drawings of aspects of life at Lucknow (examples of which survive today and offer a fascinating insight into his time there) not only placated mother, but created a personal record of his experiences and offered an outlet for his artistic talents.

Acting, his other love, would, much to his surprise, also be accommodated. One of the reasons Stephe had been so happy at Charterhouse was because his headmaster, Dr Haig-Brown, actively encouraged his boys to act and to take part in plays. This wasn't based on any desire to see his pupils take to the stage as grown-ups, but because he knew that the skills acting could instil in them – an ability to memorise speeches, to be confident in a crowd, and to gauge the response of said crowd – would be of great value to them in later life.

Play-acting is very good fun – and besides speaking clearly, the great step to success is to play your part as naturally as you possibly can, just as if you were not in front of a lot of other people but actually doing the things that you are pretending to do. (B-P, *Lessons from the Varsity of Life* 1933)

With many army bases located in places too inaccessible for theatrical companies to visit, 'in-house' entertainment was very much encouraged, however it tended to veer between short on the ground or painfully amateur. This left the men desperate for any sort of amusement or stimulation that would relieve the monotony of everyday soldiering. With little choice but to create their own diversions, anything offering even the slightest whiff of light relief was welcomed with open arms. Enter Stephe, stage right.

On joining the regiment one of the first questions asked by the Adjutant was: Can you act, or sing, or scene paint?

This struck me as curious and incongruous. I thought that he'd only care for my ability to drill, to ride, or to shoot

Later on, I realised the meaning ... [and] I began as scene-painter in our regimental theatre. (*Indian Memories* 1915)

So adept was he at creating scenery that word quickly spread and he was invited to a neighbouring garrison at Simla to work his brush magic there.

Disarmingly honest about the situation, he admitted that he was less in demand for his artistic talent than he was for his fast work rate, an important consideration when staging several productions a month. In what would become his trademark jocular take on life, he wrote: 'It was not on account of my excellence as a painter, but on account of the rapidity with which I was able to work ... owing to my ambidexterity.

It was easy for me to slam away with a paintbrush in each hand ... In this way, I did the work at double the pace of the ordinary painter; the quality may not have been good but the quantity was all there.

I even went so far on occasion to strap a brush onto each foot, and sitting on crossbar between two ladders I managed to paint a woodland scene in record time with four brushes going at once! (*Indian Memories*)

Eccentricity was Stephe's middle name.

While his regular outbursts of demonic energy and limelight hogging had already singled him out as a bit of an odd fish, a tad effete and slightly left field in everyday scenarios, it never bothered him in the least and when he finally got to play to the gallery, the men couldn't get enough of him and roared their approval.

He was a natural comic with great timing, an air of mischief, at times menace and endless reserves of pent-up energy, which was exactly what his literally captive audience craved.

Now he'd also found an outlet for his acting, and boy did he make the most of it. By gleefully slapping on stage make-up and dressing up in all kinds of wild and wonderful costumes – mainly female outfits, often those he had made himself – to perform in the company's regular shows, in no time at all he was officially the campest and most popular member of the regiment's entertainment troupe.

His, and everyone else's, favourite performances were his full-on, showy turns as the leading 'lady' in the company's light opera productions. Little Agnes' skirt dancing routine – basically now evolved into full drag – was brought into play on many an occasion to great hilarity.

Here we see further evidence of his split-personality because despite relishing every second of being in the spotlight, socially he remained reserved, aloof and distant, very much an introspective loner so that by the end of his first posting, finally heading home on extended sick leave in 1879, he hadn't made any close friends at all.

As it was customary for a ball to be held at the general's home after regimental performances, Stephe was a regular guest and he attended one just before he returned home to England to recuperate. While trying to ask an Indian waiter for iced drinks, a short, 'soldierly' man took over and gave the order in Hindustani. 'Young fellow, you will make your life happier here if you learn a bit of the language,' the man told him then asked, 'Who are you and where are you staying?' Stephe told him, thanked him, and carried on with his evening.

The following day, he received a small note with the name of a local teacher of Hindustani; it was signed 'F.S. Roberts.' The man turned out to be Sir Frederick Sleigh Roberts, who Stephe would come to know well in the future as their paths crossed again.

Back in England on sick leave, being Stephe, recuperation wasn't enough and when he returned to India the following year, he had a string of amateur dramatics performances and an impressive 1st Class with 'extra' certificate pass from Hythe's Musketry Course under his belt. He rejoined his 13th Hussars regiment in anywhere but his happy place – the dreaded Lucknow.

However, this time things were a little more hopeful. He got on well with his men, having previously fretted over whether he was a convincing leader. Unlike other British officers of the time, who only deigned to speak to their men to bark orders at them, he socialised with his, acted alongside them, had them to his house to give them advice and joined in their sports and gymnastics activities, all of which was completely unheard of at the time.

Better still, his showmanship was still in great demand and his early childhood escapades, the land-mapping, the tracking and the reading of 'sign', his term for clues to activity in an area, all of which Henrietta Grace had disapproved, were finally to be put to good use.

Having had the luxury of time to think his situation through properly while on leave, he managed to redefine his previously uninspiring role by focusing on his interests and strengths, namely his inherent talents for fact finding and problem solving, teamed with his now finely tuned scouting skills. Focusing firmly on surveillance and reconnaissance worked to his advantage, as both were niche skills which were becoming increasingly valuable to the army. Somehow, while away in England, he'd devised a unique role for himself to come back to – that of expert scout. Now he could escape to explore the uncharted areas around the station in Lucknow with impunity, relatively unshackled by the rules, regulations and strictures of regimental responsibility while honing his already considerable tracking nous as he went.

It was an immensely enjoyable learning exercise for him. He was doing what he loved and could use it to 'sell' his notion that soldiers performed far more efficiently and were more prepared for all eventualities when armed not just with guns, but with outstanding scouting techniques. He believed, in fact he knew for certain, that the skills he could teach them would be every bit as important as any other weapon in the army's arsenal and was intent on proving it.

All the time he was busy, recording and sharing significant information about the hitherto unknown territory surrounding them and he would impart his findings, tips and ideas not just to his own men but to other commanding officers, who could subsequently share it with theirs. In essence, he was a one-man reformer of the art of soldiering. And he was writing a book about it, too.

This was a huge improvement to Stephe's previous situation and he was feeling happier with his lot. When, shortly after settling back in 1880, he was informed he would be going to Afghanistan, specifically to Kandahar, he was beyond thrilled.

He would have been well aware that the region was considered one of, if not *the*, most dangerous and inhospitable of all war zones at the time; a brutal place of death and desolation, so his delight at the prospect was such a typically contrary Stephe reaction.

While others would have found this command daunting in view of the perilously volatile state Kandahar was in then, to him it represented freedom from dreary Lucknow as well as the possibility of finally seeing some real action, something he'd been itching to get his teeth into for some time.

Here, at last, was the adventure he'd dreamed of and in turn one that could earn him a promotion which would mean a higher salary. An officer's lifestyle was expensive to maintain, even in India where it was significantly cheaper than if he'd been stationed in England, and he was tired of permanently penny-pinching. Although his insistence on using the finest tailors and buying the very best British-made boots didn't help matters.

From the British Army's standpoint, the Kandahar situation was a particularly precarious one and a fair snapshot of how the so-called 'Great Game', the power struggle between the British and Russian empires, was progressing. The Second Afghan War was a crucial part of this power struggle, with strategies that saw both sides involved in a series of political and diplomatic wrangles; the object of the 'game' was to bag the ultimate prize: to have complete power over Afghanistan and swathes of its neighbouring Central and South Asian territories.

After several battles culminating in 1879 – the latter few of which the British had won, but not without cost – Major General Sir Frederick Roberts (who had advised Stephe to learn Hindustani) rounded the year off with a further attack in December. His British and Punjab force defeated an army of Afghan tribesmen in the Chardeh Valley in the fiercely fought Battle of Kabul.

In April 1880, fighting was back on the agenda when Lieutenant General Sir Donald Stewart marched towards Kabul with a division made up of Bengal and British regiments. Once there, he defeated more Afghan forces in what came to be called the Battle of Ahmed Khel.

It was a narrowly won victory for Stewart and his men, nevertheless it was a crucial one as they then went on to take Kabul. They 'retired' the existing emir, Yaqub Khan, and selected Abdur Rahman Khan as his replacement, handing him the job on the proviso that he remained an ally and allowed the British to have their way on certain geopolitical objectives, mainly of the sort that would provide obstacles to the progress of the Russians. In the July of that year, Ayub Khan, younger brother of the now vanquished Yaqub was having none of this and promptly set about raising his own army and began to march towards Kandahar to reclaim Kabul for himself.

On 26 July 1880, under the command of British Brigadier General George Burrows, a 2,500-strong force of more British and Indian troops (350 of them cavalry) was marching away from Kandahar when Burrows received solid intelligence that Ayub's army was heading there, but was close to nearby Maiwand. Burrows decided they would take him by surprise and meet him head-on with the intention of scuppering his plans. In what proved to be a critical misjudgement, he also decided they should rest first and head out in the early hours of the following day.

Had he moved immediately on hearing the news, there was a chance they'd have reached Maiwand ahead of Ayub, but being late to this particular party, when Ayub's force was a mighty mix of various regiments and Afghan tribesmen, most of whom knew the terrain like the backs of their hands and that amounted to 12,000 men, including a 3,000-strong born-in-the-saddle cavalry, was not a good move.

Approaching Maiwand, they saw the Afghans already marching towards its front in a huge dust cloud kicked up from its semi-desert location. Burrows, failing to consider the effect of the conditions, remained confident they could still get there before Ayub and urged his clearly outnumbered men forward. When they finally encountered Ayub and his men, all of whom were hellbent on avenging the defeat at Ahmed Khel, they faced unexpected ravines and a vast, exposed and dusty plain; as well as being woefully undermanned, they became immediately bogged-down in the swirling sandstorm.

Worse, a sudden and nigh-on impenetrable mist descended, leaving them utterly disorientated and, obviously, extremely vulnerable. There was no choice; the battle had to be fought 'blind' on the parched, open plain in blistering heat. Many of the British troops had nothing to eat that day and the Afghan cavalry, managing to get in front of the fighting line, cut off all supplies of equipment, water and any hope of casualties being rescued. In addition to the brutal landscape, the British were armed with entirely inappropriate, cumbersome and antiquated weaponry for which they had insufficient ammunition; they had both a literal and metaphorical mountain to climb. It was an utter disaster.

The Afghan fighters, accustomed to the atrocious conditions, surrounded the British in a horseshoe formation. Despite some desperate and truly heroic efforts by the British in the face of the inevitable, including a last stand by two officers and nine soldiers (subsequently known as the 'Last Eleven') who, finding themselves backed up against a mud wall, fought to the death using their last dregs of both fire-power and willpower until they were trounced.

It was an enormous loss; in fact it was the biggest defeat for the Anglo-Indian army in the Second Anglo-Afghan war. Of Burrows' men, 948 soldiers and 21 officers lay dead and another 177 were either wounded or missing. Ayub Khan, despite estimated casualties of 3,000, reflecting the desperate nature of the fighting, was buoyed-up by the decisive victory and carried on as intended, laying siege to Kandahar. However, in spite of their awful pounding at Maiwand, the British and Indian garrison somehow managed to hold him off until Roberts stepped into the fray once more, arriving with a fresh force and saving the day in the Battle of Baba Wali, the final fight of the war and one which the British won, occasioning Roberts to be showered in glory and hailed 'Lord Roberts of Kandahar'.

Not so Burrows, though. Reeling from the disaster at Maiwand, he and the surviving officers who were involved in the awful defeat had questions to answer; this was where Baden-Powell came in. His mission, on the back of his growing reputation for being the best tracker bar none, was to visit Maiwand's battlefield locations, analyse the aftermath, study the lie of the land, make conclusions and draw a series of detailed maps that could be used as evidence in the court-martial.

His journey from Lucknow to the Kandahar base was in the company of a vet, a subaltern and a couple of doctors and was in itself a gruelling experience. They travelled first by train to Sibi and then had a six-day march to Quetta, located close to the Pakistan–Afghan border and the main road across to Kandahar, where they had a brief rest and picked up an escort as the final leg of the trek, a twelve-day march to Kandahar, was highly dangerous and small groups were forbidden to travel any further without armed protection.

This last endeavour entailed walking in sweltering heat during the day and camping in plummeting temperatures overnight. Baden-Powell, ever prepared and a hardened camper, embraced the traditional garb of the

Afghans – wearing a thick woollen gilet with a long, padded coat – and thoroughly enjoyed sleeping fitfully under the stars. He was less enthusiastic when part of the journey involved walking through a long track running between a hill range so treacherously steep that people and animals frequently perished while attempting to climb it.

As well as the precipitous mountain slopes being covered with dead creatures in various stages of decay, the track they had to walk along was also piled high on either side with an accumulation of rotting corpses of camels, elephants, horses and even men that had slid down the sides. It was a truly gruesome 'hedgerow' and the stench was unbearable.

George Noble, a friend of Baden-Powell's who'd previously taken the same route, described how every form of carrion-eating bird seemed to have gathered around the carnage and how injured beasts were being eaten alive. He likened the scene to Dante's Inferno.

On the other hand, in his inimitable joshing style, Baden-Powell played the whole thing down, telling his mother that the consequence of the sloping track was 'dead camels on either side of the road all along and a splendid aroma'.

When he finally arrived in Kandahar he immediately realised why the place had such a terrible reputation. One of the first things he noticed was that the officers were armed all the time, walking around with deadly hog spears as well as their revolvers because they were in a permanent state of high alert from fear of being murdered by zealous Ghazis who equated martyrdom, (preferably by hanging, for killing a Brit) with heavenly rewards.

Even the simple task of fetching water from a stream next to the barracks had to be carried out with drawn bayonet in hand. According to Baden-Powell, they were 'fanatics who were only too anxious to stick their knives into a European'. Vicious floggings and other harsh punishments regularly took place right outside the main gate of the British Kandahar base. The local gallows were there too, and various people were hanged on an almost daily basis. This relentless stream of corporal punishments and executions triggered a macabre and lasting fascination in Stephe. Hangings were carried out in a spectacularly haphazard fashion. Sometimes the shoddily built gallows would just collapse, leaving the unfortunate, soon-to-be-dispatched souls (plural, for there were often multiple ropes) in the ghastly position of having to endure a prolonged and agonising wait as the platform was hurriedly reassembled or, worse, be forced to help rebuild the thing before dying on it.

One zealot, wishing to go to his maker by this unreliable method, murdered a sentry at the gate, sauntered into the army guard room, tossed his bloodied knife on to the table and demanded to be hanged immediately. Presumably, deduced the stunned personnel, in view of his earthly work now being done and a keenness to reach heaven as soon as possible to claim his rewards. Nuance and understanding did not come as standard in the hellish environment that was Kandahar, and while modern-day methods and technology may differ, in terms of motivation, the assailant in this incident carries hallmarks of today's 'suicide bombers'.

Even in the midst of this death-trap of a place, as far as Baden-Powell was concerned, the show had to go on so, unbelievably, he and whichever men from the 13th Hussars were there, staged a production of the *Pirates of Penzance*, armed with loaded revolvers and with their swords stuck in the sand to mark the 'footlights'.

When the time came to journey to Maiwand, he was accompanied by Colonel Oliver Beauchamp Coventry St John, the Chief Political Officer who had fought in the infamous battle. St John had managed to escape with his Afghan orderly, but on finding his dog had gone missing, he encouraged the orderly to re-enter the battle to find him, which he did. The 'happy ending' quality of this anecdote somewhat belies what lay ahead of them.

Reaching the battle site at Maiwand, they were met with a tableau of grotesquely preserved horror. In and around the edges of the battlefield, everything was as it had been left after the battle in which more than a thousand men had died. Fallen soldiers who had been speedily buried had been dug up by scavenging dogs and jackals, leaving partially devoured, decaying bodies and horses littering the landscape. At the location of the desperate, final fight by the band of British soldiers known as the 'Last Eleven' referred to earlier, who'd found themselves literally up against the wall and were shot, Baden-Powell noted how the wall had been pushed over on top of them, it having been decided that it was the quickest way to bury them.

Despite the endless grim sights and, of course, smells (he was unable to eat meat for a long time afterwards), being a Baden-Powell, as always, he did his duty and got down to the serious job of assessing what was now basically an open mass grave.

Along with his own instinctive feel for scouting and reading 'sign' he had also picked up a great deal of knowledge from the tough Afghan fighters. He admired their superb tracking skills, their ability to move without a sound and their courageous fighting style and he factored these into his careful deductions. Baden-Powell's talent for interpreting circumstances from clues that others simply wouldn't spot now came fully into play. Crawling around on his hands and knees, he methodically noted crucial indicators as to what had transpired on the fateful day of the battle.

Meticulously, he recorded particular characteristics of the site and the geographical difficulties that it would have posed to the unprepared men. He analysed the directions of footsteps, deducing how and where the opposing sides had moved in relation to one another to work out actions and reactions, and he studied the depth and routes of the guns' wheel tracks:

dead horses were lying about, mummified by the sun and dry air. There had been no rain at all and apparently very little wind.

Lines of empty cartridge cases showed where the heaviest fighting had taken place. (*Indian Memories*)

Although moved and dismayed, Baden-Powell would nevertheless have been in his element.

Sleuthing and reasoning, like some armed Sherlock Holmes (who, in the future, would be another of his heroes), he set about creating a comprehensive picture of what had gone on, personally and simply concluding the facts: that the British force had been far too small to cope; that reconnaissance had been totally inadequate, as had the quality and quantity of firepower.

This expedition was a defining moment in his life. Scrabbling about in the dirt, dust and bloodstained sand of Maiwand for clues, his fascination with tracking was consolidated and what had been a childhood hobby became a lifelong obsession that would ultimately form the basis of the Scouting movement.

He never did get to see any promotion-friendly fighting action in Afghanistan however, his successful mission to Maiwand was incredibly useful to him on a professional level. Not only did it bring him to the attention of St John, but of other highly influential military bigwigs, not least of which was General H.C. Wilkinson, Commander of the Cavalry at Kandahar and, most importantly, Sir Garnet Wolseley, Adjutant General to the Forces – the Holy Grail of British army connections, who took delivery of two of his Maiwand maps for use in the court martial.

The only person Baden-Powell actually shot was himself, by accident, just as the regiment was about to depart Kandahar and head back to Quetta. His friend George Noble was there: 'Baden-Powell managed in playing with a revolver to shoot himself in the leg.'

The bullet went down his calf and settled in his heel. Describing the event himself in article that he sent home to be published in the Charterhouse magazine *Greyfriar*, Baden-Powell, in typical fashion, dramatized the entire affair, blaming a servant for leaving his revolver loaded after borrowing it and therefore causing it to go off unexpectedly while he was out in the dark of night trying to catch a horse thief.

Rogue bullet still in situ, he had to travel in agony to their base at Quetta in a covered wagon over almost vertical hill formations; it was an absolutely torturous journey. Unsurprisingly, he made it back and was soon recuperating in his own private room – a tent in St John's garden. When the surgeon arrived to remove the bullet from his heel, he joked with him that it no longer hurt and that he could go away. Regardless of this humorous suggestion, the essential and delicate procedure, which he endured without anaesthetic, went ahead and he kept the offending bullet as a souvenir, referring to it as 'precious'.

At this time, enteric (typhoid) fever was running through Quetta with many of the regiment's men now seriously ill, more than half a dozen dead and cases still rising. Funerals had become so regular that the Death March was banned in a bid to prevent morale plummeting any further, especially for those in hospital, including George Noble, who no doubt wondered whether they'd be next. Noble survived, but many others weren't so lucky.

A love of camping and an obsession with the power of fresh air in preventing ill-health meant that Baden-Powell was more than happy to remain under canvas in St John's garden for the time being.

He recovered enough not only to parade, but to perform.

However, the true grace-saver, and the single most important occurrence that would end any lingering unhappiness or depression that he may still have been suffering, was a chance meeting with Kenneth McLaren, a dashing young 13th Hussar officer whom he nicknamed 'The Boy' on account of his childish good looks.

Straightaway the pair clicked and went on to form an incredibly strong (and in later years feverishly scrutinised) friendship that would endure for three decades.

Chapter 4

Mad About The Boy

'A clean young man in his prime of health and strength is the finest creature God has made in the world.'

Rovering to Success, Baden-Powell (1922)

Acting the fool or putting on a show had been Stephe's mechanisms for dealing with difficult situations since early childhood, which is why performing played such an important part throughout his life. Since winning his mother's approval had been difficult, at times downright exhausting, the applause and admiration of others, even strangers, was the next best thing. Adulation became his salvation, reassuring him that he really *was* worthwhile and likeable and successful and funny and all the other things that Henrietta Grace seemed to think he wasn't.

Still in Quetta during the fetid summer of 1880, and with enteric fever continuing to spread and deaths in camp remaining high, it was about to become more significant than ever. Fear of disease, his recent leg surgery and unresolved loneliness had left him in a melancholic mood but, with his men feeling equally despondent, duty came first as always and it was up to him to rescue the situation. Aside from prescribing plenty of fresh air (he was still sleeping outdoors), clean water and fastidious hygiene to his men, Stephe couldn't do much about the fever, so he turned to what he knew best and put on a show.

In fact, between August and September, he staged and starred in not just one but four theatrical productions. They were light-hearted musicals and dramas which, as well as giving him the opportunity to take to the stage again, would hopefully serve to cheer up his beleaguered regiment.

Two plays in particular, *The Area Belle* and *Rosebud of Stinging Nettle Farm*, would turn out to be the most significant productions he had ever done. Playing the female lead in both was a new actor, a handsome young officer that Stephe had been vaguely aware of but didn't know well. He'd first noticed him earlier that year at Lucknow in the company of a newly arrived doctor who was preparing, just as he had done, to travel to Kandahar.

At the time, judging the boy to be about 14, Stephe asked the doctor what he intended to do about his son while he was away, to which the surprised doctor replied: 'My son? This is not my son. This is an officer who has come to join the 13th!'

The 'boy' in question was Kenneth McLaren, not a teenager at all but a 20-year-old British army officer, fresh from his training at Sandhurst. Like Stephe, McLaren had taken the same trajectory of education then straight into the army, so had experienced the same rules and rigours of public-school life, but as a pupil at Harrow. Being only a few years younger than Stephe, it transpired that they had much in common, not least of which was a love of horses – and acting.

Come the summer, McLaren, or as Stephe now called him 'The Boy', due to his youthful appearance, was cast in the aforementioned plays, where it was universally agreed that he made a 'wonderfully good lady'.

In *The Area Bell* he played the toothsome 'Penelope', with Stephe playing opposite as her smitten admirer, 'Tosser'. In *Rosebud of Stinging Nettle Farm* he was 'Rose', the winsome only daughter of an adoring father, played by Stephe. Both shows went down a storm with the crowds and with the new pals, who loved every minute of it.

Stephe and McLaren's friendship was sealed and from then on, they spent all their free time together, mostly riding and hunting in the hills, followed by leisurely picnics at their favourite spots, including one they named 'The Pleasure Gardens', where they'd rest on blankets underneath the trees, read books or nap. Before long they were living in neighbouring huts and it wasn't unusual for Stephe to get back from work to find The Boy and his beloved dog, 'Beetle', making themselves at home, scoffing his biscuits or sound asleep on his bed.

Over the years there has been a great deal of speculation about Stephe's sexuality, whether this close bond with McLaren was more than just friendship, and whether it confirms that he was gay. This chapter, in which the pair first properly connect, seems as good a place as any to consider this, along with the paradoxical accusation that he was homophobic.

It is neither a forensic study – that's already been done – nor a judgmental one; it is an acknowledgement of an important aspect of his life that influenced it greatly.

Along with how the friendship developed in India, initially through their shared interests – not least of which was a voracious appetite for hunting – and then through having the freedom to share an unhindered, judgment-free life together, it will also consider how they remained close for many years, going on to fight in Africa together and later working on shared ventures when back in England, up to and beyond the birth of the Scouts.

While the chapter is mainly in a chronological order, there will be brief diversions into relevant future events. For now, though, let's head back to Quetta 1880, where the performances continued apace and Stephe's turn, in full drag as Ruth, the contralto in *The Pirates of Penzance*, was deemed a triumph.

His letters home became notably more upbeat and his previous, endless gripes were replaced by jolly accounts of his and The Boy's many adventures. It was an idyllic bubble of bucolic camaraderie, interlaced with the excitement of hunting trips; however, it was about to burst. Not long after they'd become close, McLaren's beloved mother died, leaving him absolutely beside himself with grief. Stephe too was deeply upset, though not about the deceased mother – he didn't know her – but about the depth of his friend's anguish. This can be seen in a passage from a letter he sent home explaining the situation:

> That poor little chap McLaren ... this morning I went into his room and found him on his bed crying, with a telegram, which he handed to me saying his mother had died yesterday.
>
> Poor little chap! I've been trying to comfort him as well as I can – but I break down more than he does almost – he's so awfully cut-up.

Being so young and so far from home, The Boy was inconsolable. Even so, Stephe, never one to give up, did all that he possibly could to comfort and support him in his state of grief. Finding himself floored by the situation too, and unable to bear his friend's despair, he also succumbed to tears on several occasions. This was unusual, because for years he'd been used to keeping his feelings tightly in check and holding people at a safe distance.

From the traumatising abandonments of his childhood, which despite his early protestations, he later forced himself to endure in silence to avoid further angering his mother – she once proudly wrote (clearly post-tantrum stage) 'Stephe never cries.' – to tolerating the school beatings that he both witnessed and received, nothing moved him.

As an adult, neither watching the hangings, murders and floggings at Kandahar, nor coming across the corpses of his fellow British soldiers being eaten on the battlefield at Maiwand, all highly emotive experiences, served to elicit much more of a reaction than the odd trademark Stephe wisecrack. It took this unexpected event, the ultimate agony of the loss of a mother combined with the subsequent suffering of his best friend, to finally release his deeply buried emotions and, just as importantly, his sense of empathy. Eventually, he got McLaren (and himself) back on track and as a result of the solicitude and tenderness he showed towards him, their bond grew even stronger.

They were now inseparable and when not soldiering, they'd be immersed in all the other manly pursuits considered de rigueur for colonial, Victorian gentlemen, including holding gymnastics events, playing polo and hunting. They were devoted to one another and for Stephe to at last find someone with whom he had so much in common and could open up to and be himself with, was life-changing. For the first time in his life, he'd found true, uncomplicated happiness. Stephe (now nicknamed 'Bloater') and McLaren took delight in exchanging gifts, such as personalised accessories and cologne, and when the regiment upped sticks and moved to nearby Muttra in the autumn of 1881, they set up home together in a spacious, nine-room bungalow, complete with stables to house their growing string of polo horses.

Despite considerable research, I couldn't find the reason behind the nickname, 'Bloater'. I knew of Bloater fish but ruled this out since Stephe, being largely teetotal, never drank like one. I asked biographer, Tim Jeal (*Baden-Powell*), who offered a plausible reason that did, indeed, involve fish:

> 140 years ago, fat herrings and mackerels were known as Bloaters. So, if you called someone an old Bloater, you probably meant in a facetious way that he was fat, lazy and ate too much. Baden-Powell worried all his life about always getting enough exercise, and remaining slim.
>
> Perhaps McLaren's nickname was an affectionate way of ribbing him about his fears of getting unfit and fat.

Bloater and The Boy were never happier than when surrounded by their steeds. The valuable ones they kept for riding, hunting and army life, the others were bought at a good price from local Indian dealers, trained and then sold on, ready for action, to newly arrived officers.

They named their home Bloater Park and lived in a state of perfect harmony that Stephe described as 'paradise'. Along with their horses, which would all follow Stephe around like shadows and come to him the minute he whistled, they had a menagerie of other pets to keep Beetle the terrier company, including three more dogs and a pig by the name of Algernon.

Stephe's constant complaints and requests for leave ceased entirely, and for the next three years he never once complained nor asked to escape into the hills, as had previously been the case, whenever he suffered fresh bouts of his recurring maladies of fever and diarrhoea. Having found contentment in the company of The Boy, whom he would still be calling his 'best friend in the world' twenty years later, he now decided that life in India was perfectly agreeable. Happiness, it seems, bred further happiness as it was during this period that Stephe caught the eye of his new commanding officer, Colonel Sir Baker Creed Russell, a strapping chap, well over 6ft tall, 'with the piercing eye of a hawk, a big, black moustache and a stentorian voice like a bull', who had already built a name for himself as a fighting man. In 1857, notably the year Stephe was born, Baker Russell was fighting the Indian mutiny and he'd also served under the all-important Garnet Wolseley in the Ashanti War of 1873–4.

He had spotted the young Baden-Powell's can-do approach to everything, but was specifically impressed with his reconnaissance skills, especially when he managed to track down a sergeant major's runaway horse and return it safely back to base after it had bolted during a thunderstorm.

Being a notably unorthodox commanding officer, whom fellow officers could be rather sniffy about, Baker Russell was delighted when Baden-Powell showed him a shortcut he'd discovered in the route from Quetta to Kandahar that would make future marches for the 13th Hussars considerably shorter and, later, make Baker Russell look superior to his aforementioned scoffing peers.

His maverick approach to army rules and regulations greatly appealed to Baden-Powell and, in turn, Baden-Powell's left field sense of humour and audacity appealed to Baker Russell.

At Charterhouse, sometimes his jokes had come across as awkward or too personal, but Baker Russell found it highly amusing when he disguised himself as an army bigwig in a borrowed uniform and with his moustache whitened, fooled his boss into believing he was high-ranking visitor come to surprise them with an unannounced inspection. Baker Russell was completely convinced until Baden-Powell leapt on to the stage and belted out the Major General's song from *The Pirates of Penzance*. The boss thought it hilarious and finally awarded him the promotion he had craved, making him Adjutant.

The longed-for upgrade wasn't exactly a triumph; being an adjutant involved long hours and vast amounts of laborious administrative work, but it was a promotion nevertheless and paid more money. Baden-Powell was known as the busiest officer in the 13th and was as happy as a sand-boy.

At Bloater Park, he and The Boy had become enthusiastic interior designers, creating their idea of the perfect home in the sweltering Quetta plain. Today, the place would likely be described as a perfect fusion of Indo-Bohemian colonial living, with a nod to classic Victorian gender fluidity. On the macho side, it was a paean to their sporting and hunting prowess, decorated with ranks of lovingly polished guns, gleaming polo mallets, hunting trophies and crossed hog spears.

In typical duality, the effect was softened with elegant upholstery and extravagant ferns, some large enough to be used as room partitions, thus allowing ventilation while maintaining privacy, and billowing muslin drapes.

Outside, a large area was designated for the growing of vegetables and there was a lovely flower garden. Even the stables, naturally one of the most important elements of Bloater Park, benefited from their decorative skills and, unlike anything ever seen before in the region, possibly in all of India, were beautifully painted inside. Complementing the brilliant white walls was a dado rail in a smart red and beige 'military' stripe running horizontally around the walls. This impressive stable and its superb equine stock was an 1880s' equivalent of today's toys for boys; instead of a fleet of expensive, flashy cars to play with, they had a string of magnificent ponies.

The Boy was dazzlingly brilliant at polo. Known as 'the little prince' (McLaren was certainly a magnet for nicknames) within the polo-playing fraternity, he was the best back in the entire army, leading the 13th Hussars to a hat-trick of victories at the Hurlingham Polo Championships and acknowledged as being as valuable as two men in any team. Baden-Powell, though an expert in the saddle and a solid team player, was aware that he was way out of McLaren's league and was content just to be immensely proud of his pal.

In *Lessons From the Varsity of Life*, Baden-Powell fondly recalls a speech made by Winston Churchill at a banquet in India that he was attending where the future prime minister spoke eloquently on the subject of polo, describing it, perhaps with more than a little hyperbole, as 'Not only the … finest and greatest game in the world but the most heroic and sporting adventure in the universe.'

Better still, as far as he was concerned, as well as Churchill waxing lyrical about his favourite sport, there also followed a prank:

At his peroration, we could restrain our enthusiasm no longer and greeted the [polo] statement with a round of cheering. After this, someone moved that 'this be enough of Winston,' and Winston was duly put under an inverted sofa, to be retained there for the rest of the evening while a hefty subaltern sat upon it.

But shortly he emerged from under one of the arms, with what might be taken as an historic phrase: 'It's no use sitting on me – I am India-rubber.'

So much into their polo were he and The Boy, that it's difficult to imagine they could possibly have had room for an even greater obsession – but, they did. Hunting.

So far, so stereotypical of their generation, but while big game animals may have been the target of choice for most officers, for this pair of adrenaline junkies the best hunting by far was pig-sticking or hog-hunting. This cruel and extremely dangerous chase between hunter and wild boar entailed a relentless, breakneck pursuit on horseback culminating in a ferocious finale, sometimes, though not always, with the huntsman on foot, armed with a wooden stick and extremely vulnerable; if all went to plan and neither horse nor rider was critically – or mortally – gored, the unfortunate pig was skewered with the lethally sharpened pole.

Wild boars being incredibly strong – and infinitely more so when hurt or cornered – meant it often took multiple spears to finally bring them down. If they retreated injured into the dense undergrowth, Baden-Powell and McLaren would dismount and charge straight in to the thick of it and fight the animal to the death, often stripped to the waist and wearing their shirts as turbans. They could kill up to four of the poor creatures in a day. Little surprise, then, that they needed to rest in the hills afterwards.

Rather than the gratuitous bloodlust and wanton cruelty we'd consider this to be today, pig-sticking was widely applauded by society. It was deemed to be the most extreme of all extreme sports due to the jeopardy involved; hunters and horses were regularly seriously hurt, and occasionally killed, not only due to the boar's strength nor its killer tusks, which could disembowel a pony with a slash, but more from accidental falls from speeding mounts.

So perilous was the killing of hogs, it was regarded as the ultimate proof of manliness, superiority and courage. Which is why Stephe and The Boy enjoyed it so much and, wishing to be seen as brave, romantic heroes of the Empire, joined pig-sticking groups, hunted with Indian princes and maharajas and competed professionally, winning yet more grizzly trophies to grace the walls of Bloater Park.

As guests at the Maharaja of Deeg's opulent palace for a hunting weekend, the pair were designated equally opulent accommodation. 'As we had one large, marble hall as our joint room, The Boy read a novel to me as we lay in bed till breakfast time.' A fine example of the sort of quite-possibly innocent sentence that courts rabid speculation.

In 1883, Baden-Powell won India's greatest prize for pig-sticking, the Kadir Cup and, ever prolific with a pen, later wrote a best-selling manual on the subject entitled: *Pig-Sticking or Hog-Hunting: a Complete Account for Sportsmen and Others*. That he never even contemplated the viciousness of the so-called sport and instead believed it to be both a means of self-improvement and an excellent method of military training, is clearly seen throughout the handbook:

> It teaches a man to ride by forcing him to exert to the utmost all his riding powers without any effort of mind; by making him anticipate the moves of the boar and regulate his own accordingly and to the best advantage of the ground; it teaches a man to use his wits and powers of observation, and gives him an eye for country; it trains him to decide in his course of action without a moment's hesitation; it gives him practice in the use of a weapon while moving at speed, in an encounter with a strong, infuriated boar, it teaches him self-reliance and to keep his head and his pluck in an emergency; in a word, it excels all other methods of training in essential qualifications of a successful soldier on active service.

With his taste for hunting now amplified, Baden-Powell openly relished the kill and the more brutal, the better. Here we need to pause once more, for we are now inescapably face-to-face with the basis of another accusation levelled at him, namely that he was a sadist, and in light of these gleefully excessive killing sprees, it's hard to argue with that.

In fact there is little dispute, as one letter he wrote to Henrietta Grace, in which he describes in great detail one of his many pig-sticking experiences, is now very much in the public domain.

It's a harrowing passage that clearly highlights the very different values of our times and, although it was written in an era when the hunting of animals was accepted, nay, wholeheartedly encouraged, even *he* appears to realise the exceptional callousness of his tale, as he forewarns Henrietta, albeit jokingly, that she may want to: 'close your eyes and cover your ears, mummy,' and then goes on to triumphantly describe how, in the course of the hunt, one of his sticks pierced a boar with such force that it went right through the unfortunate beast, coming out from its underbelly and impaling it to the ground.

Other big-game animals did come into his sights, including the hippo, which conversely was an animal that he was so enamoured of that he dreamed of having one as a pet. The trend for killing for pleasure can be ascribed to the entrenched behaviours of the period as well as the ignorance of any need for, nor inclination towards, wildlife preservation. These are undeniable factors; just look at any natural science archive and you'll find a raft of 'preserved' creatures bagged by trigger-happy Victorian 'adventurers'. Still, the sheer enthusiasm and the cold-bloodedness of it are indefensible.

Even more so was Baden-Powell's apparent appetite for cruelty towards the human species. Not doled out by him directly, he was only ever physically aggressive when hunting or in war situations, which so far had been few and far between, but rather in a purely voyeuristic capacity.

While always incredibly kind and solicitous towards others in his social groups, especially his siblings and the young children of fellow army officers, all of whom adored his funny, childlike ways, he is on record, including in personal letters to his mother, for having had an unhealthy fascination with the callousness of others towards their fellow men, though only those outside his immediate cohort; in other words, strangers and indigenous people.

During his early military years, particularly (and unsurprisingly) in Kandahar, then later in Africa, he is said to have actively sought out public corporal punishments and executions to watch. These episodes were always completely passive, but are a disturbing psychological facet of his personality nevertheless. He even kept records of the abominable scenes he'd witnessed through writings, sketches and photographs.

One image, drawn in the Matopo Hills during the Matabele Rebellion around 1896, depicts a man tethered to a tree and being flogged (sadly a regular sight at the time). Another, from the same year, is a copy of a photograph from Olive Schreiner's book Trooper Peter Halket of Mashonaland, (Roberts Brothers, Boston, 1897). It is a harrowing image that has appalled even the most fervent of Baden-Powell's admirers; it shows three dead black African men hanged from the branches of a tree in Bulawayo by white colonialists. According to Frederick Selous, a British explorer and hunter in Bulawayo at the time and author of Sunshine & Storm in Rhodesia (Rowland Ward & Co., 1896), they were three of a group of nine men hanged for allegedly spying and/or looting the homes of white settlers as they fled from attack. Accounts are sketchy, but Selous writes tellingly that they were 'tried in a somewhat rough-and-ready fashion'. The graphic content of the photograph, which was in Baden-Powell's scrapbook, is horrific enough, but the caption beneath it: 'The Christmas Tree' (the nickname given to it by the colonialists, not by Baden-Powell) is beyond the pale.

What compelled him to seek out such suffering? He'd certainly experienced and seen many examples of it first-hand, so was it satisfying for him to see something or someone else suffer for a change? Remember, he was living in an environment where extremely harsh punishment was pervasive – and not only in foreign regions; when he joined the 13th Hussars, the punitive and often merciless floggings of soldiers had only just been outlawed in the British Army itself. Did years of bottled-up rage towards the domineering Henrietta Grace play a part? Or his abiding memories of 'swishings' at Charterhouse, despite it otherwise being his happy place? Could the daily murders and death-threats of Afghanistan, and the awful fate of his countrymen at the hellish Battle of Maiwand, have left him not just traumatised, but immune – or even attracted – to pain and death?

Or a combination of all of the above?

Biographer, Tim Jeal, is of the firm opinion that Henrietta Grace was at the root of it: 'There must [have been] something very deep in his nature that was responsible for it. I'm pretty convinced that it was his very controlling mother who absolutely outlawed any kind of bad behaviour.'

Unlike his treatment of wild animals, when it came to his fellow man, Baden-Powell never acted upon these impulses to witness pain or suffering, nor did he allow them to take any physical form that may hurt another in any way; an expert at suppressing his feelings, it appears to have been a deeply personal addition to his store of mainly stifled emotions.

Apart, that is, from a later incident that we will come to in due course, and for which he was exonerated of blame at the time, but is widely seen today as a manifestation of his dark obsession.

Whether McLaren was aware of his friend's penchant for pain, or carried a similar lack of empathy towards human suffering, is a mystery. In fact, his opinions and thoughts on just about everything are largely unknown. Very few records of McLaren's life exist since, in later years, his personal belongings, including, presumably, his correspondence with Stephe, became thinly spread over two marriages and numerous house moves, before being mostly destroyed by both of his wives in turn. This wanton destruction of his past, much of his entire life even, has naturally resulted in further conjecture about his relationship with Baden-Powell.

Still, strong male friendships where unselfconscious displays of, if not love, then certainly a deep fondness were shown to one another, were considered normal in the late 1800s, especially in situations where there was a dearth of female company, for example within public schools and military organisations.

Their happy homemaking would have been pretty unremarkable and there would have been little, if any, judging of it; there be no question about it being anything other than two great friends of a similar disposition cheerfully lodging together. At the very most it would have been seen as a light 'bromance' in today's parlance, rather than an ardent and taboo love affair.

Baden-Powell's letters home were now almost irritatingly upbeat and dominated by tales of life with The Boy. The fact that he used McLaren's nickname in front of his friends and Henrietta Grace, who was now more than a little put out about her son's preoccupation with this man she'd never met, could either be construed as proof that he had nothing to hide (at a time when a homosexual act could result in a prison sentence, exile or even death, so simply had to be kept secret), and that their relationship was an un-gossip-worthy heterosexual one. Or, it could be seen as Baden-Powell's natural mischievousness and daring taking over in an almost goading manner that cryptically hinted at a deeper intimacy.

Henrietta Grace was irked that his blind devotion to her appeared to be shifting elsewhere and she regularly had little digs at McLaren in her correspondence. Once, when he'd told her that his chum had a funny laugh, 'like a railway whistle', she batted back at him with a snippy enquiry as to whether the sound of it was nuisance. Ignoring the lightly veiled barb, he cheerily replied in the negative, adding that his new puppy's sharp teeth were far worse. Do we detect maternal jealousy sneaking in here?

During this period, his mother was in the middle of one her most important and strategic contact-building campaigns yet, laying on entertainments at their home for important figures in a bid to further the progress of all of her sons in their various occupations and endeavours. Having pointedly failed to invite any of McLaren's perfectly acceptable brothers to any of these soirees, despite Baden-Powell's suggestion that she do so, he berated her in one of his weekly letters. She stopped writing for five weeks after that; it was their first ever outward fall-out.

Undeterred, and possibly emboldened by having his friend's loyalty and affection, his correspondence to his mother remained littered with stories of their activities, along with tales of camp fires under the night skies, hunting successes and the strong bonds being forged between men from all walks of life while 'roughing it' on training manoeuvres.

In the latter part of this sentence, he was referring to the practical training exercises he'd devised to propel his one-man crusade to impart his vast bank of reconnaissance and tracking knowledge to his men in a bid to improve their performances and, subsequently, their chances of staying alive.

Baden-Powell assessed their various strengths then fine-tuned them into invaluable tools that would give them an advantage over their adversaries. He was probably the only officer in the army thinking of his men as individuals in this way. It was revolutionary and it was also another example of his contrariness. On the one hand he wished to be seen as an exemplary officer, superior and distant enough from his men to ensure unquestioning obedience; on the other, he wanted to be their ally, even their friend, and for them to be led as individuals as opposed to the traditional mass of faceless troops.

So committed was he to his cause, he devised and presented a series of twenty lectures on subjects such as tracking, reading 'sign', camouflage and mapping, all based on his belief that 'success in modern warfare depends on accurate knowledge of the enemy.' Baden-Powell's mission was to make his men, in fact all British soldiers, as savvy as he was at spotting, interpreting and using the clues that surrounded them to gain insight into the intentions, habits and whereabouts of the enemy. To this end, he repurposed the lectures into an informative manual that was then distributed as a useful guide for troops on outpost duty.

It was an immediate hit with the officers and their men and began slowly engendering a new approach to soldiering. By the following year, 1883, it was so popular that, on some very shrewd advice from his brother George, to whom he had been complaining about being broke and lacking any real career prospects, he worked frantically to repurpose it again, this time into a book.

He had ambitions for it, but they were really more military than monetary. Acutely aware that an order had been issued for army instructors to teach reconnaissance to officers and their men, he had an idea. Even if the book didn't sell more than a few copies, it would be, he wrote home, 'a grand advertisement for me because I could send copies to all the boss quartermaster generals, Wolseleys, etc., asking if they approve of it.'

It was a bold and original work, eschewing the traditional stereotype of the obedient soldier and advocating individual thinking that could be channelled into more targeted, tactical situations.

Here was his regimental training method writ large, based on his experience of being in the company of his men and treating them as – almost – equals. Those exercises, where he'd take them into in the wilds to live under canvas and rely on one another for survival had paid off. He called it *Reconnaissance and Scouting*. It would become one of the most significant books he ever wrote.

Unaware of that at the time though, Baden-Powell fretted about even getting it published and called upon George for help once more: 'If you think the book can be published, I'll hatch out some more.' Finding a publisher wasn't a problem for the ever-resourceful George, and *Reconnaissance and Scouting* was released in all its glory in 1884 by William Clowes & Sons, Limited as a neat, bright red, linen-bound booklet, containing a dozen of his original map sketches.

The subject of the book was actually the driving force of Baden-Powell's life.

Camping and scouting had always been his favourite pastimes as a boy, and the halcyon summer days, spent with his brothers, sailing the family boat around the coast, where they'd disembark, find a good tent pitch, catch their dinner and cook it over a fire while spinning yarns under the stars, featured in many of his books. Not only had he managed to translate his hobby into a military text, he could relive those happy childhood times and, for a while, feel like the boy he wished he still were.

Later on, the civilian version, ergo the Scouts, would serve the same purpose; it would also change his life, and the lives of millions of people around the world in an extraordinary way. To Baden-Powell, camping represented living one's best life; it offered freedom, challenges, space, plenty of fresh air (with which he was now fixated, thanks to typhoid) and good old hard work. In his opinion, if it was easy, then it wasn't really camping at all.

It also helped that he was a superb handyman, generous with his know-how and never happier than when showing others how they too could be as ingenious and resourceful as he was.

Reminiscing to his mother about the holidays with his older siblings, he said: 'They were grand days,' then rather spoiled the moment by adding, 'But this [life in India or with The Boy?] is the real thing.'

So devoted were he and McLaren to one another and for so long, their partnership endured through much of their military and later, to a lesser degree, their civilian lives (even when they married) for nearly thirty years, which is why it is widely assumed the friendship was more than merely platonic and that it was, in fact, a fully-fledged same-sex relationship.

If that is the case, then its beginning would have been in India in the 1880s, less than twenty years since the abolition of the death penalty for sodomy and therefore a frightening, or at least extremely constrictive era, for same-sex couples. Strict laws on buggery remained, with fines and jail sentences doled out to anyone breaking them – unless they had enough money or the right contacts to allow them to flee into exile. Not only that, if found in a 'compromising situation', lives and reputations could be, and regularly were, ruined.

Secrecy was the norm and a Victorian proliferation of intense male-to-male and female-to-female friendships helped in that an almost passionate love of one's best friend was perfectly fine. In a nutshell, if you happened to be in a same-sex partnership, as long as there was nothing too overt about it, then on the whole society tended to turn a blind eye.

Still, rumours abound about Baden-Powell's sexual orientation. On paper, if one is to play to the stereotypes, unreliable and patronising as many of them are, then he fits the template. Playing with dolls; performing in drag (his famous skirt dancing) at every opportunity; no hint of a romantic, never mind intimate, relationship with a woman until at the age of 55 he abruptly and secretly married one in the shape of 23-year-old tomboy, Olave Soames (the 'girl Peter Pan' he'd been searching for); regularly admitting to preferring the company of men to women; describing men in flattering terms such as 'muscular', 'bronzed', 'strong' and 'fit', while referring to women in either bland or rude terms, like 'heavy', 'plainly pleasing', even 'heifers'; and, of course, living for years with The Boy, then it seems a given.

But then, having had such scant contact with the opposite sex, other than dusty dowagers and little girls (the latter with which he was comfortable and with whom there was never any suggestion of an unhealthy interest), he made few female friends and those he did, he tended to back away from once they looked likely to be seeking romance.

Add to this the fact that his main example of womanhood was the formidable Henrietta Grace and it's not surprising he was wary, if not actually terrified, of women. Or, as is widely accepted, he was simply a gay man either in denial or hiding. Or both.

And while Baden-Powell's sexual persuasion is of far less consequence today, fitting into the 'Who cares?' category as far as most people are concerned, the issue is that, despite his well-documented appreciation of the male form, preferably young, fit, clean – always clean – and stripped to the waist, he devoted so much time practically evangelising on the importance of boys remaining chaste and straight, avoiding thoughts of sins of the flesh or having a 'dirty' mind. Self-control, he told them, was all-empowering and his guilt-inducing exhortations that boys should avoid succumbing to sexual urges at a time when their hormones would be running wild, coupled with declarations that even thinking about sex (especially 'beastly' gay sex) was evil, as were relationships out of wedlock with the wrong sort of girl. All this, and with hindsight, means he is now seen as a hypocrite.

In the 'Continence' section (long since edited out) of early editions of his best-selling book, *Scouting for Boys*, subjects that were coyly phrased thus: 'It is called in our schools 'beastliness' and that is about the best name for it', now come across as sanctimonious and contrived, as well as detrimental to the understanding and normalising of gay people.

Masturbation, or 'self-abuse', also popped-up in the no-doubt well-thumbed Continence section, described as a 'most dangerous thing, for should it become a habit, it tends to destroy both health and spirits ... and often ends with [the] lunatic asylum.'

In case that wasn't enough to terrify boys into a permanent state of purity, there was also this dire warning:

> The use of your parts is not to play with when you are a boy, but to enable you to get children when you are grown up and married. But if you misuse them while young you will not be able to use them when you are a man: they will not work then.

Suggestions for fighting the temptation to take oneself in hand were to avoid looking at 'smutty' or 'dirty' books, and the slightly less obvious, to avoid indigestion or constipation.

Bathing ones nether regions in cold water immediately any of these dangerous urges arose and, bizarrely, boxing, were also both strongly recommended.

Though he agreed they were unavoidable, wet, or 'bad', dreams were 'another cause of trouble, which often come from sleeping in too warm a bed … or from sleeping on your back'. So many things to avoid, so much detail.

Most concerning was a sign-off piece of advice saying that should the symptoms persist, they must not be kept a secret and it might be a good idea for the Scout to talk it over with his scoutmaster. And there lies the root of the problem, from the protester's point of view. To be constantly maligning people for even thinking about sex, or having gay tendencies, while evidently pondering both these subjects a great deal and almost certainly having gay inclinations, albeit repressed ones, himself is not only cage-rattling, but is precisely the reason why the fascination continues even now and why some believe he was homophobic.

Basically, it all smacks a bit of the Chief Scout 'doth protest too much', and even a layman could spot signs of projection or sublimation, even if unfamiliar with the terms. It's the theory that someone who strongly criticises the actions or perceived wrongdoings of others is only being judgemental in order to assuage their own feelings of guilt, and that repressing urges considered unacceptable by society can transmute in to overzealous activity or behaviour in other fields of life…

So, gay *and* homophobic?

With hindsight today, this officious and, frankly, uncomfortable advice, some of which he created with the help and approval of Henrietta Grace (which is really unnerving), points to Stephe having an unhealthy interest in the sexual desires of boys. He is also on record for admiring the physiques of younger men and boys, in particular watching them as they swam naked (as was the norm then) in the communal pool at Gilwell Park, the Scouts' headquarters in Chingford, London.

For the sake of balance, as the Stephe side of him desperately longed to stay a boy forever (that 'Peter Pan' complex), the former advice could be seen as his misguided way of keeping boys away from girls for as long as possible in order to prolong the time they had to just be children, and the latter, simply him watching wistfully and wishing that he were as young and full of life as they were. There is no evidence whatsoever that this interest went beyond musing and observing. That said, it was musing and observing that led to his most flagrant, deeply uncomfortable and extensively reported display of impropriety regarding youngsters.

It occurred in 1919 when Baden-Powell was back in England having completed his military service and had already founded the Boy Scouts.

Now in the public domain, it is the singular and most inflammatory event used today to fuel the accusations of sexual deviancy surrounding his life. He visited Charterhouse school to see a former schoolmate, by then a master at the school, called Alexander Tod. While he was there, Tod showed him an album of photographs that he had taken, of a number of his pupils in various 'artistic' poses as part of a project recording life in the school. The problem was that the subjects were either semi- or completely nude.

In some of the images, the naked schoolboys posed in trees, akin to male versions of mythological Greek dryads; this was presumably in order to lend credence to why Tod was taking inappropriate photographs of children in his care in the first place. For the record again, there has never been any suggestion, evidence, nor accusations of anything physical taking place with any youths in connection with Baden-Powell.

However, and it's an enormous however, this overnight visit took place when he was married, had three children and was responsible for the safeguarding and wellbeing of thousands of boys. And yet, he clearly didn't consider Tod's photos objectionable nor, one presumes, express concern about the boys themselves. Quite the opposite in fact, he actually wrote the following entry in his diary: 'Stayed with Tod. Tod's photos of naked boys and trees. Excellent.'

Worse, in a subsequent note to his old Carthusian chum on the possibility of setting up a Scout group within Charterhouse, added: 'Possibly I might get a further look at those wonderful photographs of yours?' Tod had created an entire series of albums, comprising innocent and, in truth, fascinating images of life in a public school, for a pictorial record that today offers a rare insight into education of the time. Today the works are considered very important historical documents. Incredibly, the single album of abusive images was openly included in the project for many years afterwards and the entire collection was eventually donated to the school's library in 1923.

In fact, it wasn't until the 1960s that the nude album was deemed to be both offensive and dangerous (mainly to Tod's reputation presumably) and was consequently destroyed, 'out of deference to the feelings of the sons and grandsons of the boys depicted'.

* * *

Consultant psychiatrist, Sidney Crown, who appeared in a 1995 Channel 4 documentary on Baden-Powell, offered professional insight of the time:

There's no doubt at all in my mind that Baden Powell's basic sexual orientation was homosexual.

Or, if I put it in psychological terms, he was a suppressed or repressed homosexual. By that I mean he was of [that] orientation but he couldn't allow it in himself.

He liked watching male workers who were undressed.

To me, he was very homosexual in orientation I think but that doesn't mean he was in practice.

In fact, I think that there is no evidence that he was.

The irony, as previously mentioned, was that by lecturing boy scouts to avoid such proclivities, Baden-Powell came to be regarded as a rabid homophobe. According to Tim Jeal, the Boy Scout movement offered him 'scope for sublimation which Freud himself would have marvelled at'.

So, nowhere is there evidence that he acted upon his feelings in any physical or erotic way, and even when considering his relationship with McLaren, and his open admiration of strong, muscular men, Crown's opinion remained that his yearnings were from a distance and never a reality. And in true contradictory style, it appears that while he and McLaren were very happy together, so too were he and his wife Olave, who, although far younger than he, took great delight in teasing and mothering him and had three children, Peter, Heather and Betty, with him.

Jeal's is a thorough and fair analysis. Among the various experts he consulted was one who assessed the reason behind a series of excruciating headaches and disquieting dreams that Baden-Powell experienced almost immediately after marrying Olave. The headaches and dreams began when he took to the marital bed and persisted throughout the early years of the couple's marriage. They became so bad that he consulted a Harley Street doctor by the name of Jackson, who among other things, suggested that Baden-Powell should record the perturbing dreams.

When analysed, they revealed a mix of homoerotic longings and anxieties about his marriage being perceived as forced.

In one dream he was stressed because he'd forgotten that he was married and then had to prove that he was happy; in another he accidentally mistook their bedroom door for another that, when opened, revealed not Olave but a young man standing in shirt-sleeves having a shave. Others involved symbolic aspects, such as being embraced by a strange man with a 'lump' under his coat, and fending off a guardsman who grabbed at a whip that he held and asked him if he'd ever been disciplined.

After the birth of their final child, it was 'job done' and time to quit the marital bed for good. He created his own bedroom, complete with an army camp bed and a canvas blind, on an open-air balcony at the side of the house and slept there, hail, rain or shine, for the rest of the years they lived there. The headaches and dreams stopped immediately.

Throughout all of this, from their India days in the latter part of the 1800s and active service in Africa at the turn of the century and forward into the early 1900s, The Boy remained, if not always physically by Baden-Powell's side, then certainly virtually. In 1886, when the 13th Hussars returned to Britain for a while, Baden-Powell travelled straight to The Boy's home in Scotland instead of to his own mother in London, which did not go down at all well. They crossed paths and were posted together frequently after that; their final shared military experience was in South Africa in 1899 when McLaren led a force of 200 men heading to liberate the town of Mafeking, while Baden-Powell was busy leading the British defence. En route, McLaren encountered a Boer force far greater than this own and was quickly overwhelmed by the sheer number of Boers; forty of his men were killed or injured.

McLaren himself lay where he fell, seriously hurt, for sixteen hours before being found and taken to a Boer hospital for treatment. When Baden-Powell found out, he had to be stopped from rushing to see him, for his own safety, so instead sent daily notes from the barracks. He went from disparaging the Boer commander, to thanking him for looking after him.

McLaren later went on to be one the staff at Baden-Powell's Brownsea Island experimental Scout Camp in 1907, and acted as his manager at publisher, C. Arthur Pearson Ltd.'s office of *The Scout* magazine, although he resigned that position in March 1908, citing illness.

Relations between them cooled upon McLaren's first marriage to Leila Evelyn Landon, with whom he had a daughter and then more-or-less fizzled out completely with his second marriage, after Leila's death in 1910, to Ethyl Mary Wilson, who was the nurse who'd cared for Leila and who Baden-Powell considered beneath The Boy's station.

Despite the forensic analysis, there remained no evidence of a love affair. It should end there, but no.

Despite Olave Baden-Powell and McLaren's wives – and even Baden-Powell himself destroying mountains of personal papers, a rogue telegram unexpectedly came to light in 2018, with an intriguing, and many consider telling, message scrawled across it. It turned-up in an auction lot of McLaren's few remaining effects and its suggestive content triggered the eternal 'Were they, weren't they?' question yet again.

Auctioneer Chris Albury, believes it proves, or at least comes very close to proving, once and for all, that the men were involved in a loving relationship. Albury, from auctioneers Dominic Winter of Cirencester, said:

> There is a lot of evidence to suggest that Baden-Powell was a repressed gay man, but in the telegram, which is written as if suggesting a lover's tryst, there is a big hint that the relationship between the two men may have been physical after all.
>
> Of course, nothing is proven for certain and for me the most intriguing thing is that McLaren's wife who compiled the scrap albums must have known what the telegram really meant when she chose to preserve it in the albums.
>
> At the very least it shows she accepted the relationship of her husband and Baden-Powell.

The seemingly hurriedly scribbled message was part of a batch of unexpectedly remaining letters, telegrams and newspaper cuttings in three scrapbooks saved by Leila, mainly documenting Major McLaren's army service. Dated 23 July 1901, it's a rare find indeed, there being almost no correspondence nor written notes between, or even about, the pair in existence.

The lot also contained a scrapbook of sepia photographs ranging from 1899–1900, compiled by McLaren and related to the Second Boer War. It included images of British soldiers, prisoners, an X-ray of his own leg wound and images of Baden-Powell, with his signature, including one of Bloater on the ladder he used as a makeshift lookout station at Mafeking.

And the telegram's message?

It is short and to the point, in the usual manner of telegrams, and simply reads:

> Could you put me up Friday night incognito[?]
> Bloater.

Chapter 5

Dinizulu's Necklace

'Through the whole of my career in the army there was a vein ... that obsessed me and which, while adding zest to my work, came to be of use for the service. Later on, it proved the connecting link between my two otherwise dissimilar lives. This was scouting.'

Lessons From the 'Varsity of Life' (1933)

After eight years of military service, the only things that Stephe, now Captain Baden-Powell, had managed to shoot were most of the wildlife and himself – the latter by accident. His longing for active service, real fighting, seemed destined to be thwarted at every turn, and if confirmation of this were needed, in the autumn of 1884, the 13th Hussars received an order to quit India for good and sail back to England.

He was torn. Although excited about going home, it meant that now the only battle he would face would be funding the high cost of being a cavalry officer in Britain. It also meant leaving behind the domestic Nirvana that he and The Boy had created at Bloater Park.

Then there was the less than small matter of having to quickly sell off the polo ponies while organising the shipping of all his worldly goods, including his collection of trophies, sentimental items and Indian artefacts, back to the new and grander house that Henrietta Grace had managed to acquire at 8 St George's Place in Hyde Park Corner, after some deft juggling of the family finances.

Barely had the news sunk in when, on 13 November, just as the regiment was about to sail, the order unexpectedly changed. They were now directed to sail straight to Durban in South Africa for extra duty in the British colony of Natal, where trouble was brewing between the British and the Boers.

For perspective, in the relatively recent history of the 1800s, a brief period of Boer rule in the Cape came to an end when the British, after battling with France for power over the region, took control. As well as restoring order, they were now better placed to further protect the Empire's interests in what was not only a critical military location, but one rich in mineral wealth to boot. By the 1830s the British had organised a shake-up of the law courts and government, introduced numerous reforms, and decreed that English would be the official language. This all coincided with slavery being abolished throughout the Empire.

These changes greatly disgruntled the settled Boers, most of whose ancestors had first arrived at Table Bay as far back as 1652. The final affront, however, was when they were ordered to return the lands they'd settled back to their original black African owners. The repercussions were huge and although a compensation system was put in place, making a claim was complicated and long-winded; and *should* a claim be considered valid, then the pay-out had to be collected – in person – in England, making it impossible for most Boer farmers. They lost all of their slaves, of which they had many, the number usually corelated directly to the size and profitability of their farms, and they also lost the land which the slaves had worked on. This was the last straw and the catalyst for the now historic Great Trek of 1833, a mass migration of more than 11,000 Dutch-speaking pioneers, or Voortrekkers, in search of new lands where they would be free from British colonial administration.

It was a long and arduous journey with men, women and children travelling in wagon trains drawn by thousands of oxen. They settled by the River Vaal, establishing Transvaal on its northern side and the Orange Free State to the south. Natal, a British colony, abutted them both, flanking sections of their borders and incorporating Ladysmith and Colenso, with Durban, situated on the south coast (where Baden-Powell and the 13th Hussars were about to land).

Despite Natal's proximity to Transvaal and Orange Free State, the British left them to settle and granted them independence and self-rule. It was fine for a while, but after escaping the iron-fisted rule of the British, instead of finding the peaceful existence they'd imagined, the Boers attempted to expand into surrounding territories which left them facing a new enemy, namely the combined ferocity of the likes of the Matabele, Basuto and Zulu peoples. The British were on the brink of getting involved and the discovery of vast reserves of gold and diamonds in the region in 1867, completed a perfect storm for conflict between all parties.

Battles raged and in a series of horrific raids, tribal warriors defended their territories by massacring hundreds of Boers using spears and clubs. In furious retaliation, the Boers massacred thousands of indigenous Africans who were no match for the rifles the hardened farmers handled with the deadly accuracy of those born with a gun in their hands.

On the struggle went and, unwilling to be governed by either the British or even one another, the Boers wound up surrounded by more adversaries than ever. Within the Boer community itself, political and religious divisions increased, taxes remained unpaid and the currency value plummeted, resulting in bankruptcy. Their new life had effectively broken down.

Britain decided it had to step in after all and, following talks in the Transvaal capital of Pretoria, annexed the region on 12 April 1877; then on 24 May, Queen Victoria's 58th birthday, the Union flag was raised over Pretoria. Now all the British had to do was secure the south-eastern border of the Transvaal from the Zulu tribes. What could possibly go wrong?

The first of many British forces that crossed into Zululand over the River Buffalo was met within days by a terrifying horde of 20,000 shrieking Zulu warriors. A brutal hand-to-hand battle ensued, racking up huge losses, with 800 British soldiers and nearly 500 of their allied local troops slaughtered; close to 3,000 Zulu fighters, killed by British bullets and bayonets, lay alongside them on the battlefield.

Three more months of disastrous fighting continued with comparable heavy losses. Back home in Britain, people, used to hearing news of triumphant empirical victories, were now alarmed by the reports of defeats and horrendous mass fatalities. What was initially seen as a minor skirmish became a major campaign. It took 20,000 British troops to quell the Zulu armies and force them back but, at last, (for some) peace was re-established around the Cape, though, unfortunately not in the Transvaal itself. Over the following three years, the Boers grew progressively antagonistic towards British domination, with increasing numbers demanding that independence be restored.

Meanwhile, in Britain, William Gladstone was fighting a different campaign, to oust the incumbent prime minister, Benjamin Disraeli, and was being vociferously critical of the decision to annexe the Transvaal. This gave the Boers some hope that their demands might be met, however when Gladstone did defeat Disraeli and became the new prime minister, he performed a classic political U-turn and gave his support to the monarch, saying: 'The Queen cannot be advised to relinquish her sovereignty over the Transvaal.'

This was not the good news the Boers had anticipated, so they decided it was time to revolt. They declared the Transvaal an independent republic anyway and attacked the beleaguered British detachments still within their borders, defeating them left, right and centre.

Soldiers in a British relief force marching to Pretoria were killed or captured, and a thousand-strong detachment, led by General George Pomeroy Colley, suffered massive losses while trying to enter Transvaal via the Drakensberg mountains. A foolhardy return for a second attempt resulted in another routing, and Colley himself was killed along with his men.

In 1881, a truce was secured when Colley's successor, Field Marshall Sir Evelyn Wood, managed to negotiate with the Boer commandant, Piet Joubert and they signed the Pretoria Convention, which granted the Transvaalers complete self-government but under sovereignty to Queen Victoria.

Still, this was not the end.

Free-ranging Boer factions gradually began crossing the borders into British territories, causing friction in the likes of Bechuanaland (now Botswana) and around the town of Mafeking, where they attempted to carve-up lands belonging to the Barolong people, one of the region's most ancient tribes. So persistent were they to claim part, if not all, of Mafeking, that the British decided a show of force was required.

General Sir Charles Warren was called upon to show some military strength and push the itinerant Boers back by securing the British borders. He led 4,000 troops into Bechuanaland to maintain control from within, while strengthening security measures along the Transvaal's eastern border.

A further 1,000 troops were dispatched to Natal to block the Boers from progressing any further from there, with orders to immediately march into the Transvaal if required. The scene for a major defensive was set and when Baden-Powell and his 13th Hussars made their entrance into Durban on 29 November, the cavalry had, quite literally, arrived and went on to join the Durban part of Warren's Natal guard.

Already itching for a fight, this was a dream come true for Captain Baden-Powell, although there was more to his keenness than the prospect of armed combat. He was now desperate for a promotion that would elevate his status and, crucially, his pay scale, if the bills mounting up back in England were ever to be settled. Distinguishing himself in battle was the answer, in fact, it was his only option, considering that the alternative was to pass the dreaded (for him) Staff College exam, which he knew he would almost certainly fail due to his poor maths skills. Fastrack by war it was, then. Or so he thought.

In reality, after arriving in driving rain and moving into shared digs with The Boy and his other Lucknow pal, George Noble, in Pinetown, 'a poor excuse' for a town, General Warren had the nerve to start negotiating with the Boers. A dreary waiting game began. Pinetown was miles from any town or decent hunting grounds. Although, they had no horses anyway. Entertainment was non-existent and Baden-Powell found himself trapped in a boring timetable of daily admin duties, lectures and drills.

That Indian paradise now felt like it had been a dream. No more pig-sticking, no more polo and, to add insult to injury, no more The Boy, as he was packed-off to Cape Town to complete a long-winded military course. Despondent but ever conscientious, he immersed himself in the endless rounds of workaday duties while wishing the time away. He envied his brother Baden, the attention-stealing 'precious babe' of his childhood, who was by then knee-deep in active service in Egypt; he ached to join him. 'It's no good wishing,' he wrote to Henrietta Grace, 'the only thing is to try and work it somehow – but how, I don't know, as the apes seem to think we're on service here!'

The one thing keeping him going was the possibility, albeit an increasingly remote one, of action against the Boers. Being a Baden-Powell, he was never going to give up easily and, based on an encouraging early success with sales of *Reconnaissance and Scouting*, he decided to write another military guide, this one very specific to purpose and bearing the less-than-snappy title of *A manual for the use of Officers conducting a course of military instruction in accordance with General order No. 30 of 1884*.

It took just three months to complete and when he mailed it to his brother George in England, he expressed the same lack of confidence he'd felt about *Reconnaissance and Scouting*, instructing his brother: 'If no publisher cares to publish it, please have it printed because I'm certain it will sell, particularly if brought out as soon as possible.'

He needn't have worried. It was snapped-up by Harrison & Sons, London, and rushed out as a handy, 280-page pocket manual with the far more succinct title of *Cavalry Instruction*. Despite feeling trapped and miserable in his Pinetown hut and missing The Boy, the pigs and his ponies, being so profoundly duty-bound he nevertheless continued to be Baker Russell's indispensable right-hand man.

Among the scant episodes of light relief that did occur, two were to prove significant. The first was the arrival of big brother George, who'd become a bit of a father figure to him and whose advice he valued above most. George was, among many things expedient to the Empire, now regarded an expert in colonial diplomacy, having had various successes revolving around interests and assets of the crown both in Australia and the West Indies.

His seemingly spontaneous trip to South Africa was taken under no orders other than his own and, while serving to improve young Stephe's low mood, its other purpose was to increase his knowledge of the country in order to further the lofty ambition he had to become High Commissioner at the Cape.

In classic Baden-Powell style, the cost of George's journey was funded – by a commission from *The Times* newspaper to write a series of insightful articles about the region. From Pinetown, George went to stay with the influential governor at the Cape and then travelled on to Kimberley where he was the guest of the blisteringly powerful Cecil Rhodes. A ruthless imperialist and a major player in the Cape Parliament, Rhodes was amassing a fortune from the region's munificent diamond mines, while running roughshod over the native population whose lands they happened to be on. So mercenary was Rhodes in his pursuit of power, he would later go as far as manipulating laws to meet his own ends, including creating a means of exploitatively appropriating mineral-rich lands from black Africans, blocking their right to vote and consolidating their lands, ergo, their mines, into one huge concern. His concern.

Within just four years of George visiting him, Rhodes owned almost all of the region's diamond reserves and had founded his own personal empire, the world-famous De Beers company, earning him the nickname, 'The King of Diamonds'. As well as improving Stephe's demeanour, George's working holiday would no doubt have considerably improved his young brother's career path, too. Interestingly, Henrietta Grace had recently held a grand dinner for the prime minister of the Cape Colony who'd been visiting London. The stellar guest list also included the Earl of Kimberly; Sir Robert Herbert, Permanent Under-Secretary at the Colonial office; and the editor of *The Times*. Plus ça change!

The second episode was a gift.

Colonel Baker Russell needed to form a stand-by flying column of mounted men and guns that could be mobilised quickly to go cross country into Boer territory and assist General Warren's expedition, should it be faced with resistance in Bechuanaland. He had concerns about the paucity of detailed information on the surrounding Drakensberg Mountain passes that led from Natal to the Transvaal and the Orange Free State (and where Colley and his men had come to grief). He had reasonable intelligence on the two main passes used by the Boers, which would obviously be dangerous, so what he really wanted were alternative routes that the column could use in a sudden attack scenario or if asked to move towards Warren's location. The solution was right under his nose, of course. Baden-Powell's reconnaissance skills were second-to-none and he was impossibly restless. It was the perfect assignment for his bored captain, an opportunity to make use of his excellent mapping skills and allow him to see some action at last.

Had Baden-Powell been a dog, his tail would have been wagging. He was already aware of alternative passes, but they'd been blown up a while ago, ironically by army engineers, to stave off attacks on Natal by the Basutoland tribe. His job would be to find out whether any of them could be made passable again in an emergency. Better still, the whole thing was to be strictly on the hush-hush, which greatly appealed to him as it meant he would need to travel incognito and that would require dressing up and a bit of play acting.

Instantly motivated, he wholeheartedly embraced the order and concocted a plan where he'd pose as a roving news correspondent, visiting the area with the intention of possibly recommending it as a country worth considering for immigration. Cultivating a scraggy beard and donning well-worn civilian clothes, he disappeared, complete with travel-weary persona, into the mountains with just a couple of horses, one for riding and one for carrying basic rations, and essential kit.

For a month he criss-crossed the range in happy solitude, gathering crucial information on daily stints of thirty to forty miles, while living on scant rations. Some of the time he'd unfurl his blankets and sleep under the stars, other times, he'd blag a night at a farm where, thanks to his realistic disguise and acting skills, his fake identity was accepted without question. He befriended both British and Boer farmers which gave him insight into how they felt about one another, and he developed an admiration for their work ethics; even the more reticent Boers fell victim to his charm offensives.

Traversing the mountain ranges, he quickly deduced that the existing maps of the area contained many errors, rendering them useless in places. To compensate, he added surveying to his activities, then corrected mistakes as he went along, paying particular attention to any that would be pertinent from a military point of view. Studying the areas with a fresh, forensic eye and using tactical evaluations, he also made notes and recommendations for the future; one of many conclusions he came to was that, should a British column from Natal be hindered in any way while advancing northward, it should fall back to the *left* of Natal's Tugela river and avoid trying to hold Ladysmith. Fourteen years later, that sound piece of advice was ignored by British forces with catastrophic consequences.

Having ridden 600 miles in total, Baden-Powell returned to the regiment as fit as a fiddle and armed not only with the alterations required to improve missions, but completely new maps which he had created from his notes and rough sketches, delivering them to Baker Russell on 5 May, having stayed up all night to finish them by candlelight. Mission accomplished.

By then, Warren, who now had George Baden-Powell acting as his political advisor, had managed to broker a peace agreement with the Transvaal's President, Paul Kruger. So, with any hope of war action now off the table and a strong rumour that the 13th Hussars were soon to return to England, Baden-Powell decided to up the adrenalin ante and booked a big-game hunting trip, something he'd always wanted to do.

He and four officer chums joined Reuben Beningfield, a famous Durban-based big-game hunter, and travelled with him to East-Africa for a two-month safari with a party of more than seventy indigenous carriers, seven servants and a couple of cooks.

Disappointed at the surprising lack of game they found after days of tracking and ranging further into the African veld, Baden-Powell switched to default mode and went solo. He'd become fixated on bagging a hippopotamus and, having spotted some spoors beside a lake, spent several solitary (that common thread of needing to be alone which ran through his entire life) days on its banks. By lying in silence in the tall grass for hours, flat on his back with his gun resting on his groin, he finally did exactly that. There was huge excitement when the carriers collected the poor beast and hauled it to the camp and from that day, they called him M'hlalapanzi, or 'The-man-who-lies-down-to-shoot.'

A self-sketched drawing of him, legs akimbo with the barrel of his rifle jutting out from between his legs is all sorts of shades of Freudian male superego. Although proud of his macho nickname, some reports mention that when the carriers used it, they'd often giggle and even thrust or gesture towards their groins suggestively. He probably wouldn't have minded – Baden-Powell lived to make people laugh. As well as the end of the unfortunate hippo, the safari trip also marked the end of his time in Africa and yet another end to hopes for action in the field.

Back in England, despite having managed to sell a fair few books, short stories and sketches, he was still broke and, although it hadn't been the most exhilarating role in the world, being adjutant to the charismatic Baker Russell in India was far more palatable than being adjutant to a new colonel in Britain.

He missed the stimulation and bonhomie of working directly with his men so, being an expert in making the most of a rum deal, he asked to resign his adjutancy. The request was granted, gratefully accepted and he took command of a detachment of the 13th Hussars at Colchester in Essex. He threw himself into his captaincy, his mission, to turn his men into an elite troop. He trained them himself, instructing them in the ways of the scout, in how to signal silently in the style of the Afghan fighters he'd studied in Kandahar, and how to use practical skills and natural instinct to stay one step ahead of the enemy.

Word of Baden-Powell's soundless communication system spread and when the commanding general, Sir Evelyn Wood as it happens, came to inspect his men, he asked to see a demonstration of it. Even though it was a foggy day with poor visibility, the men could clearly see and respond to Baden-Powell's soundless directions and even managed to surprise another troop that was noisily shouting-out signals. Wood was impressed and he took another step towards being indispensable. Even so, a rather long hiatus of inaction followed. Never one to sit still, he used the time to garner a deeper knowledge of the many new weapons being developed both at home and in Europe.

In England, his studies involved familiarising himself with them by visiting the factories where they were being manufactured. Information on European weaponry development was gathered by spending all his available leave on the Continent, often with brother Baden in tow, and spying on armoury trials and other related activities. Naturally, this necessitated the wearing of various disguises. Most, if not all, of these espionage expeditions were unofficial and the pair did get embroiled in several awkward situations and precarious encounters, which, in truth, could well have been detrimental to British security. Fortunately, they were never actually caught red-handed, nor were they detained for very long on the odd occasions they were suspected of any undercover shenanigans and, in later years, Baden-Powell gleefully retold – often embellished – versions of the daring exploits in his book, *My Adventures as a Spy* (1915).

Fanciful or not, the book has great merit in that it is partly illustrated with his bonkers, but frankly wonderful, spying maps, all of which are ingeniously concealed within sketches of insects, plants and even stained-glass windows. And, the wandering weaponry research did pay off.

Baden-Powell and his regiment were ordered to Seaforth, near Liverpool, to plan and participate in a grand military show-of-might that was being staged as part of a raft of countrywide celebrations of Queen Victoria's Golden Jubilee. Of course, he was in his element, plotting and planning an extravaganza that would be declared a tour de force for years to come. A large crowd attended the tournament and deemed the last act, called *The Bivouac*, the best and most spectacular by far.

A highly-dramatic enactment of a cavalry reconnaissance mission in enemy territory, it was arranged by who else but the ultimate showman himself, Baden-Powell, and starred his impeccable Seaforth 13th Hussars. Ending with a full-blown cavalry charge across the entire show field, with Captain Baden-Powell riding 'Buffalo-Bill style' atop the latest new kid on the armoury engineering block, the impressive Nordenfelt machine-gun, which he'd borrowed after witnessing its power during recent trials; no wonder the scene was an absolute show-stealer.

A few days after the display, a sergeant rushed in announcing that Lord Wolseley, Adjutant General of the British army, wanted to see him. Thinking this very unlikely, an Adjutant General would hardly have reason to visit a mere captain, Baden-Powell decided that his leg was being pulled. He took his time sauntering towards the barracks' square only to find that it was, indeed, Wolseley, and he wanted to know all about his 'mere' captain's shiny new toy, namely the Nordenfelt.

Not only did Baden-Powell oblige, answering his boss's questions and assuring him that it would be an excellent cavalry gun, given that it performed superbly even on rough terrain, he even gave Wolseley a white-knuckle ride on the gun to prove it.

As well as being convinced of its usefulness, Wolseley clearly enjoyed his thrill ride, as the Nordenfelt was subsequently adopted for the army. Shortly afterwards, he received the following letter:

Dear Captain Baden-Powell,

A recent inspection of the handling of the machine-gun attached to the several regiments of the Cavalry at Aldershot was anything but a success, attributable apparently to the defective training of the detachments.

I am anxious that this defect be remedied, and I wish you, as one of the few officers of the Army who have the requisite knowledge, to do so. It will be necessary for you to be at Aldershot for about a fortnight, and I want you to let me know when it will be convenient for you to go there

Yours truly
Wolseley

This was a double delight for he was now firmly wedged into the good books of the army's highest-ranking officer, plus he'd get to see his old chum Baker Russell, who was now second-in-command at Aldershot. While instructing the men with a training plan that he'd created specifically for the purpose, he also designed a quick-release harness for the gun to replace an inadequate one issued by the Ordnance Department. Far superior, it made operating the Nordenfelt safer and improved its accuracy. The invention was patented in Baden-Powell's name and earned him a commendation plus a handy £100.

No sooner had he completed his mission to create a crack team of very-big gun slingers at Aldershot, than a new job offer arrived out of the blue. This one came from the General Officer Commanding, South Africa, who happened to be General Henry Smyth (that is, Henrietta Grace's brother, AKA, his uncle), inviting him to join him as his aide de camp.

Although he was well aware that the role of ADC was likely to be yet another pen-pushing one, Baden-Powell bit Smyth's hand off, because he saw this one as having potential for career progression. Among other things, he'd be in charge of his uncle's diary, so he would be immersed in endless rounds of social activities, such as sporting events, balls, grand banquets and, of course, theatricals.

He would also have been aware that it would see him mixing with all sorts of extremely influential people, a realisation confirmed in a quote from William Hillcourt's book *The Two Lives of a Hero*, where he says that his ADC role 'is not soldiering, so doesn't as a rule lead to better things on its merit, although of course you meet with swells whose interest may get you on'. When the time for his departure from Aldershot arrived, his men defied army regulations and staged a farewell testimonial for their boss, something virtually unheard of between differing ranks, and presented him with a personal message, printed on white satin and bearing all of their best wishes.

As the year drew towards its close, on 30 December 1887, Captain Baden-Powell set sail once more for the Cape, destination: a desk in uncle Henry's office. Unsurprisingly, his optimism didn't last long. When not deskbound, aside from the odd polo or sporting event, he was mainly caught up in an endless whirl of social hob-knobbing and avoiding would-be wives. It was war, not waltzes, battles not banquets, that Stephe craved, so he consulted big brother George, his personal guru and now the Conservative MP for Liverpool Kirkdale.

George had also been made a 'Sir', an exciting first for the Baden-Powells, in recognition of his work in areas of Imperial importance, including new, asset-rich African regions (for assets read diamonds and gold), where he was becoming deeply involved. If anyone could find him a battle then surely, George could?

Alas, even with all his credentials and network of heavyweight global connections, he couldn't find his little brother a fight; there was no choice for Baden-Powell but to make the most of his humdrum, if at least well-salaried, situation. Grudgingly resigned to his fate, it therefore came as a welcome surprise when things took a turn for the livelier on the first week of June 1888. An urgent telegram arrived at the Cape from Sir Arthur Havelock, Governor of Natal and Zululand, requesting immediate military assistance in Natal as the native Usutu tribe, followers of the vanquished and exiled Zulu Chief, Cetewayo, was rebelling and had already attacked the town of Umsinduze, besieging the home of its magistrate, Pretorius.

The uprising stemmed from a quashing of Zulu resistance in 1879 at the Battle of Ulundi led by British Lieutenant General Frederic Thesiger, 2nd Baron Chelmsford.

At the time, the powerful tribal leader, King (Chief) Cetewayo, had been urged by one of his main advisors, a Scot by the name of John Dunn, to avoid war with the British and he was willing to comply since his beef was mainly with other tribes. However, the constant aggression of Cetewayo's Usutu warriors in native territories convinced Chelmsford that they needed to be taught a lesson. The Zulus asked to negotiate, but Chelmsford was in no mood for compromise. His involvement in previous rebellions, plus the fierce and prolonged combat at Rourke's Drift, had left his reputation less than glowing and, soon to be relieved of his command by Sir Garnet Wolseley, he fancied a final stab at redemption. He headed straight to Cetewayo's royal kraal (enclosure) at Ulundi, site of the previous clash, and defeated him and his forces thanks to superior weaponry.

Although the victory resulted in the chief's loss of power, trouble continued to simmer and fighting over territories never really stopped. When Wolseley did take over as Commander High Commissioner, he divided Zululand into several 'provinces' in a bid to restore peace.

Each was run by a Zulu chief, apart from one, which had as its leader the aforementioned John Dunn, a trader, expert hunter and a bit of a maverick. He had grown up among the Zulu people, hence his closeness to Cetewayo.

Dunn was brought to Africa as a child and was adopted by the Zulu people at the age of 14 after his father was trampled to death by an elephant and his mother died soon after. He'd embraced their culture, adopting their native clothing, customs and language; he also enthusiastically emulated their polygamic lifestyle, fathering 170 children by one white and forty-eight Zulu wives.

Knowing their ways, and speaking both English and Zulu, Dunn was a natural go-between and negotiator for the conflicting sides and his unfussy style of diplomacy had secured him an enviable personal portfolio of lands, extensive cattle herds and a vast and loyal tribe to rule over.

Dunn or not, Wolseley's provincial experiment failed, it's main flaw being that the various tribes had even more reason to fight among themselves for control. Unsurprisingly, civil war reigned across the divided territories. Fast-forward to Baden-Powell's posting in 1888. Cetewayo was out of the picture by this time, but his son and heir Dinizulu had taken his throne. In the mould of his father, the new king made an impressive figure. Intelligent and powerful, he stood 6ft 7in tall and wore the tribe's sacred royal necklace of wooden beads proudly around his neck and torso. Considering Dinizulu's stature, it's been estimated from photographs that it would have been at least four metres long. There was a saying among the Zulu fighters that their strength would vanish should the necklace ever be stolen, so when it wasn't wrapped around Dinizulu, it was housed in a secret cave and guarded day and night.

Still smarting at the fate of his father, Dinizulu had started this latest uprising and, eager for a rematch, his people fully backed his plan. He also attracted a force of Transvaal Boers, equally up for a fight and doubly motivated by Diniuzlu's promise of lands in exchange for their support. With these combined forces, he soon took control of many of the neighbouring tribes; however, when the time came to dole out the promised lands to his Boer buddies, he suddenly realised that the debt owing ran to more than 2 million acres of prime, mineral-rich terrain, and balked.

Tense talks followed until the Boers finally offered to 'settle' for all of northern Zululand. And an extra strap of territory on the eastern shoreline that they could turn into a new republic. Frantic about losing so much territory, Dinuzulu turned to the British, who subsequently prevented the Boers from taking the coastal region but then allowed them settle into the remaining area where they set up their New Republic of Vrijheid. The British then annexed what was left for themselves and put Sir Arthur Havelock in charge of keeping the peace. This was not what Dinuzulu had in mind. Furious, he raised another impi (army) of 4,000 Usutus and set about attacking chiefs who were loyal to the British in an act of open and hostile defiance.

Havelock optimistically demanded that Dinizulu immediately cease his antagonistic strategy, and when it fell on deaf ears, issued a warrant for his arrest to be delivered by 200 of his Zululand police force and a group of British troops to ensure its enforcement. As soon as they arrived with the warrant, the Zulus launched a ferocious attack and they were forced to withdraw with significant casualties. News of the backdown spread, other Zulu tribes rose up in support and went on a rampage, raiding traders' stores and missionary stations and killing 200 European men, women and children before laying siege on Umsinduze.

Dinizulu had somehow raised four impi and things had reached crisis point, hence Havelock's urgent telegram to Smyth, despite the entrenched mistrust that existed between civil and military personnel at the time. So, while Havelock wanted a supply of back-up troops to support his local forces, as commander-in-chief of all Natal and Zululand, he didn't really want his position undermined by the interference of a military general.

Unaware, or unconcerned, about the finer points of these politics, Smyth formed a 2,000 strong, mixed-bag of an army, comprising British soldiers from various regiments, mounted local volunteers and a levy of local native men, and proceeded to march towards Natal. This force was boosted by John Dunn who, having since fallen out with his 'friend' Cetewayo and by dint, his son, Dinizulu for ignoring his advice, was now happy to pledge his allegiance to the British and joined them with his own impi of 2,000 loyal Zulu warriors.

When Baden-Powell first caught sight of Dunn and his fighters marching through the valley towards them, they were in three long lines and chanting what he later referred to as a 'wonderful anthem'.

I heard a sound in the distance which at first I thought was an organ playing in church and I thought for a moment that we must be approaching a mission station over the brow of the hill. But when we topped the rise we saw moving up towards us from the valley below three long lines of men marching in single file and singing a wonderful anthem as they marched.

Every now and then one man would sing a few notes of a solo which were then responded to by an immense roar of sound from the whole impi, of deep base voices and higher tones singing in harmony. *Lessons from the Varsity of Life*

This was the Ingonyama, which Baden-Powell would use as a chant for Scouts in years to come. A modern version of a similar Zulu chant, Nants Ingonyama sung by the South African music artist Lebo M, became famous when it was mixed with Elton John's song, *Circle of Life* and used as the opening track in Disney's *The Lion King*. In 2019, Lebo M performed it at the start of the opening ceremony of the 24th World Scout Jamboree in the USA.

Entranced by the chant, Baden-Powell was even more impressed on seeing the warriors at close quarters, describing them as 'fine strong muscular fellows, with cheery handsome faces … their brown bodies were polished with oil and they looked like bronze statues'. He was in awe of their physical strength and discipline and fascinated with their assegais (long, tapered spears), axes and clubs and by 'black polished rings', fashioned from a mix of wax and blood and worn on the shaven heads of the best warriors.

Knowing that there could be four such impi groups ahead just like this one, he was very glad to have them on their side and much of the future Scouting movement's songs and campfire ceremonies were inspired by Dunn's gleaming Zulu men. Before Smyth and his staff reached their camp in a place called Eshowe, the only white settlement in Zululand, one of Dinizulu's impi had already been defeated by a force led by Major A.C. McKean. Despite there being thousands of Zulus, the disparity of weaponry made it an easy victory with only six British killed.

After a punishing, fifty-mile march in diabolical weather, batting off small Usutu fighting factions on the way, Baden-Powell, uncle Henry and their diverse army arrived at Durban and travelled by train, then mule wagons to Eshowe. McKean, now in charge of all British armies in the region, combined forces with them in preparation of completing the job. Baden-Powell became staff officer to McKean and they now had a formidable flying column that included Dunn's 2,000 Zulu men, 400 horse infantry and a couple of hundred Basuto fighters.

With no sign of Dinizulu, they began to march to relieve Umsinduzu; it didn't take long for the officers to discover that keeping control of thousands of Zulu and Basuto forces was far from easy, especially when they began burning alleged enemy kraals en route. They spoke of being powerless as, by early July, up to eighty kraals a day were being razed to the ground then, on 11 July, four indigenous men were killed and a girl was badly injured when a stray bullet went through her stomach. Baden-Powell and McKean did what they could to save the poor girl's life, but the wound was so catastrophic that she died during the night.

Havelock was fuming when he heard what had occurred and berated Smyth about the killings by Baden-Powell's men. He also pointed out that they happened over the border, inside the Boers' New Republic (meaning the victims were likely to have been 'friendly') and that their deaths should be considered murders. Uncertainty still hangs over the events of that particular twenty-four hours, ditto over the specific orders that Baden-Powell gave to the men that day.

Later, under scrutiny over the incident, Baden-Powell was inconsistent, saying he hadn't realised that they'd crossed the border at the time and, on another occasion, that the maps they'd been using contained errors. The latter was true and he was able to prove it, so Havelock reluctantly took the case no further, instead telling Smyth to ensure there would never be another occurrence of so lamentable an error.

The day after the event, the looting and razing continued; however, the military priority was still to relieve Pretorius. When they arrived, the magistrate and his men were safe and surrounded by friendly Zulus and Europeans. Yes, they'd been attacked, with forty dead and many others injured, but they were in good spirits.

Now, the only assistance required in the town was of the practical kind, so they began a clear-up with Baden-Powell taking on the role of medic again to tend the sick and injured. The rest of the troops helped rebuild and refortify the town. McKean set up a protective garrison for Pretorius and his people but as low morale increased among the enemy troops, so their numbers diminished. It seemed the worst of the crisis was over.

By August, General Smyth had a reputation for ferocity that was far beyond the reality. The Usutu troops were close to collapse, with only pockets of rogue marauders at large, and the chief was believed to be hiding in his stronghold in the Ceza bush. Smyth still wanted to teach Dinizulzu a lesson, so asked Baden-Powell to create an intelligence group that could ascertain the exact whereabouts of the evasive chief. He formed a band of Zulu spies and, in no time at all, had information on his movements and confirmation that his hiding place was indeed located on the inhospitable Ceza, a place of treacherous fragmented rocks and nigh-on impenetrable vegetation.

They planned an ambush and were ready to pounce when a directive came from Havelock forbidding them to strike without his approval as he felt their action was disproportionately extreme in view of the improved situation. Smyth and his nephew put this down to pettiness on Havelock's behalf, believing the inexplicable order to be for no other reason than for him to flex his authoritarian muscle. Conversely, Havelock felt that any immediate danger has passed and that there was little point in pursuit, but after five tense days he suddenly gave the go-ahead and Baden-Powell finally led his men deep into the Ceza.

The trail led to a series of deep caves but again, Dinizulu was nowhere to be seen and all that remained was a series of abandoned huts and small rocky caves, inside one of which was what appeared to be Dinizulu's sacred necklace. General Smyth and Baden-Powell complained that Havelock's delay had caused the mission to fail, allowing Dinizulu to slip back into the safety of the Transvaal, evading them yet again. Havelock stuck to his guns on the issue but most of the British press (including titles widely-read and respected by officers) had been fed a regular diet of news of events by George Baden-Powell, based on his brothers' extensive correspondence from the Cape and so, they sided firmly with General Smyth and his men.

When questioned later about the incident of the killings of the civilians in the caves while relieving Umsinduzu, Baden-Powell said that he had ordered his men to spare the Usutus' lives and take them prisoner. Apparently, his men were considerably far ahead of him when they spotted several warriors scurrying away and what has been described as a 'short but fierce skirmish' ensued. Baden-Powell said that he was not near his men, who ploughed straight into a cave tunnel and, ignoring his orders, killed the four men and somehow injured a young woman.

He explained that as the scouts were some way ahead, which is feasible, they were out of his sight and therefore out of his control and there was nothing he could have done to stop them. They ended up taking twenty-six prisoners and commandeered 110 head of cattle, presumably with Baden-Powell's knowledge and permission.

As well as coming out of the debacle unscathed, Baden-Powell and Sir Henry and received letters from Wolseley, whose dealings with the Zulus in 1879 had caused much of the situation in the first place, sympathising with them over Sir Arthur's dreadful behaviour. In fact, Wolseley used it as an excuse to bring the role of colonial governors, who seemed to hamper rather than support military leaders in the territories, into dispute. Major McKean stepped in, too, crediting Baden-Powell for his part in the mission: 'I beg to bring to the notice of the Lieutenant- General Commanding, the invaluable services rendered me by Captain Baden-Powell. This officer's unflagging energy, his forethought and thorough knowledge of all military details were of the greatest assistance to me.' For his efforts, and no doubt thanks to McKean's endorsement, he was appointed Brevet Major.

Despite this, controversy stubbornly clings to the incident, mainly due to something Baden-Powell himself wrote forty years later where he acknowledged that the Usutu were trying to reach the safety of the Transvaal but that 'we disregarded the border and followed them up, attacked, and got them'. Adding to the sense of disquiet is a question over the true source of Dinizulu's necklace, which Baden Powell took back to England and later dismantled to use in woodcraft badges he gave to his Scouts.

Photographs of Dinizulu clearly show him wearing a necklace with hundreds of wooden beads which seems to corroborate his story; the beads were awarded to kings for acts of heroism and passed down the royal line over generations. However, another tale exists that has caused speculation that the Scouts' Woodcraft beads could have come from elsewhere.

In *The Brave Zulu Girl*, a story published years later in his book, *Lessons From the Varsity of Life* (1933), Baden-Powell recounts the time in Natal when he and McKean tried to save the life of the injured girl, who was brought to them by her uncle after being shot in the stomach by a stray bullet in the controversial raid.

He describes how they were out in the open in driving rain, but managed to dress the girl's gaping wound as best they could and how they fashioned a sack into a tunic with holes for her head and arms because 'her only clothing was a bead girdle and a necklace of black and white beans.' He continues with details of how the uncle ran off into the night, taking the sack with him, so they wrapped the child in McKean's overcoat, lit a fire and gave her 'a little soup' before placing her underneath a wagon for shelter. He concludes: 'the poor girl died before morning', then adds 'he [McKean] and I put her into an anti-bear hole and filled it in as well as we could, and threw a heap of thorn bushes over it to keep the hyenas away'.

There's little doubt that the beaded jewellery he took back to England represented a 'spoils of war' trophy, or at least a regrettable case of souveniring. Both these options are despicable, of course, though entirely standard practice at the time, but the real question is: was it Dinizulu's necklace, left behind in his rush to escape his mountain lair, or was it taken from the dead African girl? Or both?

Considering that sections in some of Baden-Powell's books make loose with the facts, not necessarily to obscure the truth but more often to render them more exciting, glamorous or dangerous, these confused accounts simply add weight to accusations that he was a fantasist or even a liar, and are why it is so difficult to get to the truth even now. Saying that, in May 2021, an investigation by the national headquarters for the Boy Scouts of America concluded that the inflammatory wooden beads were most likely to have been removed from the Zulu chief's hideout by Baden-Powell.

The finding countered one cited in 1990 by Ray Baker and Deneen Robinson from Chicago, who, having read Tim Jeal's biography, *Baden-Powell*, flagged-up a section where Jeal says that while there is no record in Baden-Powell's notes or diaries of having taken Dinzulu's necklace, he does mention appropriating the necklace of the dead African girl. Baker and Robinson, both district executives for the Boy Scouts of America at the time, raised awareness of the beads when they refused to complete a required Scout management woodcraft training course, saying that the beads – replicas of which are worn by instructors and given as rewards at end of the course – symbolised oppressed Africans. The pair, who chose to resign from their posts rather than complete the course, demanded that the Scouts embrace a more ethnically neutral symbol.

Scouting officials who conducted the investigation in 2021 agreed that the original beads were taken more than 100 years ago by Baden-Powell in South Africa in the late 1880s. 'They were indeed the spoils of war,' confirmed Lee Sneath, Boy Scouts of America's national spokesman. 'I don't think there's any way around that. Baden-Powell was a colonial soldier.' He added that the investigation, which examined Tim Jeal's research, revealed that Baden-Powell actually acquired two necklaces – one from the dead girl, the other from the chief's hut. An archivist at London's Baden-Powell House also confirmed that an intact necklace of beads (or shells) exists with a tag attached bearing Baden-Powell's handwriting, identifying it as the girl's necklace. Several other biographies mentioning his discovery of a necklace in Dinizulu's hut are also cited in the report. According to Scout officials, that's the one that was broken-up for early bead rewards for Scouts who had completed his woodcraft training course. Sneath concluded, 'I don't know if there's any, absolutely fool-proof way of saying who they belonged to.' Baker and Robinson said that regardless of the origins of the beads, they should be replaced by something other than replicas of items taken by a colonialist who fought against Africans.

Baden-Powell's African service ended in direct correlation to a semblance of order being restored in the Cape. This was followed by a series of fairly uneventful service postings, predominantly further administrative roles, including another phase as ADC to his uncle Henry, this time in Malta. To balance the tedium, he indulged his love of espionage (usually of his own volition when on army leave) in North Africa and Europe, recording his escapades and illustrating them with detailed sketches, which helped his cover story that he was an artist, capturing the beauty of the country (he happened to be spying in).

He had also finished his book on pig-sticking, his first major work, which was snapped-up immediately by Harrison & Sons again and published under the title of *Pigsticking or Hoghunting*; A Complete Account for Sportsmen; and Others. It was a luxuriously bound hardback with deep, gold embossing that went on to become a classic among pig-sticking aficionados and is deemed the undisputed authority on the 'sport'.

When he finally returned to England in 1893, he went to re-join his beloved 13th Hussars at County Kildare in Ireland and, better still, his equally beloved best friend, Major McLaren. He was happy, though still struggling to make ends meet.

He later wrote how, while in Ireland, he again managed to attract the attention of Lord Wolseley, with a quick-thinking ruse he'd devised to outwit another regiment during manoeuvres. To reach a gun battery ahead of the competition, he describes ordering a few of his men to drag leafy branches behind their horses on a dry road, thus creating a huge dust cloud to act as a 'smokescreen' (shades of the Battle of Maiwand) that suggested far more of his men were within it than was actually the case. Seeing the cloud, the other regiment headed in an alternative direction and Baden-Powell's full complement of waiting men headed straight to the gun battery and claimed it. Wolseley was full of praise, telling him how good it was to see an officer use his wits and not be tied down by Drill Book regulations.

His account and the clever conceit, if true (unlike other Wolseley anecdotes, such as the Nordenfelt gun display, there is no mention of the dust-cloud ploy in any of his notes or letters) was surely based on his memories of the British defeat.

By now, Baden-Powell's stocks of Wolseley commendations were looking pretty healthy, hopefully standing him in good stead for the future.

He didn't have too long to wait for a pay-out.

Chapter 6

Ashanti Bloodbath

'In the darkness I could see nothing, but going closer to the great gnarled tree-trunk he guided my hand as high as I could reach and I touched what quickly proved to be a human jaw-bone hanging there. And then another, and yet more. It was a fetish tree.'

Adventures and Accidents, RBP, 1934

When the hunter suddenly becomes the hunted, a prompt escape is essential. With the dust cloud now settled over his fortuitous encounters with Wolseley, Baden-Powell felt certain that an official proposal for active service was just around the corner. Frustratingly, time simply dragged on with no offer in sight and the only proposal on the horizon was the one he was desperately trying to avoid – marriage.

It was all his brother George's fault.

In defiance of Henrietta Grace's relentless edict that her sons would be best-off eschewing marriage as it was a costly affair and therefore detrimental to the success of the burgeoning Baden-Powell empire, George had become engaged. Curiously, bearing in mind her staunch anti-matrimony mantra, far from being furious with her favourite son, she welcomed the news, fully supporting, in fact actively encouraging, his union with Miss Frances Annie Wilson.

While this complete volte-face on Henrietta Grace's part initially seems bizarre, once one learns that his new fiancée happened to be the daughter, and more pertinently the heiress, to the estate of an immensely wealthy Australian landowner, it suddenly makes perfect sense.

George proposed to Annie after telling Henrietta Grace that marriage could be an excellent investment, as it would generate 'a lasting form of income'. To underpin this he added, in the manner of a man better schooled in the intricacies of finance than of romance, that there were plenty more rich girls like Annie about and all with potential to yield a return of a few thousand pounds a year. 'If we could each [the Baden-Powell brothers] pick one up,' he said, 'the family would be able to spend fifteen-thousand pounds a year, or more.'

As her maternal manipulations sprung less from any erstwhile Jocasta complex and more from her love of money, Henrietta Grace was sold on the idea; before she'd even contemplated a new hat for George's wedding, her eyes turned to the resolutely-single, Major McLaren-obsessed Stephe. The sport of bagging her second youngest boy a moneyed wife of his own had officially begun.

With no active service looking likely and the Staff College test still out of the question, Stephe was feeling under pressure; now his most important assignment was to use every trick in the book to avoid getting hitched.

There was a precarious moment when his sister Agnes (no doubt with some input from mother) introduced him to a bona fide heiress by the name of Edith Christie-Miller. As with all things Stephe, his aversion to having a relationship with a woman was more complex than simply down to any romantic or sexual inclinations. Remember that up until this extended stint in England, he'd spent most of his life in male-only company and, therefore, felt infinitely more at ease with men than with women.

He thrived on masculine discourse and macho pursuits and was as much an athlete as he was an aesthete, as interested in fighting as he was in acting and he would certainly have been much happier marching up a hill than walking down any aisle. Women couldn't join him hunting wild boar, or exploring or playing polo; nor would they relish the idea of surviving outdoors with not much more than a stick and a smile. Where was the appeal in that for a man who didn't want to grow up?

He did like Edith, just not enough to marry her, so he used his secret weapon, the inherent snobbery instilled in him by his mother, as an excuse to postpone a proposal for a while at least, telling Henrietta that although Edith's parents were both 'very kind and very rich', they were also, 'in the words of the Duke of Cambridge, very common'. Touché. Did Henrietta Grace realise she'd been hoisted by her own petard?

Edith, either disregarding or possibly being unaware of his reticence, lingered in the background and intensified the pressure, but just when he thought there was no way out, an escape hatch suddenly appeared in the form a telegram from his hero Lord Wolseley, bearing the magical words: 'You are selected to proceed on active service.'

Active service. Thirteen long years he'd waited for such an order and the elation (and relief no doubt) that he felt at finally receiving it is evident in the letter he wrote to his mother, informing of her of the wonderful news.

Well, My Dearest Mother, would you believe it – I've got my orders for going on service at last! I'm to go to Ashanti as one of the staff.

I needn't tell *you* it is a great thing for me.

At the interview, a mere formality really, Wolseley, now the army's newly appointed commander-in-chief, welcomed him like an old chum, immediately confirmed the commission and gave him the low down on it: Ashanti (now Ghana), in West Africa, was in the region then known as the Gold Coast, now the Ivory Coast, both names referring to two of its most lucrative trading resources.

Baden-Powell would be arriving at what was an early uprising by the indigenous African Ashanti people, reputed to be the fiercest, bravest and most bloodthirsty tribe on the Gold Coast. Sir Francis Scott would be in command of the expedition, leading a 2,000-strong British force and Baden-Powell's job would be to raise a local army of 1,000 men and lead them ahead of Scott in covert reconnaissance and tracking duties. While doing so, his force would hack an entirely new pathway through the jungle, all the way from the coast to the Ashanti capital of Kumasi some 150 miles away and deep inside the bush – oh, and build a road as they went.

Essentially, he and his advance levy would be the eyes, ears, pioneers and engineers of the mission and the road they were to lay – by hand – was to facilitate a swift and efficient pathway for Scott and his troops who would be following behind. It was hoped that this would enable them, if not to surprise the Crown's most bothersome of enemies, then at least to reach them fighting fit. This was the ultimate in scouting and therefore Baden-Powell's dream mission; in shades of his first army entrance exams, he beat more than 300 other candidates all desperate to bag this 'Boy's Own' adventure of a posting.

It was a big achievement for him, for the entire Baden-Powell 'corporation' in fact, as this was no ordinary appointment. It made him one of Wolseley's 'Garnet Ring', an elite, inner circle of officers the commander-in-chief trusted and favoured above all others and to whom he also referred as his 'Africans'.

In a yet more exuberant letter to Henrietta Grace, he enthused: 'I've been given the one very duty that I'd hoped for but had not dared to ask – viz to have charge of the reconnaissance work. It is a grand thing for me.' Then, remembering the most important reason that he needed action, added: 'it will be even grander if the enemy will only attempt to stand against us.'

Being monumentally ambitious, his mother was filled only with maternal pride and not concern about her son running so eagerly into jeopardy.

She was not alone, though; this was the late 1890s, the new military era where young, privileged, upper-class men, who previously would never have condescended to an army career, were being badgered into it by aspiring parents who recognised that colonial conflict was a route to rapid ladder-climbing. Most of Baden-Powell's fellow officers would, like him, have been seeking a promotion as much as a fight.

Surely Ashanti, an infamously tumultuous state near the southern shore of the Gold Coast, was a place he'd see some real action? Wolseley, indefatigable sabre-rattler that he was, had already been there in 1874, sent by the British Government to wield his fist of iron and put an end to, using whatever means necessary, decades of full-scale Ashanti invasions and killings around the area. He had viciously battled them into submission then got them to sign a contract, the Treaty of Fomena, the principles of which included agreements by the Ashanti to pay 50,000 ounces of gold (roughly the weight of a hippo) as war indemnity, relinquish sovereignty over the tribes they'd been decimating and an immediate cessation of rumoured human sacrifices. Wolseley then departed leaving a shambles in his wake, much as he'd done in the areas around Natal where Baden-Powell had subsequently been stationed. And it was a pyrrhic victory, costing the lives of 300 of Wolseley's men, yet it was only the most recent confrontation in a long series of battles with the Ashanti, who'd been seen as a thorn in the side of British and European rule and entrepreneurship for more than 400 years.

In the years following Wolseley's departure, the Ashanti King, Prempeh, broke every rule on the treaty's page and every breach was regarded as a steady weakening of the Crown's superiority. This is the situation that Baden-Powell and Sir Francis Scott faced.

Traders were still being waylaid in large numbers in the process of harvesting every lucrative resource they could lay their hands on – apart from slaves, since the practice had finally been outlawed. This made routes through the interior of the country, including ones crucial to British trade, wildly perilous, if not completely inaccessible. It was also suspected that human sacrifices were still occurring in the capital Kumasi, although hotly denied by Prempeh.

Baden-Powell was headed for what was then called the 'Dark Continent', not for the contextual geographical reason that a fair bit of it lay under the shadow of an almost impenetrable tree canopy, but mainly as ploy by the

British to suggest menace and to give the impression that it was a place to be avoided, in order to keep other explorers and traders away from mineral-rich land areas. At the same time, it gave militarists the status of heroic adventurers.

Atrocities and wars defined the Gold Coast. As well as endless tribal in-fighting going back centuries, the indigenous people were regularly under attack from outsiders, using mightier, more imperialistic weaponry and military know-how to quash, abuse and even to own them. Unsurprisingly, they had been compelled to retaliate as best they could and with equal brutality.

Their crimes? Having the temerity to fight for their own territories and for making the theft and trading of their natural resources – ivory, gold, rubber and, for a long time, humans – as problematic as possible. This generally meant ambushing ruthless traders as they transported their goods from the interior to the coastal ports and taking back what was rightfully theirs.

This resulted in the killing of countless Africans and, of course, a considerable number of white raiders – often in rather innovative ways.

Military leaders were not left out. When Wolseley arrived, the hollowed-out cranium of a previous white governor had been trimmed with gold and was being used as a ceremonial drinking vessel for Ashanti rulers, who were known to hold large stores of gold; skulls and jawbones of other captured explorers and soldiers had found posterity as decorations on huge tribal drums, rattling melodically along to their throbbing beats, for eternity.

Gold, rubber and ivory had been highly profitable commodities for centuries, but from the 1600s, these took second place to an altogether more valuable resource – slaves. The horror and misery of slavery had had the most profound effect on shaping the region. In the early days of the Atlantic slave trade, Europeans arriving at Cape Coast Castle to capture what in previous experience had been harmless, defenceless tribespeople, soon came face-to-face with warrior tribes who didn't fit the mould, especially the Ashanti, a well-established and powerful fighting force.

Notorious throughout the Coast, they were feared by all-comers on account of their reputation for the enthusiastic use of human sacrifices, both ceremonial and as a form of capital punishment. Needless to say, the Ashanti were not the first choice of 'prey' for avaricious slavers, and as the market for slaves increased around the new world, the dealers struggled to keep up with demand.

They coaxed some of the African kings to join them, with offers of treasure and extra powers over the tribes and, no doubt seeing this as an opportunity to avoid a predictable fate worse than death, the Ashanti adopted a sort of 'kill or be killed' policy and became part of the system they'd fought so ferociously against. They operated with the slave marketers, helping to gather their shameful harvests, attacking peaceful tribes and killing their children and elderly before lashing the poor remaining souls together and transferring them to the port.

By the time of Baden-Powell's commission in 1895, slave trading was illegal throughout the colonies, though its tragic and appalling legacy remained deeply embedded. His port of arrival and home to the British governor, Cape Coast Castle, would have been the last place that thousands of unfortunate native people would see of their homeland, for they were held there, in its grim dungeons to await the ships that would transport them around the globe in the worst conditions imaginable.

When the slave industry finally collapsed, there was no longer any need for the Ashanti's services, but it was believed that they continued to seize slaves, no longer to sell them but to ensure a plentiful supply of humans for their sacrificial ceremonies, of which there were many. Ashanti leaders denied this, insisting that the many prisoners they held were not for sacrifices, but were criminals brought from all over the region to the capital for the purpose of death sentences being served. While this may have been true, the whiff of sacrificial victims still lingered.

Wolseley was sending his new protégé into a place of danger, civil wars, long grudges and negative fall-out from the deeds of those who had preceded him. Baden-Powell couldn't have been happier.

The purpose of Sir Francis Scott's expedition was three-fold: First, Baden-Powell's indigenous troops would clear a way straight to Kumasi. Second, Scott and his men would arrive and quash the uprising, thus improving the lives of the relentlessly terrorised tribes. Third, this, in turn, would result in reclaiming British rule and therefore the control of some very valuable tracts of land, making it easier to deter foreign traders, like the French and Germans, who were jealously eyeing-up the area's incalculable natural wealth.

Before joining Scott and his 2,000 men aboard the British troopship, SS *Bathurst* in Liverpool, Baden-Powell enjoyed a splendid send-off at London's Euston Station. He was surprised when a large public crowd joined his brothers, Frank and Baden, in wishing him bon voyage. 'Although it was past midnight,' he said, 'they were cheering and singing patriotic songs as if we were off to fight the French.'

This was an early indication of how supportive the British people were becoming of Queen Victoria's mission to stamp her authority around the world, and a hint at far bigger things to come later in Baden-Powell's military life.

Kenneth McLaren and Sir Baker Russell also joined him for a brief farewell onboard ship. No doubt this would have been a parting of 'such sweet sorrow' from The Boy, whom he'd managed to spend some valuable time with while stationed in Britain, but McLaren's thoughtful gift of a compass to guide him through the jungle made a wonderful memento, as did the reassuring bayonet from Baker Russell.

En route to his destination, Baden-Powell was aware that Wolseley's success in quelling the immediate unrest in 1874 had incurred serious British casualties, albeit as much from malaria as conflict. Wolseley himself pre-warned him about the dreaded disease, telling him to take a double set of mosquito nets to cocoon himself in and once cocooned, to smoke a pipeful of tobacco, since the insects hated the smoke. While this was solid advice, he detested smoking. His dilemma was resolved when, despite giving it a go, he had no choice but to quit when the African climate rotted his stash of tobacco.

The voyage allowed Baden-Powell time to plan how best to construct his local levy force. According to the experience of others involved in previous Gold Coast initiatives, using only men from the same tribe could be problematic, even catastrophic, as they could easily plot rebellion, so he decided to select men from a variety tribes. Hopefully, he thought, the mix of different languages and customs would reduce the possibility of in-fighting or, worse mutiny.

When the ship dropped anchor at Cape Coast Castle, on 13 December 1895, a fleet of open boats, manned by locals, pulled up alongside it and took Scott, Baden-Powell et al to the shoreline where more locals, this time naked, lifted them out of the water and plonked them on dry land to ensure that they arrived with dry feet.

The new arrivals attended a welcome reception at the castle, courtesy of its resident, His Excellency the Governor, W.E. Maxwell, who lived in lavish rooms directly over the hellish, but by then thankfully vacant, slave dungeons and (unlike one of his predecessors) had so far managed to retain his head. After that, it was time for action. Well, almost.

Advance promises by local authorities that arrangements would be made to build an army of local indigenous men hadn't been fulfilled; therefore

Baden-Powell spent the next couple of days 'palavering' (a bastardisation of the French 'to parlez') with local chiefs to bring them on board. With agreement from six tribal leaders, he then asked them to have their men gather on the Castle parade ground the following morning.

Major Baden-Powell and his support, Captain Graham waited for their expected 1,000 indigenous troops to arrive. And waited. And waited. Frustrated, they could bear this no-show any longer and wound-up going to the villages and chivvying the men along. Recruiting eventually began around noon.

This did not bode well for the job ahead and Baden-Powell was scathing of the lack of punctuality and inability to obey what were, to him, simple orders. He is on record describing the men as 'duller than oxen' and saying that a dog would grasp his meaning in half the time – another example of his use of language we now consider highly offensive but which was standard at the time. What Baden-Powell, like most outsiders, failed to grasp was that these tribes had never used nor required structured time-tables or itineraries. Their daily lives ran on immediacy, necessity and survival, and a combination of any of those things might be needed at any given time. They worked to a different beat, like lions, hunting at night and sleeping in the day for example, and were often far smarter and infinitely more resourceful, although not as well armed, as any of their so-called 'superiors'.

As in Afghanistan and Natal, Baden-Powell at least recognised this pretty quickly and came to admire, respect and like many of the men in his levy; he used their unique expertise and skills to enhance the force's scouting ability and every new tip, skill and procedure was soaked up and retained for future use.

The thing that had begun as a tiny seed on nature walks with his mother as a child and while hiding in The Copse at Charterhouse as a schoolboy, had taken root in India's bushlands, grown on the foothills of Kandahar's mountains and then blossomed in South Africa's veld was now about to fully mature into a passion that would drive him for the rest of his life: scouting.

Once all the men were recruited, with each given a bag for food, a blanket, an old flint-lock gun and a 'uniform' that comprised a belt, and, bizarrely, a red fez hat ('it gives as much satisfaction to the naked warrior as does his first tunic to the hussar', quoth Baden-Powell), they set off. Some brought horns made from elephant tusks and others, drums made from scooped-out tree trunks and so they played as they marched towards a path they had yet to create.

Sir Francis and his troops followed as closely behind as they could, based on how Baden-Powell's advance force progressed. It was far from sweetness and light, though. The armed forces were still a fair way back and this was deepest Africa, where peace was a volatile beast and where being a couple of white men among hundreds of black tribesmen could feel extremely perilous. Baden-Powell and Graham were on constant alert, acutely aware that at any minute, their levy force could turn on them in fury over past (and present) tyrannies and they wouldn't stand a chance.

The only way to stay alive, he had been told, was a regular demonstration of power and to be, or at least appear to be, self-confident at all times. This he translated into walking and working faster and showing more agility and ability than any of his men. He also carried a whip, which he was never seen to use, other than to crack it in warning.

'In addition to the "whip that talks",' he wrote, 'I also had another moral persuader in the shape of Isiqwi-qwa, a Colt repeating carbine. This weapon could bang away from its magazine a dozen rounds if need be as fast as a man could fire.' (*The Downfall of Prempeh, 1896*). He'd either fire it off into the air or, being an excellent shot, blast a paw-paw to pieces, which seemed to have the desired effect. Even so, the pair felt particularly vulnerable at night and so hired themselves an eight-man bodyguard of trusted Sierra Leone 'hammock men' to avoid being murdered in their sleep.

Paying his African troops the same wage as British privates helped the situation, as did using the free time the men might have spent planning a revolt to train them in the traditional pioneering skills of axemanship and ropework.

Both of these were crucial, as few of the recruits had ever cut down a tree with an axe and only one tribe had rope skills (luckily, excellent ones for they were fishermen and could tie intricate knots), yet they would need to chop down trees for logs and make ropes from anything suitable they could find, such as creepers, vines and flexible sticks.

The logs would be laid on the swampy jungle floor to make Scott's new road and the ropes would be used to fasten and suspend bridges, which they also had to build (and which they'd never done before), so rope-making was a basic requirement. More important still would be their ability to tie effective knots in said ropes to securely lash the bridges together. Extensive, on-the-job apprenticeships were the order of the day while they waited for Scott and company to catch up.

The roadworks went well but early attempts at bridges did not, and when the first few were raised, they collapsed straight away. Patiently, Baden-

Powell and Graham (literally) showed them the ropes and eventually things clicked; the men quickly became very proficient, no doubt motivated by the fact that Baden-Powell's acid test for whether a bridge was strong enough, was to get the team that built it to jump up and down on it.

In all, an unbelievable 200 bridges were constructed across the profusion of intersecting streams along the way. To better hone their skills, he sorted his troops into teams of twenty to thirty, each with its own 'captain' and second-in-command and ideally both with a grasp of English, in charge, then trained them from scratch, quickly pin-pointing their strengths and letting them play to them. Little did Baden-Powell realise that this was an early blueprint for the first Boy Scout group he would form on a desert island in Dorset, a little over a decade later.

As well as the road and the bridges, they also had to stop every seven miles or so to clear areas of ground and cut down yet more trees to build shelters with woven leaf roofs in which Scott and his forces could eat and rest in safety. Working on these demanding tasks in searing heat and suffocating humidity to such a punishing schedule, they were perpetually exhausted.

Naturally, this took a toll on their physical and mental wellbeing and the men began to get sick and depressed, including Captain Graham who fell ill with malaria. 'By the end of the day,' Baden-Powell noted in his diary, 'one wants but little here below but to drink and lie down and sleep or die, you don't care which.'

Even though he was very low himself, he noticed how the troops always responded well to humour and jokes, so he larked around, joshed with them, gave them funny nicknames and put on his cheeriest face. As much as he loved singing and knew how good it could be for morale, he had to forbid it – somewhat perceptively from today's perspective – as he believed that the act of singing would spread more than the usual level of germs from their mouths.

Dog-tired and dispirited or not, they had to carry on moving still deeper into the jungle, hacking and chopping, raising and knotting as they went. There was also the small matter of getting an entire force across the River Prah and the closer they got to their destination of Kumasi, the tenser things became. While certain they would find vast stores of gold there, they also had to assume it would be a forbidding fortress, manned by many fearless warriors.

By now, any number of Ashanti fighters could be skulking silently in the dense shade of the trees and rumours were flowing back from Baden-Powell's advanced reconnaissance scouts (as well as sundry deserters) of

Ashantis armed with modern Snyder rifles, and King Prempeh gathering his ten chiefs together for a traditional pre-battle 'fetish' ceremony that lasts for about fourteen days.

Fetish ceremonies were fairly commonplace among the Ashanti at the time. They mainly stemmed from ancient superstitions, a fear of famine and a wish to appease angry gods, and marked or honoured important events in the life of the tribe. The rituals, held by the king, performed by priests and attended by notable citizens as well as the entire tribe, involved the use of various good-fortune and protective talismans or 'fetishes'. These totems did include animal and even human sacrifices at certain points in Ashanti history – but would they now? And could Baden-Powell and his men become them…?

While the Ashanti still held fetish ceremonies in the lead up to, and on the eve of war, there were also ceremonials for funerals, for dead ancestors and to honour their gods; they also performed them for legal matters, including in the case of Kumasi, the carrying out of capital punishment for the entire Gold Coast region (the reason cited by King Prempeh for the capital's numerous killings).

One of the main fetish events was the annual Festival of New Yams, as thanks for a good harvest; interestingly, this always took place around the time Baden-Powell would have been close to entering Kumasi and in past times the tribe *had* used human victims as 'new-fruit' offerings. Rumours were rife among his frightened men, but it could well have been this sort of fruit fetish as opposed to a fighting one that Prempeh was organising. Regardless, the plan then was a surprise rush on Kumasi before the ceremonials could be completed.

Despite much apprehension, in the last week of December 1895, Baden-Powell got his levy across the Prah, using an enormous dugout boat that made several journeys until the entire column and all its equipment were on the other side. Here, just days from the capital, the forest thickened, the path narrowed and breathless scouts came rushing back with the unwelcome (though to Baden-Powell, thrilling) information that the king had an army of 8,000 warriors.

Things were getting serious. They now moved only at night, an incredibly difficult thing to do as they were travelling blind, relying on the man in front's white rag for directions, using a stick to 'feel' ahead and stumbling and falling all the way. Progress slowed to a snail's space.

Suddenly, the scouts' news changed; apparently Prempeh was now saying that he was unwilling to fight with the British forces and that he wished to surrender.

This was somewhat confirmed at the beginning of January via a note from Major Gordon, who'd been brought in to assist Baden-Powell when Graham was laid low with malaria. Gordon said he'd been 'palavering' with Prempeh who had sent him a delegation which included two of the tribal chief's own small sons as hostages. Gordon described how the little boys were draped with golden ornaments which he admitted to admiring, 'I coveted the latter,' he wrote, 'but would have nothing to do with the former.' He added that he'd refused the 'bribe' and told the king that nothing could be done until Sir Francis Scott and his British force could speak to him, face-to-face, in Kumasi.

Sending Gordon his own children should have been proof aplenty of Prempeh's sincerity. It should also have been an encouraging development but, of course, it suited neither Baden-Powell nor Gordon, for both men were in full 'seeking active service' mode; they decided not to trust Prempeh, accusing him of game-playing, despite his plucky gesture, and instead chose to head for the capital, and confrontation.

Baden-Powell did relay the details of Gordon's meeting to Sir Francis Scott, however Scott had his own agenda, a face-saving one, in that he didn't want to be the leader of a high-profile, high maintenance and long-drawn out mission that ended with no military action whatsoever. The vested interests of these three men could have prevented certain aspects of intelligence from getting back to the main force in an effort to deny Prempeh a peaceful conclusion. It seemed that the restoration of peace held less glory than ignoring the facts in favour of a fight did.

On 15 January, now two day's march from Kumasi, Prempeh sent yet another band of representatives, again offering complete and unconditional submission to Gordon but he and Baden-Powell claimed to be unconvinced. 'In spite of all assurances, we cannot trust to what the Ashantis say,' wrote Baden-Powell. And so they ploughed on, with the levy now moving in three columns on separate paths with him leading the central one. This was to facilitate a synchronised arrival, at precisely the same time on the same day and from three directions.

Scott's outfit would follow directly behind and specific orders were to use moral force, rather than guns, if possible, ideally with a quick display of strength, followed by negotiations.

Tension and excitement levels were sky-high. Were they or were they not heading for an almighty fight?

Close to Kumasi, Baden-Powell's column came face-to-face with a startling sight. A row of wooden dolls, all planted firmly in the ground and facing towards the coast from whence he and his troops came. There was no doubt in the levy mens' minds that this was a portent of doom, an unmistakable fetish warning, telling them to turn around or face the wrath of the gods.

Or, as Baden-Powell with his trademark divergent joviality in times of danger put it: 'A fetish hint to turn around or the gods would be exceedingly unkind to us – if not absolutely brutal!'

While extremely unnerving to his soldiers, Baden-Powell cynically regarded the wooden figures as a bit of a cop-out on Prempeh's part because they were a watered-down version of the usual Ashanti warning. Prempeh wanted to scare them, but to Baden-Powell it was clear that he also wanted to distance himself from accusations of human sacrifices, for, as intimidating as this fetish was, it wasn't nearly as powerful a deterrent as the traditional version where the 'dolls' would have been humans, such as enemies, prisoners or slaves, buried alive in the ground up to their necks and then 'left for the ants to do the rest …'.

After this alarming discovery came a 'weird sound' that gradually built into the recognisable throbbing of many drums; the native levy confirmed they were alarm drums – they'd been spotted! Baden-Powell describes the moment, saying that his men were up, alert and smiling and there being a sense of great expectation in the air. Out of the blue, the drumbeat altered and he was informed that they were now 'speaking'. Stock still, they listened in silence while an orderly deciphered the drum message, translating it for Baden-Powell as: 'Ashanti blood fella say talking to white fella. Don't want a fight. Sit down palavertalk.' They complied.

'Out of the dark, soggy depths of the jungle we came, for the first time in four weeks into the open and sunshine.' said Baden-Powell in *The Downfall of Prempeh*. It's hard to imagine the shock to the system that being hit by harsh, dazzling sunlight and even fiercer heat after endless days of darkness must have been.

Directly before them was a parade ground of sorts and beyond that, endless thatched dwellings that went all the way back, as far as the eye could see into the jungle behind. There was absolutely no sign of life, other than the relentless drum beat. And the fabled Ashanti 'stronghold' turned out to be just a village. No ramparts and no fortifications, just a lurid reputation.

For effect, Baden-Powell and his men paraded and he waved the union flag on the end of a hog-spear (what else?). As they performed, the other two levy columns joined them, wearing matching fezes and playing their instruments. Kumasi was officially surrounded.

In response, the drumming instantly got louder, more insistent and was soon accompanied by deafening roars. Next there was movement and a crowd of singing people appeared, holding brightly coloured umbrellas that bobbed about above their heads as they approached. Some played elephant horns, others huge drums decorated with the skulls of the hapless adventurers. At the parade ground they stopped and watched as Prempeh and his chiefs were carried in on chairs then placed under the jolly umbrellas, like interesting objects in a bazaar.

A long and silent wait followed, as Prempeh, resplendent in gold jewels and clenching a solid gold nugget in the shape of a bean pod between his teeth – a symbolic talisman to prevent him from saying the wrong thing – took in the scene.

Then two things happened that turned what was a rather anti-climactic day into a surprisingly surreal one. The first was the emergence from the jungle of three Royal Engineers (today, the Royal Signals) and some levy troops hauling a large communications cable reel. They proceeded to cross right in front of the royal party, rolling out the cable as they went.

They then set up the necessary kit and actually transmitted confirmation that the British had arrived; the news spread through the jungle, down to the coast and straight to England. This practical demonstration of the famous bush telegraph in action elicited a rousing cheer from the men. What the Ashanti thought of it is not on record.

The second event involved one of the cable reelers who, while lingering by a clump of trees, happened to take a look behind them. His action triggered agitation among the Ashanti people, which piqued Baden-Powell's interest. He ordered his scouts to go deeper into the trees and investigate what was causing their disquiet. It wasn't long before he found out; the scouts soon came flying back out and announced that they'd discovered a copse piled high with decapitated corpses and skeletons.

This harrowing mass grave may well have held all the region's condemned prisoners who'd been executed in the customary manner of decapitation, and their heads put to other use.

However, the spectre of human sacrifice loomed large over Kumasi, casting shade over what was truth and what was fiction, so in the heightened atmosphere and with the British looking for a reason to condemn Prempeh, the terrible graveyard was deemed absolute proof that the chief and his people had wilfully ignored the Fomena Treaty's order to desist from the barbaric practice.

When the British troops turned up, in three columns and in tandem, Prempeh reiterated to their leader, Sir Francis Scott, that it had always been his intention to surrender to Governor Maxwell of Gold Coast Castle. Scott apparently told the Ashanti leader to 'dry up', and to wait for Maxwell's arrival in the morning, then he could offer his surrender.

Baden-Powell still doubted Prempeh's honesty and during the night he and some of his men hid and observed the comings and goings near the chief's dwelling. Prempeh stayed where he was, nothing suspicious occurred and Baden Powell's group only succeeded in scaring a number of the king's counsellors on their way home to their huts. Apart from a light, and probably unnecessary tussle with one of Prempeh's lowliest servants, there was simply no action to be found.

Later that night, however, there was a sudden flurry of excitement when some scouts rushed to tell Major Baden-Powell of another discovery. Pumped and ready for anything, he followed the excited men into a wooded area that was pitch black and as he grabbed a branch in a tree to steady himself he touched what turned out to be a human jawbone. Then another and another. They had stumbled upon a sacred ceremonial place and Baden-Powell was holding on to a fetish tree. Moving on from his grizzly find, he noticed the men were now gathered around a bulky object on the ground which, on closer investigation, was a very large metal bowl.

'I realised that the bowl, a brass one about four feet across and eighteen inches deep, was just of a size to make a glorious tub for me.' (*The Downfall of Prempeh*) . He decided the bowl would make a splendid bath and since he hadn't had proper wash for more than a month, which would have been torturing the clean-freak in him, he ordered his men to lash it to some poles and take the thing to his digs.

The next day Scott paraded his men on the square then, on the arrival of Maxwell, summoned Prempeh to come and palaver. Scott and Maxwell, seated on old biscuit tins, ordered the proud chief to kneel in full view of his people and hug Maxwell's knees in supplication. Members of the tribe were visibly shocked to see their great king obey and be humiliated in such a way.

When Scott insisted that he then pay the outstanding Treaty of Fomena's 50,000 ounces of gold, it was Prempeh's turn to be shocked and when he refused, saying that he could only afford 700 ounces, Maxwell arrested him, along with his mother and father, his brother and several other family members and advisors. This was contrary to advice from the colonial secretary, who said that if the king couldn't pay, then so be it, as long as he surrendered and peace was achieved.

It was no good; the discovery of the headless torsos in the copse, which Prempeh still swore were the result of executions, had strengthened the resolve of the British to punish him. Later that day, Baden-Powell searched for the legendary gold stores and found none. Even a row of sacred metal coffins containing past tribal elders, where he was sure it must be hidden, were empty of both precious metals and precious bones.

He also oversaw the destruction of all the fetish places and admitted to feeling no guilt in burning them down. 'It was not done with any idea of sacrilege or want of respect for any religious convictions of the people, but because for more than a thousand years it had been the scene of horrendous human sacrifices.' He then he also wrote to his brother Frank, now a successful artist, offering some of the victims' skulls for use in his portraiture work. Joke or not, Frank declined.

Returning to Kumasi's centre, he found a crowd of British men grouped around his new 'bath', which it transpired was the infamous 'Ashanti Blood Bowl', mentioned by an explorer back in 1817 and used to collect the lifeblood of human sacrifice victims as it flowed from their necks. So wide and deep was it, that, according to Baden-Powell's The Downfall of Prempeh, it took the beheading of at least twenty men to fill it up for the high priest's ceremonies, including one where he used the blood to 'clean' the bones of Ashanti ancestors. This happened every three months, equating to eighty men a year. Add the yam festival's 'first-fruits' offerings, and the figure could reach a hundred deaths.

Re-assessing his find in the cold light of day, Baden-Powell noted that its interior was a 'horrible' shade of rust brown that created a sinister tide-line alluding to its macabre purpose.

He decided that it wouldn't make such a good bathing tub after all, though he still had it swathed in a sheet with poles and carried all the way to the coast, on to his ship and then home.

With Prempeh under arrest, a 150-mile march back to the coast loomed and feeling thoroughly fed up at not having fought – again – he complained to Wolseley that his was 'a very sad camp indeed'.

Prempeh lived in exile in the Seychelles for twenty-five years after his arrest and embraced Christianity, attending church in a top hat and frock coat.

By that time, one of his sons was a Boy Scout.

Chapter 7

Incident at Matabele

'Don't expect to find any man perfect; he is bound to have defects. Any ass can see the bad points in a man. The thing is to discover his good points and keep these uppermost in your mind so that they gradually obliterate his bad ones.'

Baden-Powell *The Scouter* (1929)

A plaque in the nave of London's Westminster Abbey 'gives thanks for' Robert Baden-Powell and his wife Olave, and on the abbey's website, there's an explanatory timeline listing major milestones in his extraordinary life. Along with his remarkable scouting achievements, it also includes a roll call of his notable military campaigns. Apart from two: the Ashanti campaign of 1896 and the Matabele Rebellion of 1896/7.

That his Ashanti campaign was short and swiftly concluded with a peaceful surrender (surely something worth celebrating?) by Chief Prempeh might explain its absence, however, Matabele is a glaring omission, one might deduce designed to avoid stirring up the hornet's nest of controversy surrounding his commission in the South African province, where he ordered the execution of a tribal chief, disregarding the fact that his surrender had been accepted on the condition that his life would be spared. Of course, its exclusion only serves to encourage further scrutiny.

As well as his macabre 'blood bowl' souvenir, Baden-Powell left Ashanti with a campaign medal and a promotion to the rank of Brevet Lieutenant Colonel. His extraordinary feat of creating a 150-mile-long road out of not much at all, through uncharted jungle, with a team of inexperienced but industrious men – in four weeks – and then assisting his commander in securing the surrender of Chief Prempeh, had not gone unnoticed.

No sooner was he settled back in Britain, than General Sir Frederick Carrington invited him to return to South Africa, this time to the Cape Colony, to act as his Chief Staff Officer in Matabeleland (now Zimbabwe), where an uprising of indigenous tribes was ensuing. Aged 39 and frustrated at still having no decent active service tucked under his belt, he was itching for a fight and grabbed Carrington's offer with both hands.

Arriving at Cape Town on 19 May 1896, he embarked on a three-day train journey to join General Carrington at the Cape Colony's railway terminus of Mafeking, which he noted was, despite its important role, a small settlement with 'a few low-roofed tin houses'. Little could he have guessed that three years later, the insignificant little town would be the stage for one of the most important roles of his life.

From there, Baden-Powell, Carrington and several other staff set off on the 587-mile trip to Bulawayo, in Matabeleland, using the only transport available at the time, oxen-pulled wagons and some mules. It wasn't ideal, since it meant they would be travelling at an infuriatingly slow pace of two miles an hour. And this was not the worst of it; Rinderpest, an uncontrollable and vicious cattle-slaying disease, was raging through the Cape, so the poor beasts were literally dropping dead in their harnesses and had to be replaced at various stops en route.

Their dismal journey was punctuated with dreadful reminders of the gravity of rinderpest, as abandoned wagons with countless dead oxen still attached lined the route; it was reminiscent of the sickening sights of dying and decaying animals and men that Baden-Powell had witnessed in the mountains and battlefields of Kandahar.

It took the group ten days to reach Bulawayo, where they joined relief forces striving to deal with a critical situation. Shortly before their arrival, almost 300 white civilian settlers, including women and children, had been brutally massacred by the local Matabele tribes, the majority led by Chief Uwini.

The unexpected killing spree was the consequence of a pressure cooker of resentment that had been building ever since Boer settlers had forced the Matabele from their own lands, pushing them northwards to Bulawayo and commandeering most of their cattle herds. At that particular time their leader was King Lobengula, who integrated the neighbouring Mashonaland tribe into his and created a new Matabeleland in the area of Bulawayo and its nearby Matopos Hill range. The new homeland wasn't a great success; there was friction between the native tribespeople and exploitative Boer farmers and the British and European settlers, most of whom had come to the area hoping to make their fortunes from the vast gold reserves discovered there.

The Matabeles' situation was further exacerbated in 1895 when their lands were violently confiscated, via an unscrupulous and truly condescending ruse played on the now-deceased Lobengula by empire-builder extraordinaire, Cecil the 'Diamond King' Rhodes.

Not content with having appropriated most of the region's diamond reserves for his De Beers company, Rhodes, who'd been made the Cape's prime minister, and his associate, a flamboyant opportunist called Dr Leander Starr Jameson, had been purloining mineral-rich lands at a steal from naive indigenous tribes and, when possible, Boers, then keeping the areas they favoured before dishing the remains out to friends. Rhodes' avaricious drive for wealth (ergo power, the thing he craved above all else) reached a new low when he coaxed King Lobengula into agreeing to a deal that gave his mining company complete control of all of Matabeleland's valuable natural resources.

Lobengula trusted Rhodes and signed the inequitable contract, which gave the delighted entrepreneur carte-blanche ownership. Upon signing, Lobengula gave:

> complete and exclusive charge over all metals and minerals in my kingdom … together with full power to do all things that they may deem necessary to win and procure the same and to collect and enjoy the profits and revenues, if any, derivable from the said metals and minerals. (from the Moffat Treaty, 1888)

In exchange for all the gold and minerals in what was an immense swathe of prime mining land, the Matabele chief came away with £100 per month, 1,000 old guns, with ammunition, and a steamboat on the Zambesi river.

Rhodes called his new bargain the British South Africa Company and, having excellent connections in exalted places, managed to get a royal charter for it, signed by the then British prime minister, Lord Salisbury.

With Matabeleland sewn up, he then sent a team of 'pioneers' to next-door Mashonaland, where a Union flag was raised at an area he christened Salisbury, in honour of the accommodating charter signee, and left his accomplice, Jameson, or 'Dr Jim', in charge as Administrator. When it dawned on Lobengula that he'd been conned, he contacted Queen Victoria, as a fellow royal personage, to complain about Rhodes. This was pointless, since some of the Diamond King's profits would indubitably find their way into the Crown's coffers.

Victoria replied with lofty contempt, via an aide: 'The Queen advises Lobengula not to grant hastily concessions of land or leave to dig, but to consider all applications carefully. … A king gives a stranger an ox, not the whole herd of cattle, otherwise, what would other strangers have to eat?'

The chartered British South Africa Company now had the minerals rights but still this wasn't enough. Rhodes wanted the land through which they ran.

He raised a chartered company fighting force, entered Bulawayo and went in for the kill. Armed only with spears and their outdated guns, the Matabele stood no chance and hundreds were killed. Lobengula fled and later died of smallpox. His tribe's lands became part of Rhodes' seemingly unstoppable conglomerate; by 1998 the Cape and English newspapers would be calling the area, roughly the size of Spain, Italy and France combined, 'Rhodesia' in honour of the man who'd 'liberated' it for the white settlers.

In 1895 though, Rhodes and Starr were still not sated and set their sights on lucrative Boer lands in the Transvaal. Unable to find backing to simply confiscate them, but supported by a large group of 'reformers' within the British settlers, or Uitlanders as the Boers called them, of Transvaal, Rhodes and 'Dr Jim' devised a convoluted plot.

The British reformers would 'unexpectedly' revolt against the Boer government in Johannesburg over various grievances, including not having a vote. They'd then seek assistance from Jameson, who'd raise a force of more than 1,000 men and rush to their aid, crashing through the Transvaal border. Once inside, Jameson would hold the government in check until Rhodes arrived from the Cape to negotiate and restore peace; a compromise would follow, et voilà, more land assigned to what would become Rhodesia. What could possibly go wrong?

Well, everything.

The raid, based entirely on a manipulation of truths, was an epic failure. Dr Jim didn't bother to get enough troops, the reformers began arguing among themselves then got cold feet and halted the rebellion, and when Jameson's men attempted to cut through a telegraph line to prevent communications, they accidentally cut a fence wire instead – leaving the Boers with full and advanced insight into their illicit intentions.

The Boers raced in large numbers towards Jameson's force, immediately defeated him and arrested him and his cronies. It was a total embarrassment to the British government as an investigation quickly revealed that their man, Rhodes, was involved up to his cravat in the conspiracy. Consequently, Rhodes had to resign his role of PM and was kicked out of the British South Africa Charter Company.

The farcical episode has forever been known as the 'Jameson Raid'; all involved were shipped back to England to be tried. All except Rhodes, that is, offering proof that money (or having dirt on important people) does indeed talk.

Chaos then ensued; the Matabele's way of life was increasingly under threat as their natural resources were plundered further by all-comers and their remaining lands and herds either settled on or stolen. They were terrorised by the white police force and browbeaten in a variety of ways by the rest of the settler population. They'd also suffered a series of extreme events of biblical proportions, including a severe drought, a plague of locusts and unsurprisingly, a famine.

The arrival of the rinderpest disease at the end of March 1896 was the last straw; they decided enough was enough and consulted their god, M'limo. The god 'told' them that since the white intruders had caused most of their misfortunes they should be attacked, at the 'place of killings', the tribe's name for Bulawayo, established by the late chief Lobengula and where their people were slain by Rhodes' forces, so the symbolism was clear.

Embracing M'limo's advice, they launched a shock attack; rather than going straight to Bulawayo, however, they were so hyped-up on anger that they invaded outlying farms en route, callously murdering any tenants they came across. Witnesses at the time spoke of small family groups trying to fend off hundreds of Matabele and fighting to their last bullets, before being battered, gored or burned to death. Word of the raids spread fast and so the remaining white population raced to Bulawayo for refuge, gathering in the main square and hunkering down behind hastily formed barricades made from covered wagons.

Out of a population of around 3,000 mainly Boer farmers and settlers, the enraged rebels killed more than 300 in revenge for years of mistreatment. At the makeshift Bulawayo fortress, 15,000 Matabele warriors circled menacingly for hours, only deterred from storming the wagon battlements by the death-dealing power of the settlers' modern firearms, including a powerful Maxim gun.

With the Boers fortified and fighting back in earnest the warriors retreated, but lingered just out of firing range. A relief force of Salisbury residents from Mashonaland arrived to assist, as did a troop of 800 men raised by Colonel Herbert Plumer in the Cape Colony. General Carrington, who would command the entire situation, and his new Chief Staff Officer, Baden-Powell, were on their way.

Many of the Matabele rebels however, knowing that they were out-armed if not outmanned, had returned to their strongholds, in the nearby Matopos

Hills by the time the party arrived from Mafeking. Still, the fury in the air, due to the horrific murders of the women and children, was tangible and, emboldened by the Matabele's lack of defence against their guns, the settlers and armies began a series of raids designed to quell any remaining Matabele groups and hopefully capture their leader, Chief Uwini.

It wasn't easy; the Matabele's hideouts were dark, warren-like cave systems deep inside the treacherously jagged hills, making combat dangerous and ridiculously complicated. Finding the caverns between giant razor-sharp rocks was a hurdle in itself, but then, if they thought they'd found a hiding enemy, the soldiers would have to fire a round of bullets into the blackness and wait for sounds before diving into the cramped holes, praying their target, if there was one, would be disabled or killed.

It really was fighting blind and if there were a warrior lurking and who happened to be alive, it was unlikely that the soldiers would be for long.

Enter Baden-Powell, stage right.

So cheerful was he at being somewhere with such superb potential for conflict, that a letter he sent to Henrietta Grace reads more like a holiday postcard from Bournemouth than news from a blood-drenched war zone. 'Am getting on splendidly here. Grand climate, interesting time,' he joshed. 'I am Chief Staff Officer to Sir Frederick Carrington and am overcrowded with work. All office work at present, alas.' Adding: 'I hope the general will himself take the field very shortly and we will have at least one good fight.'

It wasn't long before he got his wish, but first, he had something equally exciting (to him) to do: a series of scouting missions in the heart of enemy territory. He was delighted. 'These reconnaissance became the joyous adventure of my life even if they were a bit arduous.' (*African Adventures*, 1937)

In the course of these excursions, Baden-Powell met and befriended an experienced Stetson-wearing American scout by the name of Major Frederick Russell Burnham, who introduced him to many of his North American Indian woodcraft skills. Although he only had a few days in Burnham's company, Baden-Powell learned a great number of skills and would come to incorporate some of Burnham's woodcraft lessons into his Boy Scout movement years later.

Being able to use the new skills practically in the course of his reconnaissance, combined with the very real possibility of coming face-to-face with what he described as a foe of 'special cunning, pluck and cruelty', was, he admitted, thrilling. The degree of danger involved in the job meant that one of the most important skills was avoiding being seen and for that reason he took only one assistant, a friendly Zulu commissioner called Jan Grootboom, who spoke English, and whose scouting prowess he admired; Baden-Powell trusted Grootboom with his life. Spooring, or tracking the trails of animals and people, were their main methods of intelligence gathering; they'd travel half way to enemy sites, scouting by day but waiting until nightfall to complete the task under the cover of darkness, when they'd creep in silence, amassing precious information.

Being excellent scouts themselves, the Matabele people were well aware of Baden-Powell's nocturnal prowling but they never managed to capture him and so were very wary of him, which he loved.

While tracking one day, Jan spotted a damp leaf on what was otherwise completely treeless and dry ground. He showed it to Baden-Powell, drawing his attention to sets of footprints at the location where he'd found it. The prints were small and appeared to have taken shorter than usual steps. They both knew the size indicated that they belonged to women, but Jan explained that the short strides implied they had been carrying heavy objects.

He then offered his boss the leaf and asked him to identify its smell. Baden-Powell correctly guessed it to be local beer. Between them they then deduced that a group of Matabele women had walked that way transporting pots of beer on their heads. Beer pots were traditionally 'stoppered' with leaves to prevent them from dripping, hence the random appearance of the leaf, which must have come loose as the women walked.

This led them to the assumption that Matabele men must be nearby and that they would soon be drunk, as the fact that the leaf was still wet indicated that the women must have travelled past the spot fairly recently. Predicting that the ale would have made the men sleepy and likely to let their guard down, they followed the tracks and, completely undisturbed, managed to get a raft of intelligence on their whereabouts and the lie of the land, plus a rough idea of numbers, all based on the evidence of a single mahobahoba leaf.

Now armed with critical insight far beyond anything hitherto available to the army, and desperate for action, Baden-Powell was the obvious choice of both General Carrington and Colonel Plumer to then lead a series of advance commands into the Matopos Hills, ahead of their main British forces.

By now, all the men in camp were in a bloodthirsty state and hellbent on revenge. Especially Baden-Powell, whose attitude, somewhat predictably, was now that of a full-blown, entitled colonial stereotype. He was in charge of a couple of corps comprising 'Cape boys' (the name the army gave to English-speaking indigenous men), mixed-race Cape Colony men, 200 friendly (or possibly bribed) Matabeles and a score of mounted white troops, all of whom regularly charged into the treacherous kopjes (hills), unearthed any rogue Matabele impis (armies) and systematically drove them out or killed them in their caves until the areas were mainly cleared.

The greater the danger, the better Baden-Powell liked it, relishing the fight and attacking the tribespeople with gusto and at all times of day. They came to refer to him as 'Impeesa', translated by Baden-Powell as 'the wolf that never sleeps', and a title of which he was inordinately proud.

As with so many of his adversaries, Baden-Powell conversely disliked yet admired the bravery of the Matabele warriors, who often fought to the death, possibly some of them still convinced that bullets could turn to water as their Chief Uwini believed. The irony that they had little choice than to be brave in the face of modern weaponry was lost on him and he often referred to their fearlessness in the face of Maxim gunfire and how they'd continue to attack right up to the muzzles of the guns.

Fighting and routing continued, as did Baden-Powell's advance missions, one of which, on 11 September, the anniversary of his twentieth year in the army, would prove to be of enormous import. Riding across the veld to meet his troops, he suddenly received word that the British force had captured the main prize, Uwini.

In an audacious raid, deep inside the enemy's territory and 100 miles from Bulawayo, 350 soldiers had been on a mission to corner the chief in his rock-enforced underground domain. According to reports, when a few brave soldiers descended into the narrow tunnels, which were described as being like dank drains, one was immediately killed and four badly injured.

Other soldiers carried on searching and, spotting traces of blood, followed their trail to a far-off cavern, where two troopers, called Halifax and Davis, volunteered to enter, holding candles to light their way. They were given revolvers but were under orders to only use them in self-defence.

Hearing a Matabele voice calling out, they quickly got an interpreter to stand at the cave's entrance and after a great deal of animated shouting, Uwini, badly hurt from a gunshot wound to his shoulder, agreed to come out. Proud, fearless and having long claimed to possess the magical powers that protected him, Uwini was beside himself at being caught, and worse, shot; nonetheless, he agreed to surrender on the one condition that his life would be spared.

The troops gave him their word and it was at this conjuncture that Baden-Powell arrived; he was informed of the agreement and Uwini was taken prisoner to await trial by the civilian authorities, in accordance with the rule for prisoners of war. However, Baden-Powell reneged on the promise, allegedly because Uwini was so badly injured that he felt he'd never survive the long journey to court, and instead ordered him to be tried by a court martial, which, according to records discovered later, wasn't in possession of the full facts surrounding the chief's capture and the subsequent promise made to him. A few days later, the court found Uwini guilty on all counts and sentenced him to be shot at sunset. Baden-Powell signed the warrant.

Come execution time, to leave the Matabele people in no doubt about their leader's lack of protection from bullets, magical or otherwise, all those in camp were brought to watch as he was killed by a firing squad.

The sight of their brave chief lying dead from a rally of bullets caused those Matabele present either to surrender or flee, therefore ending further conflict in that particular pocket of the region for the time being. While this could be – and indeed was – presented as a victory, it will forever be seen as an awful miscarriage of justice.

Upon hearing about the controversial incident, the High Commissioner at Cape Town, Lord Hercules Robinson Rosmead, who had explicitly directed that prisoners be handed over to local authorities, was furious. He sent a telegraph to General Carrington, insisting on Baden-Powell's immediate arrest, saying that the officer's actions had been both illegal and immoral. Carrington, despite also having given his men printed orders to ensure prisoners were dealt with in civil settings, saw this as interference in army affairs and declined, telling Rosmead that 'Colonel Baden-Powell should be spared the indignity of arrest as an officer who had done so much excellent service.'

Even so, his officer in chief still had to stand before a court of inquiry on 30 October, where he claimed that the badly injured chief had been firing at his soldiers, and that Uwini had sent his people to attack 'friendly' Matabeles, as well as ordering the deaths of white settlers. His excuses for killing Chief Uwini instead of delivering him to the correct authority included: an impractical travelling distance to the nearest court with an injured prisoner and that the killing of the chief in front of his people was to teach them a lesson. He also claimed that as it had brought about their surrender, it had saved many lives.

In the late Uwini's defence, it was argued that if he fired a gun from inside the cave, then surely it was to defend himself as he believed that the soldiers would kill him; it was also emphasised that the chief had ardently denied the other two accusations levelled at him during the controversial court martial.

Baden-Powell with his African koodoo horn. (*Scouts Heritage*)

Baden-Powell in gauntlets and high British boots taken by David Taylor in Mafeking, 1900. (*Australian War Memorial*)

Baden-Powell in Mafeking
in 1900, signed photograph.
(*Scouts Heritage*)

Chief Scout of the World with stave.
(*Scouts Heritage*)

Statue on Poole Quay.
(*Lorraine Gibson*)

Statue and Brownsea boat kiosk.
(*Lorraine Gibson*)

Crate protecting the statue and Brownsea boat kiosk. (*Lorraine Gibson*)

Baden-Powell's mother Henrietta Grace Baden-Powell. (*Public domain*)

Baden-Powell's father Rev Prof Baden Powell. (*Public domain*)

Baden-Powell with siblings.
(*Charterhouse Archives*)

'Stephe'
(alias Robert)
Frank   Warington
Agnes   Baden
al Rosenheim
1866

Charterhouse in rifle cadets line up (centre). (*Charterhouse School*)

Baden-Powell on the left in Charterhouse Box and Cox play.

Baden-Powell family. (*Public domain*)

Charterhouse Druids title sketch by Baden-Powell with bathing towel and periwinkle. (*Charterhouse School*)

13th Hussars new recruit, 1878.

A CARICATURE OF B.-P.
SKIRT-DANCING, 1893

Skirt-dancing caricature. (*Scouts Heritage*)

Baden-Powell as clown (right) in 13th Hussars panto at Lucknow, 1877. (*Public domain*)

13th Hussars pig-sticking group; seated (middle row, left) Col Baker Russel on BP's right, Baden-Powell with McLaren standing on his left.

Kenneth McLaren, aged 20 in 13th
Hussar uniform, 1880. (*Public domain*)

McLaren on polo pony.
(*Wikimedia commons*)

Baden-Powell and McLaren, India. (*Wikimedia commons*)

REPLIES SHOULD BE ORDERED "VIA. EASTERN."
THE EASTERN TELEGRAPH COMPANY, LIMITED.

EASTERN TELEGRAPH CO., LD.,
WESTMINSTER OFFICE.
41 & 42, PARLIAMENT ST., S.W.

LONDON STATIONS:
CHIEF STATION: 11, OLD BROAD STREET, E.C.
BRANCH STATIONS:
LEADENHALL STREET, E.C.   206a, WINCHESTER HOUSE, E.C.
GREAT TOWER STREET, E.C.   41 & 42, PARLIAMENT STREET, S.W.
37, HOLBORN VIADUCT, E.C.   Foreign Auction Hall, COVENT GARDEN, W.C.
And 449, STRAND, W.C.

REMARKS.

Tal

No. _____   23 *July* 190*7*

The following TELEGRAM Received at 3 24 p.m

From *Funchal*   via "Eastern."

Foreign No. ____ No. of Words *15* Dated 23 Time 8 30a ,, m.

To *Mclaren Sa Constabulary*
Colional office London
Could you put me up
Friday night incognito Bloater

Telegraph from 'Bloater'. (*Dominic Winter Auctioneers*)

Dinizulu with his wooden necklace. (*Public domain via Wikipedia*)

Man who lies down to shoot. Hunting hippo sketch by Baden-Powell. (*Scouts Heritage*)

Ashanti's King Agyeman Prempeh. (*Wikipedia*)

Baden-Powell sketch of the Ashanti blood bowl and fetish tree.

Ashanti blood bowl. (*National Army Museum*)

Baden-Powell scouting Matopos Hills, Matabeleland, 1896.

King Lobengula with Cecil Rhodes. (*Africana Museum Jo'burg*)

Sir Leander Starr Jameson.

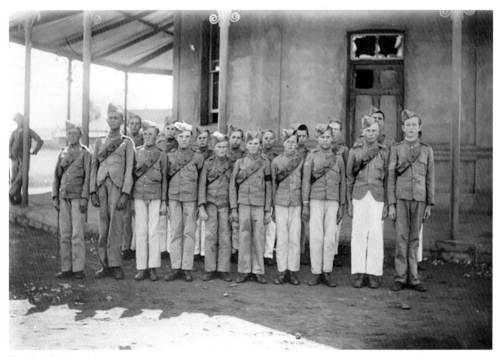

The Mafeking cadets.

Baden-Powell and his officers, Mafeking November, 1899. (*Scouts Heritage*)

Wolf howitzer made in Mafeking. (*Public domain*)

Newspaper boy with Relief-of-Mafeking bill.
(*Wikipedia*)

Brownsea first Scout uniform.
(*Wikimedia commons*)

Brownsea campsite. (*Scouts Heritage*)

Brownsea camp games. (*Scouts Heritage*)

Charles Van Raalte memorial at Brownsea.
(*Lorraine Gibson*)

Brownsea Castle, 2021. (*Lorraine Gibson*)

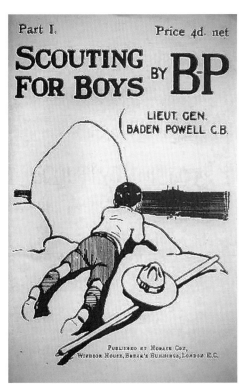

Scouting for Boys cover, 1908. (*Scouts Heritage*)

Girl Guides, Crystal Palace, 1909. (*Scouts Heritage*)

First encounter with Olave Soames aboard the Arcadian, 1912. (*Public domain*)

Olave Soames in 1912. (*Public domain*)

Baden-Powell, Olave, Peter, Heather, Betty and dog outside the White House, Gilwell Park. (*Scouts Heritage*)

Arrowe Park Jamboree, 1929, with new Rolls Royce and the famous braces. (*Scouts Heritage*)

Baden-Powell's balcony bedroom at Pax Hill.

Lord Baden-Powell of Gilwell, Jagger Portrait 1929. (*Scouts heritage*)

Baden-Powell's grave near Mount Kenya with the Boy Scout trail sign for 'I have gone home'. (*Public domain*)

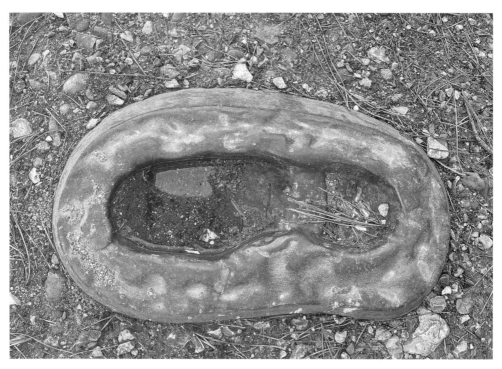

Baden-Powell's footprint impression on Brownsea Island today. (*Lorraine Gibson*)

Bear Grylls.

In what has been called a classic, old-school-tie cover-up, Baden-Powell's corner laboured the point that Uwini had fired a gun, therefore proving that he was a rebel and two local, anti-Uwini commissioners with whom B-P had discussed the potential execution with at the time, fully endorsed his actions.

Baden-Powell was exonerated and walked free, his reputation undamaged – for now.

Adding weight to the miscarriage of justice accusation was the discovery in 2009 of more than fifty documents and witness statements pertaining to the Matabele incident. The personal collection of General Carrington, they confirm that after being wounded, Uwini did surrender with the agreement that he would be allowed to live. Baden-Powell had contested this, claiming that Uwini had opened fire on his troops, a crime punishable by death. Witnesses begged to differ.

The papers, sold at an auction by Dominic Winter of Cirencester, also show that Baden-Powell did authorise an illegal execution, and that he falsified evidence and changed entries in his personal diaries to cover up incriminating facts, which today would almost certainly constitute a war crime and would have ended his career. Not only had he escaped punishment, he'd managed to experience the ultimate goal in terms of execution gratification. His own letter, in which he attempts to justify his actions, reads:

> In my defence I rather confined myself to the legal point that according to military law I had the power to exercise my own judgment if I was over 100 miles from a superior authority.
>
> I was over 100 miles from my general and over 1,000 miles from the governor, though had I been only 50 miles away I should have acted in the same way since summary punishment in the presence of his own people had given one the exceptional opportunity of smashing their belief in [their god] M'limo.
>
> It also gained their surrender and thereby saved the many lives which would have been lost, both among our own men and among the enemy, if we had had to continue our attack on … their stronghold.

Talking to the *Sunday Times* at the time of the discovery of the papers, Tim Jeal, author of *Baden-Powell*, said: 'When he arrived on the scene, he would have been told that Uwini had been promised his life. This makes his decision to execute the chief rather worse than it has so far been thought to have been.'

Not so for Baden-Powell, who it seems never had any doubt, at least outwardly, about his indefensible decision. Writing to Henrietta Grace about it sometime later, he defiantly said: 'Well, on looking back at it, I should do exactly the same thing again (though it sounds brutal, doesn't it) but it was the means of saving a large number of white lives as well as of black.'

During the October 1896 inquiry, while things looked precarious for Baden-Powell at times as his deeds and his account of events were hotly contested, he still managed to avoid any punishment for this shameful act.

Had this lamentable establishment cover-up not taken place and had all of the facts been correctly presented, the outcome would have been very different indeed.

Chapter 8

The Making of a Hero: Mafeking 1899–1900

'The whole thing was and had to be a game of bluff from start to finish.
It was not what you would call a proper military feat of arms, but just a
minor episode in the course of the greater campaign.'
Robert Baden-Powell BBC radio programme *I Was There, 1937*.

If ever there were a time when the conflicting sides of Baden-Powell's personality were evident, it was during his most famous military assignment at Mafeking during the second Anglo-Boer war. At the age of 42, he had no idea that his defence of the small South African town close to Johannesburg, which was besieged by thousands of Boer homesteaders, would be his last major military commission. He could not have known that it would end in a blaze of glory that would make him one of the world's most famous Englishmen at the start of the twentieth century and an international hero, universally lauded for his leadership and ingenious military strategies. Nor could he have imagined that it would see the dark shadow of war crime accusations hang over him once more.

The Siege of Mafeking, as it became known, began on 14 October 1899, when negotiations on the rights of British settlers or Uitlanders between the British Army and the Boer's President Paul Kruger collapsed.

With an inexperienced force of 1,500 men comprising volunteers, native tribesmen and Mafeking residents, inadequate weaponry and supplies, and uncooperative bosses who, when not obstructing him or railing against him personally, were fighting with one another, Baden-Powell somehow managed to hold up to 10,000 armed, experienced and angry Boer fighters at bay for 217 days.

His orders were to stop them from attacking the town and to preoccupy them with a series of attack 'bluffs' that would keep them away from other vulnerable British Army battle zones and to retain British authority over the locals, to boot. One could say that the siege made Colonel Baden-Powell the first modern celebrity, since the Boer War was the first conflict to be reported in great detail by the British and international press; his escapades, for reasons that will become apparent, were avidly followed by readers who were anxious about the instability of the Empire and craved good news, in the midst of tales of doom and gloom coming from far-flung places where their loved ones were stationed.

As the years have passed, however, the narrative around the Siege of Mafeking has shifted; what was a glorious victory at the start of the twentieth century became a cause célèbre, regarded by some historians and authors as an exaggerated and unnecessarily long-winded example of imperialist histrionics.

Apart from questions over how Baden-Powell even came to be in the town, rather than carrying out his initial order to patrol volatile colonial borders in Rhodesia and Bechuanaland (Botswana), there are also charges that the siege was intentionally protracted for Baden-Powell's own gratification/vanity/agenda, call it what you will.

Further and more serious allegations levelled at him are that he exploited and even caused the deaths of African people among both those who fought with him in the defence of Mafeking and the intransient tribespeople who eked out a living on the town's perimeters, some of whom died of hunger or were killed by Boer rifles as they left Mafeking under the orders of the British Army. Opinions and accounts vary enormously and there has been copious analysis and discussions of the events over the years, so it's best to consider the facts – where possible, since, as is typical in war situations, even those can be contradictory.

What is certain, though, is that by 1899, Baden-Powell's relationship with Sir Garnet Wolseley, commander-in-chief of the British Army, was fully-forged and he had become Wolseley's protégé. He'd also been promoted to a colonel, an extraordinary feat that made him the youngest colonel in the British Army. Equally well documented is that during the first week of July that year, a meeting with Wolseley in London culminated in Baden-Powell being sent to South Africa to head up a somewhat clandestine and experimental mission to protect British borders in the Transvaal Republic, where war was looking increasingly likely.

How this directive came about has become the stuff of legend, often presented, including by Baden-Powell himself, as some sort of happy accident or twist of fate.

However, as Wolseley was notoriously fastidious, and also worried about a potential second Boer war in the Cape, which he felt would be calamitous for the British who, in his estimation, would be outnumbered by about 40,000 to 7,000, then surely it was less of an impulsive whim and more likely a meticulously thought-out plan? This is further established when one learns that a month prior to the fabled meeting, Wolseley was already considering Baden-Powell as leader of one of several defence plans over which he had been deliberating.

Added to this, on closer inspection the 'chance encounter' was actually between Baden-Powell and Wolseley's Aide-de-camp, George Gough. Surprised to see the colonel lunching at his Naval and Military Club in Piccadilly, Gough went over to his table and said: 'I thought you were still in India, I've just cabled you to come home – the commander-in-chief wants to see you.'

Baden-Powell polished off his meal and went straight to Wolseley's office in Whitehall, where the chief, who made a sport of springing surprises on his men to test their mettle, told him: 'I want you to go to Africa.' Baden-Powell obediently replied 'Yes, sir.' Wolseley then mischievously added: 'Well, can you go Saturday?' (it was then Monday). Used to playing, and being the butt of, many a Charterhouse prank, Baden-Powell was an expert in handling bombshells then batting them back into the protagonist's court. 'No, sir!' he replied.

When Wolseley barked 'Why not?', he quipped, 'There's no ship on Saturday. But I can go on Friday.' Wolseley found this example of his young colonel's more mischievous side most agreeable.

After this exchange Wolseley became serious. Baden-Powell was to go to Rhodesia and take command of an elite band of twenty hand-selected (by Wolseley, not Baden-Powell) officers and, with their assistance, raise a couple of local mounted volunteer infantry regiments to defend its north-west borders in case of war. And should war break out, he added, they were to divert as many Boers as possible away from main British forces' locations by whatever means necessary. The challenge appealed to Baden-Powell's now mile-wide adventurous streak so, man on board, Wolseley took him directly to the office of the Secretary of State for War, Lord Lansdowne, who gave him the lofty title of commander-in-chief, Rhodesian Frontier Force.

While thrilled by the prospect of intrigue and action, Baden-Powell, the born risk-taker, also felt overwhelmed, especially as en route to see Lansdowne, Wolseley had confided his fears that war was inevitable – and why it could be disastrous. It had also dawned on Baden-Powell that he would be commanding the first ever group of British Army special services officers to be sent out to South Africa. And on hearing Lansdowne's more detailed orders, also realised that the risks were higher than he'd first supposed. Being the die-hard militarist, he would not permit himself to voice doubts and so, of course, he accepted the assignment.

Baden-Powell's dual personality soon took over and his misgivings gave way to great excitement about heading to the heart of the action. Now his fear was that something should go wrong before he even got there; he admitted to being as 'nervous as an old lady crossing the street for fear of being run over', in case he should break an ankle or become unwell. Perhaps the jitters were about 'impostor syndrome', which he suffered from regularly, or because his previous engagements had all fizzled out before a fight. Whatever the reason, he was terrified that his most important commission to date wouldn't happen.

Hurried farewells to friends and family done, Baden-Powell visited his old Charterhouse head, Dr Haig-Brown, telling him he was praying 'we shan't hear at Madeira that Kruger has given in'. He needn't have worried on that score.

The list of special officers chosen for Baden-Powell's Rhodesia Frontier Force read like a copy of De Brett's Peerage. Henrietta Grace, possibly England's most tenacious social mountaineer, would have been beyond delighted but to Baden-Powell it would have been quite daunting. Included was Major Lord Edward Cecil, son of the British PM, Lord Salisbury, as his Chief of Staff. Baden-Powell knew of him, but didn't particularly like him, thinking him an anti-social, literary snob. His Intelligence Officer and Press Censor was Lieutenant the Hon. Algernon Hanbury-Tracy, Horse Guards and son of Lord Sudeley.

He met both these men for the first time just before leaving England.

Also in the group were Colonel Herbert Plumer, who'd led the Matabele relief force in 1896, and Major Alick J. Godley, who'd served in Mashonaland; both men he knew and liked.

Lieutenant-Colonel Charles Hore, Captain Charles FitzClarence (a descendent of William IV) and Lieutenant-Colonel Courtenay B. Vyvyan, who stood in for him in Matabeleland when he had to lead another column, he'd never met. Baden-Powell would have preferred to select his own men, but he was at least allowed to choose a few: his first recruit was Kenneth McLaren, who'd jumped at his invitation to go to the Cape, despite having recently married a woman called Leila Landon, who was now heavily pregnant.

Meanwhile in South Africa, relations between the British and Kruger had reached stalemate with both sides disagreeing on various things, most of them related to the control of land, power, or both. As well as a string of victories, the British had also suffered some costly defeats at the hands of the Boers and yet, rather than learning from them, still looked upon them as just another group of locals needing to be controlled. Accustomed to winning wars against indigenous tribes, who, no matter how large their numbers, had only stabbing and clubbing weapons that were no match for guns, the British ignored the fact that this wasn't the case with the Boers and continued trying to control more territories. The Boers had other ideas and insisted that they were the rightful rulers and owners of the region and were now more willing than ever to fight for it again if need be.

This had little effect, for despite the conflicting interests and clashing agendas between Britain's political and military leaders, most of them shared one common purpose – empire-building.

Backed by powerful investors, including a still-lingering Cecil Rhodes who, predictably, considering his portfolio, was still in favour of uniting the lucrative lands that equated to a geographical version of the golden goose, the British continued to pressurise the Boers to back off.

The main prize was control of the vast region that incorporated Matabeleland (Rhodesia) and Bechuanaland (Botswana), essentially the heart from which ran the richest veins of gold and desirable minerals in the country. And so, in full colonial-acquisition mode, the British belligerently carried on claiming ownership. As did Kruger and the Boers. Exacerbating the situation was the same group of reformist British settlers who'd bailed out of the Jameson Raid at the eleventh hour. Still disgruntled at not having a vote while forking out higher taxes than the Boers themselves, they were looking to the British Army for a solution.

Joseph Chamberlain, the British Colonial Secretary, who'd encouraged the raid and then quickly backtracked when it failed, was getting impatient. Motivated by the lure of vast wealth and of winning equal rights for the Cape-dwelling British, who could then give him a say in who owned what, he appointed Sir Alfred Milner as the new High Commissioner to replace Lord Rosmead (gone in the wake of the Jameson Raid). Milner, former Chairman of the British Board at the Inland Revenue, could give Cecil Rhodes a run for his diamonds when it came to an inflated sense of supremacy and was of the opinion that a threat of military action was the only way to convince Kruger to alter his stance.

Chamberlain put Milner in charge of delivering the vague threat to the Boer leader that military action was a possibility, should British Uitlanders who'd lived there for at least five years still be denied a vote. It was hoped this 'feint' would kick-start negotiations and ultimately lead to a compromise. Anything but war, since, like Wolseley, Chamberlain knew that the British troops were outnumbered.

Kruger agreed to meet Milner and conceded that if British settlers were to first become nationalised, then they could have a vote after a set period of time. Instead of accepting, Milner persisted with his demand that the Boer leader should automatically give the vote to all Uitlanders who'd been there five years. Knowing that this would diminish or worse, end, Boer control and his people's lands would be taken, naturally, Kruger declined the excessive demand. Unhappy at the president's refusal, on 5 June Milner abruptly ceased all talks.

Chamberlain was incensed by Milner's heavy-handed approach, believing that Kruger had already given enough ground to move negotiations towards a peaceful settlement. Before the impasse could be rectified however, Kruger, wrongly thinking that Chamberlain was of the same mind as his aggressive representative, rather than giving ground, took Milner's threat seriously and prepared for battle.

Up until then, the British Army's success was largely down to the kind of enemies they faced. Zulus, Afghans and other tribes could fight as bravely as the fiercest soldier and even win small battles, but were usually overwhelmed when on a grander scale. This was different. The Boers had already won the first Boer war in 1881. With no formal military group, and influenced, rather than ordered, by Field Cornets (civilian officials, similar in rank to military officers), they created a force driven by their strong sense of community – and dislike of the British. After a series of bloody battles, a large contingent of Boers resoundingly defeated Sir George Pomeroy Colley's British force of just twenty-two officers and 627 men in the concluding Battle of Majuba Hill, which gave independence to the Transvaal and the Orange Free State. Of Colley's recklessly small force, 283 men were casualties. Boer casualties are not known but would, in comparison, have been trifling.

Fast forward to 1889; although the Boers didn't have a standard army as such, they still had their deep-rooted gun culture. Boers' rifles were their identity, a metaphor for their survival and their freedom. As good as born with guns in their hands, target shooting was a national sport, with one war journalist at the time comparing its popularity to the game of billiards in Britain. Again, apart from the likes of forensic strategists such as Wolseley, this seemed to have been overlooked by the army.

The Jameson Raid had already signalled to the Boers that war with the British was inevitable, and three months prior their Commandant General, Piet Joubert, went shopping – for guns; lots of guns. Thirty-thousand Mauser magazine rifles to be precise, and he distributed them among his people. A number of the latest field guns from German armament manufacturer Krupp and French firm, Creusot, completed the arsenal.

Now, on the verge of potential conflict, Kruger's men were as well armed as, if not better than, the British Army, and thanks to their love of gun sports, were generally far more accomplished marksmen, too. They were more than ready to defend what they regarded as theirs, should the need arise.

Another greed-driven plan had backfired.

Britain's leaders were in a quandary. Ditching Milner would be embarrassing and would also mean ditching all hope of achieving their ultimate objective, a British South Africa.

Bizarrely, they still thought they could progress with their procurement plans simply by containing Boers at the borders and if that failed, then there was nothing else for it but to step-up the military threats, cross their fingers and hope that the Boers would capitulate.

This was about where things stood when Baden-Powell stepped back on to South African soil. The deeply volatile period he'd not long left behind in Matabeleland remained, but this time the focus of the conflict, for the British at least, had shifted from troublesome tribes to unsettled settlers.

He was at a low ebb personally, having recently buried his older brother and surrogate father, George, who'd died of cancer of the liver, leaving behind his wife, Frances, daughter Maud and son, Donald. Baden-Powell the soldier had also endured a sedentary period of service, including an unremarkable command of the 5th Dragoon Guards in India, where he had at least got to build on his scouting nous.

Even his earlier military engagements that had been so full of promise, the Zulu uprising with King Dinizulu; the Ashanti campaign and King Prempeh's refusal to fight; and the battle-light, not to mention controversial, Matabele uprising (with the injudicious execution of Chief Uwini) had all failed to deliver the all-out blood-and-balls battles he still craved. He was now impatient for a fight.

On the voyage, Baden-Powell had passed the time compiling a list of requirements, such as horses, transport, boots and, of course, arms, based on Lord Wolseley's written instructions.

He was anticipating a full-scale, adrenalin-rush of an adventure. What he wasn't anticipating was the outright hostility shown to him on landing at Cape Castle, the very place his Uncle Henry had once overseen. Instead of Milner welcoming him as he'd supposed, Baden-Powell was directed to the office of the Cape's latest governor, Sir William Butler who, rather than welcoming him, treated him with ill-concealed derision, scoffing at his list and lecturing him on how little he knew about the Cape's current political status.

The problem – of which Baden-Powell was completely unaware – was that Butler saw him as living proof of the army interfering with governance. He was Wolseley's new pet, an upstart, an inexperienced protagonist, come to do some warmongering and that didn't suit Butler – not just yet. The governor gleefully warned him that he'd have little chance of recruiting men from the colony or from Bechuanaland as locals would never leave good jobs to work for him. From the request for supplies, he conceded only to guns, but refused horses and transport, which Baden-Powell would need to move the weapons.

Shaken by Butler's open animosity, his hope now lay with Milner, whom he felt sure, after his failed talks with Kruger, would be more supportive. Wrong. When he met him, Milner was every bit as hostile and un-cooperative as Butler, his reason being that he had not been informed of the mission and was therefore extremely irritated. Again, Baden-Powell was oblivious to this.

His assignment was unconventional to say the least. It was devised not by the military, but by Colonel John Sanctuary Nicholson, whom Baden-Powell knew from Matabeleland and who was now commandant general of the Rhodesian Police. Nicholson had discussed the Boer 'contain and divert' idea with Milner's Military Secretary, Colonel John Hanbury-Williams, as possibly being suitable for use in the event of war. He recommended that 250 Rhodesian mounted volunteers should be raised and if required, could invade the Transvaal and hold a large Boer force, allowing British forces a better chance elsewhere.

The Secretary of State for War, Lansdowne, had considered Nicholson's idea to be feasible but risky and that for such a mission to succeed, it would need an audacious leader.

Hence the deployment of the British Army's secret weapon, the gung-ho, super-keen, Colonel Baden-Powell, who was also unaware that no army department had been willing to touch his seemingly foolhardy mission with a barge-pole.

It could be seen as insensitive, or warmongering, and it was only after much debate that the Colonial Office finally took it on, with the directive that Baden-Powell and his special officers must maintain a low profile, ditch their army uniforms and instead wear mufti to avoid 'precipitating war by arousing the animosity of the Boers'. Another man might have found this cloak and dagger approach odd, but it was music to Baden-Powell's ears and he immediately hit the dressing-up box, donning the alternative uniform of what he referred to as the 'flannel-shirt life' brigade, ergo, a khaki shirt, civilian trousers and a wide-brimmed hat (a sort of hybrid of the Boer's floppy variety and his American scout friend, Major Burnham's Stetson). To complete the ensemble, he added a neckerchief for mopping up unavoidable sweat. Without realising it, he'd created the first Boy Scouts' uniform.

After escaping Cape Castle's frosty atmosphere, Baden-Powell arrived in Bulawayo, scene of the Boers' wagon sanctuary during the Matabele revolt. He marvelled at how much it had changed since he'd last been there. Where previously he'd slept on a board and bathed al fresco in a tub, there was now the Grand Hotel, with running water, electric lights, and even a dining room. There he was joined by some of the officers of his Rhodesian Frontier Force, reuniting with his friend from Matabeleland, Colonel Herbert Plumer and, best of all, his 'best friend in the world', Captain Kenneth McLaren.

Reunions complete, it was time to assess the 650-mile-long frontier. Seeing it for the first time, Baden-Powell immediately decided it needed two entirely separate headquarters in different locations if it were to be made secure. Milner agreed and Baden-Powell tasked Plumer, with McLaren on his staff, with raising a force in Rhodesia, setting up camp at Bulawayo and an outpost at Tuli on the Limpopo river.

He ordered Colonel Hore to do much the same, although his volunteers would be from the Bechuanaland Protectorate with a base at Ramathlabama, which was little more than a railway-stop of a place, but at least under British Colonial Office control.

Baden-Powell would have preferred Mafeking with its plentiful storage potential to tiny Ramathlabama as a base, however it was under Cape control and any sudden increase in military activity there would alert the increasingly twitchy Boers. Nevertheless, he got agreement from Cape Town to use Mafeking as a general supply centre. In between organising all of this, he was constantly battling against hostility and subterfuge from the older, more entrenched officers who were in high dudgeon that such a young nonentity of a colonel had been trusted to deal with such a crucial situation.

Back in London, Wolseley was anxious. He recognised the gravity of the situation in the Transvaal, now that the Boers were armed to the teeth and circling the towns of Ladysmith, Kimberley (the diamond capital) and Mafeking, while any extra British forces, of which there were few, remained in Britain. He also knew what formidable fighters and superb horsemen the Boers were. The majority were countrymen who'd been running farms from the backs of ponies with rifles in one hand. These rural homesteaders brought a lifetime of marksmanship to the war, an important edge, further exploited this time by their consignment of magazine rifles. Add strong fieldcraft skills and high mobility and you had a natural mounted infantry.

At that time, most British soldiers came from the lower classes and joined the army, less out of patriotism than to escape grim and impoverished lives. They were plentiful but they had to be trained from scratch, even in the most basic aspects of warfare. In contrast, when not fighting, the Boers did just about everything on horseback; all of them owned at least one gun and one steed. They could outride and outshoot all-comers, and the speed and dexterity with which they could gallop over vast expanses of their familiar veld (open grasslands) terrains while firing with great precision, had left previous British soldiers speechless. A testament to the Boers' equestrian and weaponry skills is that Winston Churchill, a correspondent in the Boer War, was so impressed with their capabilities that he adopted their Afrikaans word for military units, 'commando' and used it for his own, newly forged Special British Forces in 1940.

With all of this in mind, Wolseley had previously asked Lansdowne to send 10,000 troops to South Africa as a matter of urgency; his request fell on deaf ears as the war secretary, who was barely on speaking terms with him, refused point blank, arguing that it would be akin to declaring war and would incite the Boers to rise and attack Natal.

In the end, all he agreed to were some artillery additions to the existing Cape forces, extra to Baden-Powell's twenty Special Services Officers and their diversion plan, who by then were already in Rhodesia. Baden-Powell, kept in the dark about so much, had no idea about the struggle going on between Lansdowne and Wolseley as they swung between favouring negotiation and a peaceful outcome, to all-out war and forced taking of the regions. He was just eager to carry out his new role and so, despite being underfunded and short on kit, he began recruiting his taskforce of local volunteers as instructed.

Whatever the old army brigade may have thought of him, and despite his own pangs of self-doubt, Baden-Powell was by now a very capable and incredibly ambitious officer. Always the maverick, instead of just manning the borders, he decided off his own bat that, since trouble was definitely brewing, he should amass stores and provisions and place them in the storage areas he'd been permitted to use in Mafeking, and subtly turn it into a potential garrison town, which could attract Boers away from fighting areas, while still being defended and ultimately, liberated. Forever looking for the next big adventure, this was right up his street.

Throughout August and September, he never stopped. While staying abreast of the endless correspondence and orders flying in from the Cape, he constantly traversed the road between Ramathlabama, Bulawayo and Mafeking, personally overseeing the raising and training of both his new regiments, all the while building supplies of horses, guns, food and ammunition as he went.

Mafeking, the railway terminus that he'd found so unremarkable on his previous trip, was settled by a small British population but was coming under increasing pressure from the large presence of armed homesteaders stalking its perimeters. Being less than 200 miles from Johannesburg and therefore within the holy grail of gold-rich land masses, the Boers were hell-bent on wresting control of it. Their main objective was to raid the town, secure its gold reserves, which they believed were theirs (and which the British believed should be theirs) and control the railway.

By September, Baden-Powell's men were as trained and ready as they would ever be and, should the need arise, he had enough provisions to last about three months. He now had official orders to attract and keep Boer troops distracted at Mafeking. He got further permission from the Cape to set up a force there in order to protect the stores which he and other parties, sensing war, had created. And as they hadn't stipulated how many men that force should be, he moved Hore's entire Ramathlabama regiment straight in. He now had two solid and strategic bases.

At this point in 1899 Britain was the wealthiest and most powerful nation on Earth. Britannia ruled the waves and Queen Victoria ruled over a third of the world's entire population.

For years the country had enjoyed a sense of invincibility, but that had been shaken by the speed of events rapidly unfolding in the Cape. There was now a sense of panic and insecurity as news came in that the republic of the Transvaal had had enough of British colonial influence and were preparing forcibly to seize control of South Africa's mineral wealth.

Britain's cast-iron control of much of the Earth's riches appeared to be weakening; the bubble of complacency had burst and the widely held belief that the whole affair would blow over in a couple of weeks was fading fast.

The Boers' ultimatum that the British should cease building up their forces in the region (which was ignored), coupled with the deadlock on the political status of the Uitlanders, meant there was nowhere to turn. After refusals and various decision reversals, the British finally mobilised and sent more men to South Africa, including troops from Canada and Australia, New Zealand and India. Eventually, 400,000 soldiers would be involved.

Talks were hopeless now, and on 11 October 1899, war broke out. It was to be another bloody struggle between English-speaking and Afrikaans-speaking whites, and the early weeks were disastrous for the British, with high casualties and few gains. The Boers, hearing news of British troops rallying around the Empire and young men in Britain flocking to join up, knew that they had only a small window of opportunity to strike before reinforcements arrived. They didn't waste it. In a show of strength, and to let the British see that they meant business, they carried out a handful of short, sharp surprise attacks and laid siege to Ladysmith, Kimberley and Mafeking.

It was the defeat of their first British force at Lombard's Kop on 29 October which led to the Ladysmith siege at the start of November; it lasted until February the following year.

On 25 November, they were repelled by Major General Lord Methuen's force in the Battle of Enslin (or Graspan) and suffered considerable losses; however, Methuen's men were left depleted, utterly exhausted and desperate for water. Heedless of this, Methuen recklessly ordered them to continue marching to relieve Kimberley, now also under siege; they suffered heavy casualties en route at the River Modder on 28 November, followed by another disastrous defeat with severe losses in the Battle of Magersfontein on 11 December. This was their second battle in a week that became known as 'Black Week', the first being the Battle of Stormberg over 9 and 10 December, where Lieutenant General Sir William Forbes Gatacre suffered a terrible defeat in the Northern Cape colony.

Rounding off 'Black Week' with yet another trouncing on 15 December, was General Redvers Buller, whom the Boers called 'Red Bull' on account of his generous girth and puce-ness of face – and his force. Attempting to cross Natal's Tugela River to find a different route to relieve Ladysmith, his poor planning, errors and a series of unfavourable events ended in another loss, with more than 1,000 casualties and the loss of ten field guns to the Boers, whose losses, again, were slight.

Buller was clearly a firm advocate of the old adage, 'if at first you don't succeed, try, try again'; on 24 January he attempted a second, and again disastrous, crossing of the Tugela. Then a third, which also failed, and finally a fourth on Valentine's Day, which at last led to Ladysmith (and the penned-in British troops) being relieved and the Boers retreating from Natal.

Another victory for the British followed on 27 February 1900 at the close-fought Battle of Paardeberg, where General Piet Cronje, one of the most troublesome Boer leaders, was forced to surrender.

All the while at Mafeking, Baden-Powell was in full juggling mode, as by 14 October it was completely surrounded and cut off from the rest of the world. The siege had begun and at some points the town was being circled by about 10,000 Boers. In comparison, Baden-Powell's regiments, the Rhodesians and the Protectorates, even now that they had joined together in the town, amounted to just 1,500 men.

His instructions were to stay put and draw as many Boers as possible away from the coasts to ensure a safe landing for the additional troops coming from around the world. He was also to continue to protect British subjects in the vulnerable areas of Rhodesia, Bechuanaland and, of course, Mafeking and – just for good measure – maintain 'British prestige' among the local tribes, including his old adversary, the Matabele.

Mafeking was surrounded by stony veld as far as the eye could see with the occasional 100 ft-high hill. Otherwise, the only relief in the unforgiving landscape was a rare tree or two, so rare, they had names such as Jackal Tree and Game Tree.

It wasn't only populated by white settlers. A 7,000-strong Barolong tribe co-existed alongside them. The white, predominantly British residents of Mafeking sweltered inside unextraordinary, rough brick houses with corrugated tin roofs that made a hellish racket when it rained. All streets led to a central market square with shops, a hotel, a bank, a library, a printing firm and a lawyers' office, where Baden-Powell set up his HQ. According to a census taken by him, the white population stood at 1,708.

To the north was a convent and hospital, to the west, the British South Africa Police (BSAP) barracks and west of those, the native staad or large town where the Barolong tribe, led by chief Wessels Montica, lived in hundreds of round, thatched, wattle-and-daub huts.

The train came into the station from the south-west and ran between the stad and the white quarter.

So, a pretty insignificant place. Apart, that is, for its location and the fact that it had been the springboard for the Jameson Raid (still a thorn in the Boers' side and a reason for revenge).

Worse, from the point of view of Mafeking's, rumours were flying that if Mafeking fell, it would be the clarion call for the entire Dutch Cape to rise up, taking the war all the way to Table Bay.

Baden-Powell and his diminutive army may have been pluckily improving the war effort remotely by keeping this large enemy force from fighting elsewhere, but they still found the situation daunting. Nevertheless, orders were orders and the essence of the mission had always been to act as a holding agent or decoy and in view of the recent flash British attacks, for some reason the Mafeking garrison, while woefully outnumbered, seemed to be bucking the trend for losing.

Here was Baden-Powell, staring what appeared to be certain annihilation in the face. He was underfunded and poorly armed with a regiment that amounted to a handful, in relative terms, of random and half-trained troops of mainly local volunteers, and of whom he complained that despite his best efforts at speed training, were little more than 'an organised crowd of recruits mounted on ponies. They are bad riders and bad shots.' Which did not bode well when faced with a large army of aggrieved Boers who fired guns for fun and rode as though they and their horses were a single, well-oiled machine.

On the other hand, he relished a challenge, so he was also motivated by the prospect of a fight and took it as a personal compliment that President Kruger had sent him none other than 'Honest Piet' Cronje, also known as 'The Lion of the Transvaal' whose men threatened to 'eat them up as crows do lice off a cow's back'.

The paucity of support from the British military hierarchy continued, as did the inadequate supply of arms, in more than one case due to critical clerical errors, including one memorable instance that Baden-Powell never quite forgot.

Just before the war began, I had telegraphed to headquarters at the Cape to say that we must have some good artillery if we are to hold the place.

The answer came in code language that two large 4.7 [howitzer] guns were being sent up by the next train.

This news was widely publicised and would, no doubt, have also been picked up by the Boers.

The garrison flocked down to the station to meet the two monster guns that were going to make our attackers sit up.

When the train rolled in, there was no outward sign of these guns. I asked the guard 'Where are our guns that you were going to bring up?'

'Oh yes sir, I've got them in my van.'

In the van was a couple of little nine-pounder guns and old ones at that.

One of the men that had worked with me at Matabeleland recognised one of them. 'Why,' he said, 'if that isn't old 'Crooked-Tail Sal.'

Crooked-Tail Sal was a badly damaged gun that was virtually useless to them. It was incredibly disappointing and frustrating but the one saving grace was … The report had gone out that we had the big guns.

From a recording of BBC Radio's *I Was There*, 1937

This fake news, which Baden-Powell became quite an expert in broadcasting, helped the fact that in reality he was in command of this small force of only fairly capable troops while up against a Boer army that ranged from 7,000 to 10,000 and comprised war-hardened generals, experienced soldiers who had all grown up on the veld. And all of them with deep dislike for the British. He knew he hadn't a hope in hell of raising the cavalry 'feints' or bluffs that Wolseley had ordered from afar, let alone launch an attack.

Against orders to perform sham attacks to deter the Boers from heading en masse to beleaguered Pretoria, he took matters into his own hands. There was nothing else for it but to fight from the ground, from trenches. They simply had to be dug in, for if they were mounted, the Boers would wipe them out with ease, thanks to their unparalleled hillside vantage point and their murderously accurate marksmanship.

This very real fear of a massacre is a good place to stop and consider an aspect of the accusation that Baden-Powell ill-treated some of his native forces based on him making the men, particularly from the local Barolong tribe, fight from trenches. That there were more black soldiers than white on the front line, there is no dispute. Foot-soldiering, whatever a soldier's colour, was out of the question and the volunteer indigenous fighters had no mounted combat training so riding wasn't an option, let alone highly inadvisable.

The perimeter had to be secure and if anyone was to have a chance of surviving, then dug-outs and trenches were the only answer.

Baden-Powell had another important weapon in his almost non-existent arsenal – his cunning. All the wiles and guiles and practical skills he'd acquired in the field over many years as he honed his scouting, reconnaissance and camouflage knowledge came to the fore. All he had to do was channel these into convincing the Boers that they were facing a huge company of men. With trademark understatement, when relating his hopeless situation in a letter home to Henrietta Grace, he wrote: 'with 7,000 Boers camped within ten miles of us, I have just a little bit of responsibility'.

There were rays of hope, albeit slightly contradictory ones. On the downside, the war and the ensuing difficulties it caused at borders plus the likelihood of attacks on the main railway had stirred up rumours of massive hikes in taxes for commodities. On the upside, Mafeking, being a well-maintained 'European' town, with its own railway and buildings, became more than just Baden-Powell's stockpile hub, it became a one-stop-shop for both military and civilians who were laying down their stores.

On the downside again, the Boers knew this, which gave them yet another incentive to attack.

The upside of this, though, was that while military muscle was in short supply, essential goods were not, giving Baden-Powell and his troops the luxury of time to hold their nerve as well as the town. This fine balance between good and bad scenarios triggered his inventiveness, inspiring him to ever more ingenious ways of fooling the enemy into believing Mafeking was a formidable fortress.

Having found these few positives – and being a child at heart – it was time to play some games. 'Bluff the enemy with show of force as much as you like,' he told his men. 'Do not always wait for an order, if you see the situation demands action. Don't be afraid of making a mistake, a man who never made a mistake, never made anything.' In this aspect, he was in his element and from his headquarters, turned what often seemed like a hopeless situation into a battle of wills or, as he described it, a 'game of bluff', that lasted for months.

He took great delight in coming up with tricks to fool the foe. He had his men erect posts along the town's extensive outer trenches and then act as though they were stringing barbed wire along them. There was no wire – they didn't have any – but they made a great show of stepping gingerly over it. From the Boers' far-off hill position, this was entirely convincing.

Another ruse was to rotate the same groups of troops around the trenches, creating the illusion of far greater numbers of soldiers than the reality.

And again, in full view of the Boers, he got his men to overtly bury explosive mines very carefully around the front of the town in broad daylight, warning his local troops, who were unfamiliar with handling such things, to carry them with the greatest of care and cautioning them about the 'disastrous explosion that would follow should they drop one of them'.

Using whatever 'wires' they could fashion, the mines were then connected to Mafeking's central observation post. There were always spies in the town, so he explained: 'Notices were posted in English and Dutch warning the inhabitants that if they allowed their cattle, or their children to wander there, it would be at their own risk.' From a recording of BBC Radio's *I Was There,* 1937

Little did the enemy, the townsfolk, nor even some of his own troops for that matter, realise that the mines that had been so cautiously laid were just old food containers filled with nothing more hazardous than ordinary sand. He was in his happy zone and not content with what was already an ingenious deceit, he took things a step further:

> We gave notice that on a certain day, a trial would be made with one or more of the mines to see that they were in working order, so people were warned to keep clear of the East front between twelve and two.
>
> Between twelve and two, with everybody safe indoors, Major Panzera [the artillery expert of Baden-Powell's British special officers] and I crept out and stuck a stick of dynamite [the only one they actually had] in an old ant hole. We lit the fuse, ran like mad and took cover until the thing went off, which it did with a splendid roar and a vast cloud of dust.
>
> *I Was There,* 1937

The ruse worked a treat and the Boers were convinced that Mafeking's entire perimeter was now a lethal mine field.

Fate then took a hand in furthering this conviction when, out of the dust, appeared a man who just happened to be cycling by, and who then pedalled off as fast as he could for the Transvaal, eight miles away and 'where no doubt he told how by merely riding along road he hit off a murderous mine'.

If this all sounds rather Boy's Own, with tall tales of derring-do, it's because it was. And while Baden-Powell was definitely a bit of an odd cove, with his slight but wiry frame, precise mannerisms, almost obsessive need to regularly scrub himself clean (a lasting legacy of disease-ridden Lucknow and Africa's mosquito-plagued jungles) and his acerbic, often off-putting form of wit, most of his men idolised him.

As good as abandoned by the British leaders who were still fighting (often with each other) and short on ammunition, these acts of bluff turned out to be their main means of defence.

If they had to be stuck in the veld, outnumbered and outgunned, then their commander's staggering ingenuity made him the best leader they could hope to have. Larking, problem-solving and finding ways to survive was how Baden-Powell worked best and any success in putting one over on the enemy buoyed all of them, calmed their fears and gave them desperately needed confidence.

War correspondents gleefully reported on many of these antics and Mafeking was soon famous. His wizard wheezes were not the only reason that this town in particular was constantly under the spotlight of the world press, though. Winston Churchill's aunt, Lady Sarah Wilson lived in the town and, of course the British prime minister's son, Lord Cecil was there as one of the special army services officers.

Bearing in mind that retrospective accusations of Baden-Powell manipulating and elongating the Mafeking siege for his own gains, personal promotion, or both, came largely from military quarters, where there remained deep animosity (deserved or otherwise) towards him for garnering far more attention and admiration his part in the Boer War than his superiors did, made his wish to play the whole thing down at the time all the more interesting. This has been explained in recent years by the likes of biographer Tim Jeal, whose meticulous research for his book, *Baden-Powell*, makes him one of the world's experts on the man.

He refutes the self-indulgence tag and says accusations that Baden-Powell deliberately prolonged the siege or was cowardly for choosing to hunker down in the town for so long instead of fighting in the field – where his men would clearly have been defeated – are unjust:

> In September he twice begged Sir Alfred Milner to relieve him of the command of the Frontier Force as soon as his two regiments were up to strength, so that he could command the 5th Dragoon Guards when they came to South Africa.

Jeal adds: 'He *longed* to be able to "engage the enemy in the field". Milner and the War Office declined his request.'

It is well recorded that Baden-Powell's original orders were changed from manning vulnerable colonial borders to acting as decoy in Mafeking. He may have been a maverick, a boundary pusher, even a showboater, but above all, he was an incredibly obedient officer whose strings were being pulled by a variety of multi-invested and superior puppeteers, not least Wolseley and Lansdowne. In *Baden-Powell*, Jeal exposes this and highlights the great danger, depravation and disadvantage surrounding Mafeking.

Baden-Powell himself regularly understated the importance of the siege, often citing it as almost insignificant in the bigger picture of the Boer war. He also downgraded his own role, as though genuinely embarrassed by the attention he got, and, no doubt, to minimize the resentment of various officers. For example, he explains that it was really just one out of the many tricks he devised that had, purely by chance, singled Mafeking out for some of the disproportionate attention it received back in Britain.

> One thing which put Mafeking overmuch in the limelight during the early days of the siege was that we sent out exuberantly cheerful messages to Lord Roberts, our Commander in Chief.
>
> He was anxious to know how we were getting on and to show him that all was well, we sent him such messages.
>
> But it was also done for another reason. The messages were carried by native [Baden-Powell's word] runners who had to creep through the Boer lines at night and in the event of them being captured, our messages were then read by the enemy.
>
> *I Was There*, 1937

The runners scrunched the messages into tiny balls and wore them on a string and if they looked in danger of being caught, they'd rip them from them off and scatter them on the ground as they went. This way, if they *were* detained, they had no incriminating evidence on them. The upbeat messages were then read by the Boers as they came upon them later. Those that actually did reach Roberts, also reached British shores.

> We never thought that the messages would be then sent to England. As it was, they arrived there just at a time when our forces in other parts of South Africa were suffering some nasty setbacks at the hands of the Boers.

Anything that relieved the gloom set up by these was welcomed at home just then with exaggerated joy.

I Was There, 1937

Hardly the bragging of a self-centred egotist – although that's not to say he didn't have had a considerable ego.

In October, after a few daring sorties by Mafeking's British troops, including a surprise-cum-bluff attack on a small Boer force using one of the two armoured trains from Mafeking's railway, things got serious. The Boer contingent was forced to fire on the train, causing an enormous explosion which, despite ending with no casualties on either side; being unexpected, it rattled the enemy.

Baden-Powell decided to follow this up some time later with a bold move after having received intelligence that a large group of Boers were heading straight towards them from the north. He sent the remaining armoured train down the line with seventy troops and orders that they should rush the Boers and pour heavy fire on them. He told his men, 'I want the first blow felt by them to be a really hard one.'

As soon as they spotted the train, the Boers had it under heavy fire with lead scattering everywhere. Aware that there was a danger that this fighting could allow a separate Boer force into the town while they were away and otherwise occupied, he took the daring step of commanding more of his already thin-on-the-ground regiment to come and join them.

It worked. This first engagement was fought out for four hours at Mafeking's gates, where the British were vastly outnumbered. Even so, they managed to force the Boers back with what Baden-Powell proudly described as 'a spirit and dash worthy of highly-trained troops'.

The fight saw four of Baden-Powell's men dead while the Boers lost fifty-three and had 150 wounded.

Further Boer shellings were largely ineffective since having watched Baden-Powell's men 'mine' the perimeters far from the town, they deemed it out of range most of the time. A jolly note of reassurance to his friend, Plumer, now elsewhere in Rhodesia, read: 'All well. Four hours' bombardment. One dog killed.' This turned out to be one of the notes that Plumer would send to England where it confirmed Colonel B-P's (as he was now being called) spirit of resilience to the nation.

A string of skirmishes endured and Boer bombardments continued daily, apart from on Sundays; this unexpected Boer veneration of the Sabbath gave Mafeking a day's respite.

Even on weekdays, the Boer guns were often so far away, the townsfolk generally had enough time to dive for cover when the alarms sounded. The Sunday rest day meant that Mafeking's community went to church, played sport and held social events – including 'beautiful baby' shows and concerts.

Of course, there were theatricals and it's not hard to guess who was the star of the show and enjoying every minute of it. It had been a long time since Baden-Powell had slapped on the greasepaint and enjoyed the roar of the crowds, so he pulled out all the stops, building a theatre, sourcing costumes and regularly putting on shows, where he recited favourite monologues and sang songs from the operas. He would dress up as a clown to play the fool and as a ringmaster to run sports events, much to the delight of his men and the wider Mafeking townsfolk. Was it utterly self-indulgent? Of course it was, but it also gave a huge boost to the morale of his troops and the residents who especially loved his comedy capers and the boisterous and stirring music shows.

Imagine for a moment, if you will, thousands of surly, God-fearing Boer farmers looking on, no doubt nonplussed, from the surrounding hillsides while B-P regaled the crowds as Madam Butterfly.

Bluffs continued. Nights were fraught due to the impenetrable blackness of the veld, which made them very vulnerable to attacks after sundown, so Baden-Powell decided they needed floodlights. With a single acetylene lamp and a metal cowl made from repurposed biscuit tins, he and his men managed to fashion one. The tins and light were combined, strapped to a long pole then taken at night to a certain spot. Next, the lamp was lit and manually twisted slowly back-and-forth to look like a high-tech, oscillating spotlight. The Heath-Robinsonesque contraption was then carted around the outskirts of town on rotation and fired up at various locations, leading the Boers to believe that any movement on their part at night would trigger a great bank of floodlights, and make them sitting targets.

To compensate for Crooked Tail Sal, the old sub-standard field gun sent to them in error, they embarked on the ultimate upcycling job and built their own. It was designed by officer Panzera and a Mafeking railway engineer using a steam-pipe from a railway engine, reinforced with molten iron railings and anything else they could find.

The carriage was made from train parts and the ammunition was made from melted metal forged into cannonballs using holes in the sand as moulds. Once they had the big gun they needed, they mounted it on the wheels of an old threshing machine and would trundle it out at night, its wheels muffled by straw and sacks, and surprise the enemy.

Baden-Powell was still known by the indigenous people as Impeesa, 'the wolf that never sleeps', so the new gun was christened The Wolf Of Mafeking and is today stored at the Royal Artillery Historical Trust in Salisbury, England.

Unbelievable as it seems, in the middle of all this hectic schedule of survival and stage shows, Baden-Powell would regularly rise early to spend a couple of hours reading the proofs of a little book he'd written about the training system he used with his men in the 5th Dragoon Guards in India before coming to Africa. When he'd returned home from India, he offered the book to a distributor of Indian military books who turned it down, the publisher himself writing to him to explain that he felt there would be too few sales to justify its publication.

Undeterred but without his agent, big brother George, he handed it to his other brother, Frank, to see what he could do with it. In August 1899, Frank sent the book to Gale & Polden, publisher of the popular *Military Series*. They snapped it up and agreed to pay the author 'a royalty of £5 on each thousand copies sold after the first two thousand copies had been disposed of.' B-P agreed but asked to see the proofs prior to publication; when it arrived in Mafeking, he corrected a few errors, added some extra anecdotes and revised a chapter. Happy with it, he then popped it back in the same wrapping it came in and sent it back to England on what turned out to be the last train out of Mafeking with the casual message, 'Publish it.'

The book was *Aids to Scouting for N.-C.Os. & Men*, which would eventually go on to be reworked as *Scouting for Boys* in 1908 and become not only the bible of the Boy Scout movement, but one of the world's best-selling books, at times outsold only by the Bible and the Qur'an.

The hastily proofed instruction manual wasn't the only thing in town that would later influence the Scouts. So too, would the Mafeking Boy Scouts, an army of white local boys of fighting age now used to stand guard and carry out errands such as delivering instructions to outlying forces, usually at great speed on their bicycles.

It is often wrongly reported that Baden-Powell set up this force of boys, but it was already in existence and Cecil, one of his special services officers, then took command of them to fine-tune their duties. In the Mafeking Cadets chapter in early editions of *Scouting for Boys* Baden-Powell writes:

Every man was of value, and as their numbers gradually got less, owing to men getting killed and wounded, the duties of fighting and keeping watch at night got harder for the rest.

It was then that Lord Edward Cecil, the chief staff officer, [and the British PM's son] got together the boys in the place and made them into a cadet corps, put them in uniform and drilled them; and a jolly smart and useful lot they were, too.

We had till then used a large number of men for carrying orders and messages and keeping look-out, and acting as orderlies and so on. These duties were now handed over to the boy cadets, and the men were released to strengthen the firing line.

In reality, Baden-Powell didn't have very much to do with them during the siege; however, they clearly made a good impression, since he later praised the courage and the level-headedness with which they carried out their jobs, citing them as excellent role models in a chapter of *Scouting for Boys* (1936 edition): 'Would any of you do that?' he asked loyal young British readers. 'If an enemy were firing down this street, and I were to tell one of you to take a message across to a house on the other side, would you do it? I am sure you would. But probably you wouldn't much like doing it.'

Baden-Powell's casual mention of a gunman firing shots down a boy's street and asking whether he'd be brave enough to deliver a note to his neighbour despite that, reveals a lot about, a) how real people's fear of coming under enemy attack was, and b) just how much children's literature has changed since then.

With fewer men and supplies dwindling, the siege lasted longer than anyone had thought it would and things became more serious. Away from the town, 'The Boy', who was fighting with Plumer, had been injured in a losing battle and lay, left for dead, on the veld for hours. He was eventually found by a Boer fighter, who in a twist of fate, somehow discovered that they were both Freemasons and so decided to spare him, taking him prisoner and delivering him to the Boers' hospital.

On receiving this news, Baden-Powell, who had kept a framed photograph of McLaren on his desk at all times since their days in India, was distraught and had to be implored not to risk his own life by riding out of Mafeking to rescue him. Eventually, common sense prevailed. Baden-Powell had been corresponding on an almost daily basis with General Cronje, exchanging letters that were polite, even jovial at times, but always with a subtly bellicose undertone, they were enemies after all.

So, rather than get shot, he made do with sending friendlier, more placatory messages to Cronje, asking if he would please take care of his very good friend, Major McLaren. Once reassured, he wrote to 'The Boy' every day and sent gifts, such as a hair brush, toiletries and other items that he might find comforting. Knowing that his letters would be read first by the Boers, they contained nothing of a military nature, nor of their special relationship.

Things then took a further turn for the worse. The Boers stepped up their attacks and were inching closer to being within range. Shelling was serious and casualties rose. Baden-Powell's men never wavered, they fought back with furious gunfire and any other means they could and most of the time the Boers would eventually retreat. The consensus was that perhaps the Boer general had begun to think that Mafeking wasn't really worth losing too many men over.

A bleak Christmas and New Year came and went and, come January 1900, the town was utterly beleaguered. The war situation overall, though, was looking a bit brighter for the British. Field-Marshall Roberts had been given supreme command and had already arrived in Cape Town with Major General Lord Kitchener of Khartoum as his Chief of Staff. Roberts and Kitchener had much to address and unfortunately for Baden-Powell, any hoped-for early relief of Mafeking was dashed on 8 February when a message he described as a 'bombshell' arrived from Roberts telling him that there was little hope of Mafeking being relieved until 'well into May', and so he should ensure the garrison's supplies could last at least that long.

Having digested this disheartening communiqué and knowing that the supplies were already inadequate, Baden-Powell forced himself to take his own advice and remained calm. As well as his garrison of white and Barolong fighters, the Mafeking townspeople and the non-combatant members of the Barolong, there was now a group of around 2,000 displaced or 'outside' (as the Barolongs called them) African Shangaan tribespeople who, fleeing a war, had taken their chances in a settlement on the edges of Mafeking, rather than be killed fighting. Somehow, all of these groups of people had to be fed. Baden-Powell's earlier calculation for a sufficient supply of food was based on an early relief within two months. Robert's directive meant that it would now be more like four.

With emergency rationing already introduced to manage the delay in Mafeking's relief, they had fed everyone for far longer than the first estimate, based on an even earlier end to the siege, but the continued delay had now seriously depleted stores. With the latest news from Roberts, he knew things could quickly become desperate.

He made his superiors aware of the dire situation they faced and in response, Kitchener ordered him to begin a 'leave or starve' evacuation of the

Shangaan people, sending as many women and children away as possible. Throughout the siege, the Boers had been adamant that the war should be a 'whites-only' fight and had even written to Baden-Powell scorning him for having the audacity to arm black Barolong fighters.

As this was their stance, he was able to negotiate with them, agreeing a safe passage for the Shangaans that would move them into nearby British-held territory, accompanied by a military escort and a food wagon. They attempted to move the refugees but as they progressed, Boer snipers opened fire on them and 'decimated' the group. The truce had been ignored. Baden-Powell realised he had been naive in trusting the enemy and that he had made an awful mistake. Those who were not killed returned to Mafeking and he commanded an immediate abandonment of the plan. Kitchener's orders had been followed and, although he'd never before have dared to defy him, enough was enough.

In *Mafeking: The Story of a Siege* (Covos-Day Books, 2000), Edmond Yorke and Malcolm Flower-Smith of the Royal Military Academy, Sandhurst, insist that Baden-Powell has been unfairly tarnished with claims that he committed a war crime in this instance. Having undertaken what they describe as the fullest study and analysis so far made of diaries kept by garrison soldiers and civilians during the siege, they say that 'other writers have previously used these selectively to attack him.'

Also using Baden-Powell's staff diaries as a source, they believe that the mass evacuation policy was an order and a blunder under immense pressure, 'the product of naivete and misjudgement rather than any concept of premeditated murder'. Even B-P's critics within the garrison credited him with quickly taking 'extensive remedial measures'. Yorke does admit that Baden-Powell was far from perfect however: 'We don't want to portray him as an angel,' he says, 'but these were not the actions of a war criminal.'

There was now nowhere near enough food to go around, so rations were reduced further.

In *Scouting for Boys* (1936 edition) Baden-Powell says:

Our food towards the end was limited to a hunk of pounded up oats, about the size of a penny bun, which was our whole bread supply for the day, and about a pound of meat and two pints of 'sowens', a kind of stuff like bill-stickers' paste that had gone wrong.

On the whole, the men and the Mafeking residents had been supportive of Baden-Powell's endeavours and adhered to this well, but he'd left the administration of it to his subordinates and there was a lack of control over racketeering and hoarding. Once he found this out, Baden-Powell and his men became dab hands at unearthing 'surplus' supplies and anyone caught hoarding was duly punished. Still the lack of food was a major concern.

Unsurprisingly, considering the era and the entrenched mindset of superiority in most colonials, particularly those in the military, Baden-Powell's priorities were the welfare of the British soldiers, followed by the Europeans under his command. However, when he was informed that the outlying Shangaans, who the Barolong had little concern for, were starving, he made a difficult decision.

Although it pained him greatly, he gave the order that the horses were no longer to be fed and instead were to be used for food. Eternally practical above emotional and having read somewhere about how meat-packing firms in Chicago were utilising every part of slaughtered animals, Baden-Powell decided that if the horses were to be eaten, then every part of them should be used, too. They set to work:

> The meat was minced; the interior arrangements were cut into lengths and used as skins for the mince; the hide, after having had the hair scaled off was boiled with the head and hooves to make brawn; the bones were collected and pounded to dust and used for adulterating the flour; the manes and tails were used to fill the mattresses at the hospital.
> Everything pertaining to the animal is utilised.
>
> *Baden Powell: The Two Lives of a Hero,*
> William Harcourt with Lady Olave Powell, 1964

His harrowing yet thoroughly clinical description of how to dismantle a horse is pure Baden-Powell duality. The jarring juxtaposition between his love and empathy for horses and the callous brutality with which he could despatch wild animals, could lead one to the conclusion that if anyone had to organise such an onerous undertaking, then it might as well have been him.

Horse comestibles at the ready, he set up four large soup kitchens to feed everyone. All remaining grain stores and those previously used to feed the horses, along with the paste-like equine 'soup', would be the main sources of food for the native peoples, now that increased shelling bombardments had prevented them from rustling the Boers' cattle, a precious commodity to the tribe.

Despite these actions, many of the Shangaans who had managed to survive the Boer attacks still starved. Exactly how many perished due to the shootings or the hunger is unknown, though some years ago, an expert at Mafeking's Museum guessed 'hundreds'.

In his book, *The Boer War* (Weidenfeld, 1993), historian Thomas Pakenham wrote that Baden-Powell's actions to resist the Boers cost the lives of African soldiers and civilians, including members of his own garrison. Pakenham states that B-P drastically reduced the Barolong's rations in the garrison to ensure that his soldiers had enough to eat. It is known, however, that his own men were on basic emergency rations and in his 1989 Baden-Powell biography, Tim Jeal, a master of deep and balanced research, used factual records and sources and had, even before Yorke and Flower-Smith, already come to an entirely different conclusion to Pakenham's. Jeal said: 'By carrying out a virtual audit of all the food in Mafeking I cleared B-P of starving the African residents.'

In 2001, after further records showed that while many indigenous people left Mafeking under pressure and with a promise of supplies in nearby Bechuanaland (Botswana), others are said to have left because of a taboo against eating horseflesh, Pakenham changed his position and completely withdrew the charges.

On the last day of March, the British Army high command finally turned its attention to Mafeking, but with lessons still not learned and Baden-Powell's advice about mounted soldiers being vulnerable against the Boers marksmanship clearly ignored, Colonel Plumer tried to fight his way into the town with a Rhodesian force. The Boers, now under the command of General Snyman, whom Baden-Powell detested and called a coward for bombing Mafeking's hospital, easily repelled them and Plumer suffered a heavy loss of men.

On Saturday 12 May, acting on intelligence that a large advancing British force under Colonel Mahon was on its way, the Boer Field Cornet, Sarel Eloff, launched the most significant assault on Mafeking yet in a bid to capture the town before it could be relieved. By now, few of the Boer burghers, or leaders, were prepared to take part in such a foolhardy expedition.

The operation began with a feint assault on the eastern defences of the town by Snyman. Eloff then attacked through the Barolong town and captured the police barracks in the centre of Mafeking. His men set fire to native huts as they passed through, gifting the Mafeking garrison with an instant alarm. The plan was that Snyman would launch a further attack on the town's defences, thereby subjecting the garrison to assaults in front and rear, but this did not materialise.

Throughout the rest of the day, fighting raged around the barracks, until Eloff was forced to surrender and the attack collapsed. Eloff, however, got to carry out his boast to his fellow Boers that he would breakfast at Mafeking's Dixon's Hotel the morning after the attack, unfortunately for him, he did so as a prisoner. The following Wednesday, 16 May 1900, the cavalry did finally arrive, as Colonel Mahon's flying column of Imperial Light Horse and Royal Horse Artillery regiments rode into Mafeking, after an epic ride and the siege, which had lasted for 217 long days, was over.

For Baden-Powell, Mafeking was pivotal for two reasons. First, he finally got to experience the military action he'd craved. Second, it was where his idea for creating young scouts in Britain sprung from.

He returned home to a hero's welcome and was absolutely astonished at the hordes of people crowding the streets, waving flags and banners and cheering his name. Even in his opinion, in military terms, Mafeking wasn't a hugely important battle, but the papers had been in overdrive, hyping-up the triumphalism and exclaiming Baden-Powell to be the embodiment of British heroism. Mafeking was seen by some as the first real victory against the Boers and so, to them, he was a god. Major or minor, the episode made him a worldwide name.

Predictably, there was little focus on the deaths of the black African people involved. One thing is certain, far more black people than white died in the siege and in the Boer War in general; tragically, in the colonies in that era, this was commonplace.

On the war memorial at Mafeking, alongside the names of British soldiers, there is a plaque commemorating, with no names, 'the Black Watch'. It is gratifying that in 2021, the Commonwealth War Graves Commission apologised for denying black African soldiers and civilians war graves for their service to the British Empire and it is now working to address the issue. Also in 2021, British Defence Secretary, Ben Wallace said:

On behalf of the Commission and the government both of the time and today, I want to apologise for the failures to live up to their founding principles all those years ago and express deep regret that it has taken so long to rectify the situation.

While we can't change the past, we can make amends and take action.

Baden-Powell managed to get medals for Mafeking's boy scouts. He also officially requested that the War Office award medals to his Barolong fighters for their bravery and loyalty.

His request was refused.

Chapter 9

The Brownsea Experiment Parts I and II

Part I – Brides and Boredom

'A main step to happiness in this direction is to select the right kind of girl. There are women and there are dolls.'

Baden-Powell on marriage *Rovering to Success* (1922)

After the euphoria of the relief of Mafeking in 1900, Baden-Powell had remained in Africa, first as a commander in Western Transvaal and then as Inspector General of the New South African Constabulary, however in 1903, he was ordered back to England.

He may have been the all-conquering Hero of Mafeking, with a room full of gleaming trophies and universally adored by millions, but back in England for good, he was still living with his mother. Worse, while Henrietta Grace publicly swaggered with pride at her son's fame, in private, she continued to make it clear that she found him wanting.

Now Inspector General of Cavalry, he was stuck in London and working in the War Office, which he found stultifyingly dull after Africa's endless skies and wide-open expanses of veld, and he sorely missed being his own man with important, manly things to do. Pen-pushing and cavalry-inspecting bored him, and in many of his other duties he was self-consciously out of his depth, as he admitted in this honest and insightful passage in *Lessons From the Varsity of Life:*

> I was fully unfitted, both physically and intellectually, for the position of I.G. Cavalry.
>
> Physically because I had long had a loose leg as a result of a shooting accident [when he shot himself in Kandahar] … and I could not supply an example of hard-riding horsemanship. Intellectually I was deficient because I had not gone through the Staff College and my knowledge of strategy and military history was merely scrappy.

Scrappy. From the man who transformed disinterested, wet-behind-the-ears recruits into skilled, reconnaissance-savvy soldiers, turned mixed-bags of volunteers into armies and unwilling workers into pioneers and engineers, and all in unforgiving locations such as the bush, the desert, and even uncharted jungle.

Baden-Powell was perpetually plagued by this sort of insecurity, but in London it became amplified and it doesn't take a genius to work out that the cause of his unease was twofold. First was the lingering and open disdain, even jealousy, shown towards him within the military establishment after his Mafeking capers and the resulting adulation. Imagine, for instance, the gloating by some over his inability to demonstrate riding techniques to cavalry troops. Sensitive to a fault, Baden-Powell would have been fully aware of this.

Second, of course, was Henrietta Grace. Thanks to her, his longed-for high-ranking status had turned out to be a house built on sand. His mother, still committed to an impossibly extravagant lifestyle, had taken out a long and very expensive lease on 8 St George's Place. George was dead and his other brother, Warington, was now a balding, portly and sickly 56-year-old bachelor, his single status due to Henrietta Grace putting paid to a decade-long relationship with a woman called Hilda, with the callous explanation that 'Warington and Hilda have been long attached, but neither has enough money to live upon.'

Tired of the military life, younger brother Baden had decided to produce a science journal using his own money, and Agnes was a furiously unwilling hostage to spinsterhood. With the exception of Frank, previously an impoverished although excellent artist, but who then married a rich New Zealand girl, their 'Stephe' was now the highest wage-earner in the family home and, therefore, the main breadwinner. His 'dream' promotion earned him £3,000 a year and Henrietta Grace knew exactly where the majority of that would go. Now that she fully endorsed love at first bank account, she was also determined to get him married as soon as possible

Despite probably struggling with punitively repressed sexual feelings towards men, since Victorian mores still lingered even after the death of the queen, and in the wake of the Oscar Wilde trials of 1895, this was still in an era when homosexuality was considered an illness or proof of insanity, there followed a string of forays into something far more daunting than facing 10,000 armed Boers – the world of dating real women.

As we've learned, Baden-Powell was afraid of most females, apart from girls and grannies, partly based on his belief that prostitutes in the colonies 'contaminated' soldiers, both in body and in mind (never the other way round, though) and that a sexually keen woman could ruin a good man by distracting him from his loyalty to his duty – whatever that may be.

Again, another hangover from the Victorian period where the done thing was to corral upper-class boys in schools, treat them harshly, deprive them of female company, vilify (yet inconsistently engender) same-sex attraction and condemn masturbation, before herding them into the army for more of the same and then unleashing them on an unexpecting world (AKA, the colonies) bursting with pent-up frustration, among other things.

Predictably, Baden-Powell's dates were mainly forced and, therefore, failed. However, some were down to a mild interest in marriage, since enjoying the time spent playing games (and being a child again) with George's children, he now hankered after being a father. He also needed to escape the role of head of the family which he was now finding very hard to live with.

For years, the general view was that Olave Soames, who became Baden-Powell's wife, was the first woman he noticed, let alone proposed to. Anything but.

From 1903 to around a year or so before he married Olave, he saw several women and even asked some to marry him; all politely declined, including Edith Christie-Miller, who, if you recall, he'd snobbishly dismissed, describing her family as 'very kind, very rich, but ... very common'.

The most significant proposal of all was to Rose Gough. Baden-Powell was in a relationship with her from 1903 until December 1905, when his diary entries about their courtship end rather abruptly, presumably after she rejected his proposal in order to marry a naval captain.

What makes Rose significant, is that in spite of her declining his proposal, Baden-Powell continued seeing her regularly after her marriage. Even more interesting is that shortly after he married Olave, he introduced Rose, now Mrs. Kerr, to his new wife as a 'friend' and invited her to help Olave with the Guides. One must assume that Olave, who was a rather jealous wife, had no idea they'd been so close.

Part II – Island of dreams

'Our desire is to help the boy – and mainly the poorer boy – to get the fair chance, which in the past has too often been denied him, of becoming a self-respecting, happy and successful citizen, imbued with an ideal for service for others.'

Robert Baden-Powell on the Brownsea experiment (1907)

'All the world is made of faith, and trust, and pixie dust.'

Peter Pan, J.M Barrie, 1904

Mission: You have been selected to sail to a deserted island on a top-secret assignment with a group of boys. There, you will join a world-famous adventurer who needs your help with a special project. You'll eat outside, listen to ripping yarns around a campfire and sleep in a tent every night. Days will be spent exploring, swimming, scouting, playing games and learning how to do very clever things, such as building rafts, saving lives and making bread in your coat.

To today's youngsters this would be an exciting enough prospect, but to boys from the poorer classes in the early 1900s it would have been the stuff of dreams. School had only been made compulsory in 1870 for children from 5 to 10 years and so, many children, including the very young, were still working alongside adults on gruelling, often life-threatening jobs.

In 1907 and now aged 50, it was also the stuff of Baden-Powell's dreams; the idealistic scenario of boys living in the wilds and having a marvellous time was the basis of a bold social experiment he'd devised. Inspired by his wish to help hard-done-by children to live happier, more fulfilled lives, it's aim was not only to test whether the dream could be made a reality, at least for a few children, but to see whether it might work on a larger scale and help yet more.

Four years prior, the Hero of Mafeking, as he was now constantly called, was one of the twentieth century's most famous and venerated figures. However, his fame had brought him little joy. Baden-Powell was back in England, trapped in the War office, hounded by the press and troubled by the social malaise afflicting his country.

The dawn of the new century, and a new king, Edward VII, signalling the start of the Edwardian era, hadn't wrought much change and many of the draconian practices that had marked Victoria's reign still ruled supreme. This was especially the case with lower-class children, many of whom lived in abject poverty. Worse, the workhouse was still a real and terrifying prospect for the most vulnerable and the government's 1891 Elementary Education Act, making education free for all, was in its infancy. It wasn't until 1918 that school attendance was fully implemented and recorded and the leaving age increased to 14 years.

The more time Baden-Powell spent in Britain, the deeper his concern grew over the future of the next generation, especially the boys, as all things were anything but equal in the gender department at the turn of the century; he knew it was they who would be called upon to defend the country in the event of war.

This was a time when the average British childhood was as far removed from bucolic scenes of running through fields and laughing with friends as it was possible to get. At best, poor children would receive drill-style lessons in the three 'r's in schools so strict that they almost made the workhouse seem preferable. This was followed not by a weekend of rest and play, but by more of the same, with added fire and brimstone at Sunday schools, followed by chores and caring for siblings.

At worst, children would live a bleak existence of abuse or hard graft, sometimes both, due to the need to bring money into poverty-stricken households struggling under the weight of societal ills. Low wages, too many children, scant welfare and inadequate housing were the norm and absent, sick or deceased parents often meant that the children became the breadwinners. Astonishingly, this dire scenario was an improvement on the previous generation's lot; in the 1870s, only a third of all children in England and Wales went school at all.

These relentless hardships were why so many young British men of service age flocked to volunteer for the Boer War; when being on a battlefield is preferable to being at home, it's clear that life is no bed of roses.

In Baden-Powell's world, the Mafeking siege had been the most significant period in what he later came to call his 'first' life; this sorry picture of deprived childhood would be the catalyst for 1907 becoming the most definitive year of his second.

The tedium of his War Office role had made him move to the position of Honorary Colonel of the Southport Cadets and 1st Cadet Battalion of the Liverpool Regiment where he carried out training, inspecting and advisory jobs, often aligned to motivate new recruits.

Although he was back doing what he loved, working with young men to help them reach their full potential, and he was one of the army's most popular leaders, Baden-Powell was feeling despondent.

The official post-mortem on the Boer War had made grim reading, its findings casting a cloud of despair over, among other things, the shockingly poor levels of fitness in the lower-class British recruits who presented themselves for duty. More than half of them had failed to pass what were rudimentary medical exams that revealed them to be scrawnier, sicklier and shorter than their middle- to upper-class counterparts.

This hadn't entirely surprised Baden-Powell. He'd witnessed first-hand the lack of physical stature and wellness in his poorer soldiers which he knew were the result of a toxic blend of terrible working conditions, bad housing, poor diet, and a legacy of excessive smoking and drinking. He also knew that the solutions', decent food, better healthcare and more exercise were beyond their reach.

Even before returning to England from South Africa for good in 1903, post-Mafeking, his mind was on children's welfare, no doubt due to his new role as Inspector General of the New South African Constabulary which, combined with his widespread fame and his heroic tales of the Mafeking scouts, had made him a hugely popular speaker at teachers' conferences.

His speeches promoted healthier lifestyles and scouting, citing adventures outside the confines of the classroom as great motivators. 'Children should be brought up as cheerfully and as happily as possible,' he told his adult crowds and advised that their roles, in an ironic change of priority, should be less about making good soldiers and more about making good citizens. This was a significant departure from his war lust of old, suggesting that, having just experienced a 'real' battle, his focus was no longer on military might but on the wellbeing of the next generation.

Even when promoting the army method of scouting as a means of enhancing observation at a teachers' conference in Johannesburg, Baden-Powell advised observing others to gain an understanding of 'all types', which, in turn, encouraged empathy. 'This kind of sympathy or love,' he told them, 'is the one great principle for which we ought to live.'

He was also being asked to add his patronage to boys' groups around the world, most of which he supported gladly, but insisted they teach the perils of an unhealthy lifestyle, especially denigrating the evils of smoking. So significant were his opinions on this, that a raft of unofficial anti-smoking movements sprung up, the first of which he heard about in a letter from a Reverend Stables of Weston-By-Runcorn, England. Stables had formed a boys' group called The Baden-Powell Anti-Cigarette-Smoking League, and hoped that Baden-Powell might permit them to use his name. He agreed and even offered to answer letters from the boys.

Big mistake. The group quickly ballooned, other branches were added and its membership grew to such an extent that Henrietta Grace, back in England, had to manage the mountains of correspondence. Mother would not have been amused; however, here was the first hint of the power that Baden-Powell's words had on boys in need of a hero.

It confirmed his belief that a lack of good role models was rife. Some blame lay with a woeful social system that ran on beleaguered, uneducated parents and some with the public-school system for upper-class boys, where parents were largely excluded and gentleness and compassion regarded as unmanly and weak.

If only he could break the cycle and find a way of instilling the basic life skills that boys needed to become upstanding, if not outstanding, adults.

The man who, as a child, was only truly happy and fulfilled when exploring, hunting or making something and preferably outdoors, believed that if boys could experience the things that he had on a regular basis, the situation could be reversed.

That's not to say that Baden-Powell disregarded girls; he respected (most of) them, but in the way one would one's mother or sister. And, considering his recent, half-hearted and failed attempts to get married, he'd occasionally even enjoyed their company, although he preferred it when they were 'safe', as in sexually indifferent or unaware.

He preached chivalry towards them and frequently praised their sterling work in keeping Britain – and Mafeking – going behind the scenes (as though they had any choice in the matter).

Still, to him and countless other men of his buttoned-up, female-starved class, women were an enigma and girls – well they were just girls. Back in England in 1903, reality hit and Baden-Powell was torn. Yes, he wanted children to be jolly and carefree, nonetheless, he was, first and foremost, a devoted citizen of the Empire with a real dread that his beloved Britannia was facing a dangerous, future deficit of good fighting men. He knew the importance of efficient soldiers but his appetite for death and destruction had morphed into a wish to breathe spirit and self-respect into rudderless boys and make them brave enough to end wars altogether.

To a lesser degree, his concern also included those privileged boys without the guidance of loving but firm parents that was crucial to military, or any other useful, development. Cue visions of Henrietta Grace shoehorning him into the British Army at 19, despite his loathing the idea. Regardless of the focus, someone had to do something, so Baden-Powell decided that it should be him; the Hero of Mafeking needed a new cause and societal revolution was as good as any.

Coincidentally, this was around the time he learned that his haphazardly put-together army instruction book, *Aids to Scouting for N.-C.O.s and Men* was unexpectedly selling well to the general public. Written in India and proof-read in South Africa in the depth of the Mafeking siege as bullets whizzed overhead, the manual for the development of scouting and reconnaissance skills in soldiers was already immensely popular in military circles since, canny as ever, Baden-Powell had arranged for a signed copy of the guide to be sent to every important commander in the British Army.

This was a stroke of genius. Well-received, it became a bible for training, not only by the British but by other armies, too, including the French. Part of the book's ubiquitous appeal lay in the fact that it was a bit of mish-mash, full of Baden-Powell quips and anecdotes, but also packed with hints and tips, advice and detailed instructions and, of course, his excellent illustrations.

Above all, for the civilian reader, it was its easy-to-read, chatty delivery on how to be a good army scout, that proved so appealing. That and the fact that its author happened to be a famous hero. As well as Baden-Powell being the original public celebrity, one could say that his *Aids to Scouting* was the first celebrity best-seller.

Presenting subjects like observation, camouflage, tracking, stealth, equine care, map reading, first-aid, sketching and reporting as essential but easily mastered skills proved a winning formula. More gratifying still to Baden-Powell was that teachers, youth organisations and boys up and down the land were using it off their own bats. And even more exciting, many were forming their own scouting groups based on the content, which was exactly the pure escapism and happy boyhood stuff that the youth of the era craved.

A boy-at-heart, they were the things Baden-Powell longed for, too. That the humble field-skills manual written in haste and posted off to England on the last train out of Mafeking had reached a far wider readership than he could ever have anticipated was telling him something.

It cemented his belief that children not only needed, but longed for, adventure and to be outdoors. All the things that had informed and cheered him since the age of three, when, after his father's death, Henrietta Grace had continued taking him and his siblings on the nature treks that their dearest papa no longer could; then later, when he and his brothers navigated their boat around the English coast, pitching up where they pleased and sleeping outside, were the same things that boys needed now. But how he could provide access to them?

There was another, possibly deeper, motivation for all of this contemplation. Memories of the joy he'd found in childhood larks had never left him and it could be said that Baden-Powell spent his adult life attempting to relive those happy times spent in what he considered to be the best classroom in the world: the great outdoors.

During his lowest ebbs, failing to shine in school and coping with his mother's blatant displays of disappointment in him, or when forced into army life in particular, it was scouting, in its most literal form, that lifted his spirits. He would probably say that it had saved him from going mad.

It makes perfect sense that, after being discouraged from this sort of escapism by professors, commanding officers and, of course, the indomitable Henrietta Grace, who was determined to force academic genius upon him, he should want to embrace it as a grown-up.

Not only did Baden-Powell do so, he made up his mind that it should be the means by which he save this generation of boys and, thanks to his drive, his lofty position and his excellent contacts, he would soon have the wherewithal to make some dreams come true. With all the zeal of a new curate, he was on a mission. As his military role increasingly took him around the Midlands and north of England, he noted that the lifestyles of people living in cities were particularly detrimental to both their physical and mental health.

He'd address this problem and the lack of support from worn-out, poorly paid or disengaged parents by introducing a scheme that would encourage self-sufficiency, good health and give boys the tools they'd need to grow into fine, reliable fellows, just like himself.

On top of his concern for disaffected boys, Baden-Powell also realised there was the potential for much bigger problems beyond Britain's shores. Lord Roberts, formerly his commander in Afghanistan and now commander-in-chief of the British Army, shared these concerns that should further wars break out in the colonies, the likes of Germany could easily invade the British mainland, since the majority of her troops would be otherwise engaged in the Empire.

Now Baden-Powell didn't just have to save Britannia's boys, he had to save the country itself, and if anyone had the can-do spirit to carry that lot off, Baden-Powell did – in spades.

In his mind, reform was now a matter of urgency for both poor and upper-class boys, whom he saw as equals in need, if not in upbringing. It was time for some research.

He looked into various boys' groups, many of which already had mottos, badges, uniforms and pledges of some kind, although none were that successful. He attended a Boys' Brigade demonstration in the Albert Hall in 1903 and was impressed by their discipline and healthy demeanour. In a speech, he told them about the splendid work of the 'white South African boys', whom he referred to as the 'Scouts of Mafeking', and how he felt that British boys could play an equally important part in helping their country.

As mentioned previously, despite claims that Baden-Powell founded the Mafeking scouts, in reality they were the town's cadet group before it was besieged and were never trained in scouting at all – not even when Lord Cecil, one of his special services officers, took charge of them at the height of the Boer offensive.

Nevertheless, Baden-Powell had recognised their usefulness, not to mention their bravery; he also noticed how much the tales of their activities appealed to these young lads in London.

He left the Albert Hall intrigued by the quasi Christian-cum-military style of the Boys' Brigade (BB) and immediately invited its founder, William Smith, to dinner at his (make that Henrietta Grace's) home in Prince's Gate, where they talked into the wee small hours about the Brigade, 'lost' boys and Mafeking 'scouts'. By the time they were done, Smith had invited Baden-Powell to be honorary Vice President of the Boys' Brigade, which he happily accepted. Afterwards, while discussing concerns over good quality soldiers and the vulnerability of the British coast with Lord Roberts, it was decided that Baden-Powell would begin inspecting local BBs as part of his army duties.

In April 1904, while at Yorkhill Barracks in Glasgow to inspect Smith's Boys' Brigade on the drill ground, he was captivated by the show they put on; marching past him, heads held high, step-perfect, in quarter columns, wearing pristine navy-blue uniforms, pill-box hats and armed with guns (not unusual in Britain in an era where extreme jingoism had instilled a deep fear of invasion), came a 7,000-strong battalion of 12 to 18-year-old boys and 400 officers.

Admittedly, Glasgow was the birthplace of the Boys' Brigade, but even so, it was quite the spectacle. That Smith had been a former Sunday school teacher before joining the crack 1st Lanarkshire Volunteer Rifles explained the BB's curious synthesis of fervent evangelism and fondness for all things martial. It was all a bit 'onward Christian soldiers' for Baden-Powell, who disliked organised religion and thought drilling to have little merit on the battlefield. What the showman in him recognised, though, was how the uniforms, the band music and what Smith called their esprit de corps, amounted to an intoxicating blend for impressionable young boys. And he liked Smith's main purpose: to give 'ordinary' boys the same opportunities to which public-school boys were automatically entitled.

As the two men, now friends, stood on the drill ground, Baden-Powell congratulated Smith on a marvellous show, telling him he was impressed with the marching and the boys' obvious physical fitness. However, he then added that he was surprised at how, after more than twenty years, the organisation hadn't attracted more members.

Perhaps, he suggested, the addition of more interesting tasks other than drilling might make it more popular and attract more boys. Blunt as ever. Slightly miffed, Smith asked Baden-Powell what *he* would do to improve the Boys' Brigade: 'I suggested scouting, which had proved so popular with my recruits in the army,' wrote Baden-Powell.

The terms 'scouting', 'scouts' and even 'boy scouts' were already being used by some groups since scouting was in common parlance thanks to in-depth press coverage of wars, Baden-Powell's *Aids to Scouting* and his personal escapades in South Africa. None, though, had the potential to bring about the sort of universal change that he envisaged.

And Smith's reply? Not, as one might think, a defensive justification of his M.O., he simply suggested that Baden-Powell adapt his army scouting book to suit boys. The book to which he was referring, of course, was *Aids to Scouting* and so, on an unremarkable parade ground in Glasgow, the first small step in Baden-Powell's journey to create a motivational scheme for boys that would go on to attract at its peak 54 million members worldwide was taken. A truly defining moment and even today, most Scouts will tell you that, without that fortuitous conversation with William Smith, there would be no Scouts.

With his head already spinning with ideas for happy boys, there was another motivational episode for Baden-Powell when, later the same year, he went to see a new play by J.M. Barrie at London's Duke of York theatre. The play was Peter Pan. He was utterly smitten by its endearing, ethereal charm and immediately identified with its theme of lost boyhoods and the search for eternal youth. So taken was he by Barrie's play, that he went to see it three times in its first week, no doubt seeing himself in Neverland's playful and mischievous, though thoroughly heroic, Peter.

Raving about the show to a woman friend, Baden-Powell cheerfully told her how he now realised that the partner he was looking for should be 'a sort of girl Peter Pan', and, in typical style, mused on the lack of a female version of the name Peter.

He was inspired. What boys needed was to fly free. He began mulling over how his book could be used as part of a scouting training initiative, then set to work, not on rewriting *ATS*, but using it as the basis of a paper on how military and pioneering scouting could be adapted to suit civilian boys and help make the Boys' Brigade more appealing to them.

He forwarded several ideas to Smith and a few other relevant boys' groups, but they weren't seriously implemented. Undeterred, and ever the strategist, Baden-Powell regrouped and wrote a new paper, outlining in detail how scouting could work.

It was full of phrases such as 'by giving, under the name of 'scouting', an attractive form of training in manly qualities' and, interestingly: 'might also be applied to girls'. The report also referred to 'woodcraft' (the knowledge of woodlands, their wildlife and habitats and survival skills) and he expressly stated that the scheme 'could be applied to existing groups', so at that juncture, he was only proposing that his ideas be taken up by existing organisations, rather than to form a separate movement; he had neither the time nor the money for such an endeavour.

Baden-Powell sent his report to a wider group of public and military movers and shakers, including to the desk of Cyril Arthur Pearson, a well-connected, populist publisher and owner of the *Daily Express* and *Evening Standard*. Like Baden-Powell, Pearson was a man of two sides. On one hand he was a hard-nosed millionaire media mogul who Joseph Chamberlain described as 'the greatest hustler I have ever known', and on the other, the benevolent sponsor of the Fresh Air Fund, a charity that arranged days out in Epping Forest for deprived children from London's East End.

In July 1906, the magnate responded to the paper by inviting Baden-Powell to be a guest at one of his famous weekend house gatherings in the Surrey countryside, where notable figures would network over wonderful food. During his stay, Baden-Powell had very encouraging conversations and got to see Pearson's magnanimous side when he quietly slipped away to visit a home for disabled children.

Two weeks later, he was now writing a slightly different blueprint. It mentioned leaders, troops and patrols in his method to educate 'boys as scouts', and that it would incorporate a handbook. This was the first mention of the book, presumably a result of discussions at Pearson's weekend. He was another step closer to creating the Boy Scouts.

Many meetings with Pearson followed until, in June 1907, they reached an agreement that the Boy Scouts scheme had merit and that Pearson Publishing would back it on the condition that Baden-Powell began writing at least some of the chapters of a Boy Scouts handbook immediately.

Baden-Powell wanted to test-run his scheme first, but it would need the manual – as in, the book – to ensure it was fit for purpose and that his techniques would work. To this end, he decided it needed a summer camp, ideally somewhere far from the madding crowd, and then began frenziedly writing what would be the most important thing in his life, the source of the most successful, non-religious movement the world has ever known.

Reliving the experiences that he'd gained in combat and drawing on the success of the Mafeking scouts, he devised a bold experiment. It would be somewhere remote, involve about twenty boys from different backgrounds – he was now determined that scouting should be for all and not just a privileged few – and last about a week. Mixing classes in this way was, in itself, an incredibly ground-breaking thing to do in Edwardian times.

In a nutshell, it was to be an exercise in purposeful fun that involved taking boys aged about 10 to 16 out of their familiar environments and transporting them to a secluded campsite, where they'd be thrown together in unknown territory, with basic survival essentials, a programme of learning skills and activities and then be left to get on with it. And it would be top secret.

Camping would also have seemed a very unconventional thing to do in 1907, when sleeping outdoors in a tent was done out of necessity and was the reserve of campaign soldiers, hunters, explorers or frontiersmen.

Baden-Powell notwithstanding, the need to escape into the woods only really became popular a few decades later, growing exponentially with a sharp increase in urban living and the constraints that brought. In fact, it was only really after the Second World War that camping became a popular pastime in Britain.

By using tents, Baden-Powell wasn't just aiming for novelty, though, after all, it was he who said 'if camping is easy, it's not camping'. By creating a canvas village, not only would he encourage a sense of community and social interaction, he'd be giving the boys jobs to do. It was they who would be pitching the tents, making the fires, cooking, cleaning and generally being self-sufficient.

He was curious to see whether allowing 'boys to be boys' and to live in this freer way, while still having responsibilities, would result in them bonding together. Would they be more inclined to use their own common sense in what would, hopefully, be an environment of camaraderie and shared purpose? Would they even get on? Would the experience inspire and motivate them to become better, more conscientious citizens, well-prepared for whatever life might throw at them?

There have been claims that Baden-Powell's experiment was to test whether he could turn boys into bloodthirsty warmongers for the Empire. There's no doubt that his fear of enemy invasion of England was very real and informed his original concern over the plight of Britain's boys.

However, by 1907 he was well versed in the sad reality of what boyhood often meant for the lower-classes and his emphasis was less on making them war-ready, and more on making them life-ready. It wasn't to make a bunch of combatants out of children, but to show them things that could help them become adults with the physical and moral strength not to start but to stop wars.

In camp, Imperialism would be reduced to tales of derring-do around a campfire, the virtues and heroism of indigenous colonial peoples would be held up as good examples to the boys and clear messages of inclusion and respect would form part of the proceedings.

It was not about indoctrination, it was about preventing lost childhoods. 'Boys are full of romance,' Baden-Powell wrote, 'and they love "make believe" to a greater extent than they like to show.' The experiment offered a return to innocence for them, but it served a second, more subliminal purpose, that of unleashing Baden-Powell's inner Peter Pan by facilitating not only an escape for the boys, but a return to his own boyhood. For a while, he could personally, and vicariously through his young 'guinea pigs', relive the halcyon days that he so missed, free of his dull job, his overbearing mother, his cumbersome sexual conflict and from reality itself.

While his handbook was still a work in progress, his camp blueprint was ready.

He'd even found his 'Neverland', thanks to a twist of fate. Among his inestimable talents, Baden-Powell was a superb fly-fisherman and in May 1907, in between meetings with Pearson and looking for camp locations, he took an angling trip to Ireland where he became friendly with a man called Charles van Raalte and his wife, Florence.

By sheer coincidence, van Raalte, a wealthy stockbroker, was the owner of Brownsea Island in Poole, one of the very spots along the Dorset coast where Baden-Powell and his brothers would drop anchor and camp, without permission, during their sailing adventures years before.

Delighted to discover this and on hearing Baden-Powell's ambitious plans, van Raalte, a family man with three children of his own, immediately invited the general to visit the island, legally this time, and to use the place for his project should he wish.

The van Raaltes had owned Brownsea since 1901 and entertained on a scale that would have turned Henrietta Grace green with envy. From Battenbergs to Bourbons, Europe's royal families visited their island for house parties where they played golf on a nine-hole course or shot unsuspecting pheasants.

The island's residents, whose families had originally come there to work in a pottery that had closed down prior to the van Raaltes' arrival, were re-employed by the family as servants and paid what was reported to be a good wage for the time.

This troop of grateful attendees not only looked after the guests' every needs, but at the end of a hard day's slog, pulled on bandsmens' uniforms and played for them on the terrace. A milk herd fuelled the dairy, a cluster of hothouses provided tropical fruits and at the laundry the castle's linen was cleaned, as was that of the guests and the van Raaltes' house in London.

Today Brownsea Island is owned by the National Trust (NT), and according to Debbie Moore, one of the NT's Visitor Experience team on the island and whose ancestors lived there, including her great-grandmother who was born there, the importance and magnanimity of the van Raaltes cannot be underestimated.

'The van Raalte's time on Brownsea really was the golden age for the island. It's always been a paradise,' she explains, 'but under their ownership it was also a happy time for the staff. The van Raaltes had incredible wealth and connections but were also kind employers and universally loved by the islanders.'

Debbie also solves a puzzle (for me) over the island's name: 'One of the van Raaltes' most lasting legacies is the island's name. When they arrived it was called Branksea Island.

They often hosted their wealthy friends from London who became confused on arriving at Branksome Station two stops from Poole [and the island] and left the train there, requiring 'rescuing' from somewhere far less salubrious than their intended destination. So to avoid this confusion they renamed their island Brownsea.

And asked about the band-playing villagers, she replies: 'Charles van Raalte had a huge collection of musical instruments and set up the island band – prospective island employees were asked if they played an instrument and were expected to join, which provided entertainment for the van Raaltes' lavish parties.'

Baden-Powell couldn't have been happier. Brownsea was part of his own childhood and since it was completely cut-off from the mainland, it guaranteed refuge from the media attention he was still getting on the back of their reinvention of him as the Hero of Mafeking.

The 500-acre, largely windswept tract of land in Poole Harbour was exactly what he needed. It sits in the middle of the natural harbour (the second largest of its type in the world) and is far enough away from dry land to be accessible only by boat; back then, it was heavily obscured by tall trees, dense foliage and bushes, making it a perfect scout's hideaway. And being an island, of course, made it a thrilling prospect for adventures with a hint of jeopardy and an air of mystique. At the time, its population was just 100.

It's small, just 2km long by 1km wide, with far-reaching views across the water and out to sea. Its village with twenty cottages was Maryland, the pottery workers' homes at the west end of the island, which is now in ruins. The houses on the quay, by the castle and at the farm, are lived in by National Trust and John Lewis staff, and the two at the end of the quay, called *Agents House* and *Custom House,* are holiday homes.

The campsite is also still there and is still used by Scouts and members of the public from all over the world. In 1907 the twenty boys arrived by boat at Pottery Beach and Pier, close to where Baden-Powell had already partly set up camp near the ruins of the old factory.

Three sides of the large, flat field that their 'general' had selected were hugged by trees, interrupted by zig-zagging paths full of promise. The fourth side faced the shore where they'd landed and offered direct access to a sandy beach and the harbour.

Gazing across the water they'd have seen the ruins of the famous fortress of Corfe Castle, on a hilltop rising above the Purbeck Hills; from other locations they would have seen Poole Quay, where Baden-Powell's twenty-first-century bronze statue now sits staring back, un-toppled after the 2020 debacle.

Considering its size, Brownsea was – and still is – home to a staggering variety of wildlife, so they would have had plenty to study, including pipistrelle bats, many varieties of moth, herds of sika deer, wild peacocks, dragonflies and a sea of migrating birds drawn by the abundance of fish in its wetlands and surrounding waters.

By the end of the week, the boys may even have become proficient enough in tracking that they spotted a member of what is one of the most successful and rare red squirrel colonies in Britain. It's not completely clear how long the 200 or so reds have been on Brownsea, nor how they got there, however, according to Dr Phil Cox, Senior Lecturer in Anatomy at the Centre for Anatomical and Human Sciences Department of Archaeology and The Hull York Medical School, based on what research there is, they're likely to be the descendants of the original red squirrel population that would have been resident from at least Victorian and Edwardian times.

There was also the working farm, a church, a school and the luxurious castle, originally built by King Henry Vlll, as part of his coastal sea defence strategy. Somewhat ironic, considering B-P's [as the arriving boys immediately took to calling him] paranoia on that score. These days, the Castle is a subsidised holiday hotel for staff of the John Lewis retail partnership.

Hardly surprising then that Enid Blyton's Kirrin Island, which appears in the first of her *Famous Five* books, *Five on a Treasure Island*, and then in *Five on Kirrin Island Again*, was inspired by, and is an amalgam of, Brownsea Island and Corfe Castle. Never mind the Famous Five, though, Baden-Powell was about to create the 'famous twenty'.

He finished a rough draft of the handbook and got an agreement from C Arthur Pearson's that the book would be published after the trial. This was in July and just in the nick of time since he'd already booked Brownsea for the first week of August and sent out invitations to the boys, all of whom had accepted immediately.

In a letter to George Walter Green, an officer at the 1st Bournemouth Boys' Brigade, inviting the groups to participate, Baden-Powell wrote.

Sir,
I am thinking of having a small camp of boys for a week in Dorsetshire early in August 1st to 8th.

I should be glad to include six boys from the Boys' Brigade if you care to send them. I should not charge them anything … I propose to teach them my new form of Scouting for Boys – and they might therefore be of use in demonstrating some of the games afterwards, in your battalion should you like to try them.

Perhaps you would give me some advice as to whether I could hire bell tents and some flooring in Bournemouth or Poole, for that week, and at what price.

Robert Baden-Powell Lt. General

Another, last-minute equipment request was wired to Green by Baden-Powell the night before the camp, asking whether he could get hold of some harpoons for a game.

Green replied: 'I don't think it's the sort of thing you'd find in a small seaside town.' Much to his credit, though, he did find a blacksmith who. quickly made some.

Imagine the excitement of the boys chosen on being told that they would be heading off across the water to spend a whole week on a secret island, learning skills from the Hero of Mafeking. The twenty who eventually landed on Brownsea that August comprised ten upper-class boys from Charterhouse, Eton College, Harrow, Cheltenham College and two home-tutored students. All were sons of Baden-Powell's army friends or other acquaintances; the other ten came from Dorset Boys Brigade Companies, seven from the 1st Bournemouth, Winton, and three from the 1st Poole still thriving and meeting today.

It has sometimes been said that there were twenty-one or even twenty-two boys in camp, however, in *Why Brownsea?* (2002), Brian Woolgar of the Brownsea Scout Fellowship and his co-author, Sheila La Riviere, explain: 'There were twenty boys for the whole time with Simon Rodney arriving at the end to collect his [three] brothers, hence the confusion.'

The twenty-two figure is reached when incorporating Donald, Baden-Powell's nephew, who went to help his uncle.'

Their first sighting of their hero would not have disappointed them. The island was his new stage, the boys his audience and so, naturally, he'd dressed for the show. Baden-Powell's 'uniform' may have been a hotchpotch of military and civilian clothing but he'd put it together with such panache that, even at 50 years of age, he looked every bit the adventurous leader.

His old khaki flannel South African Constabulary shirt had been given a new lease of life by the addition of a white collar and a tie and was teamed with a pair of shorts, something unheard of in England at the time. The long 'shorts' ended below his knees, just above a pair of high golf stockings worn with sturdy brogues. A jaunty trilby, instead of his trademark bush-hat completed the look. Regardless of class, all the boys were immediately besotted with him and couldn't wait to begin what would be an unforgettable experience.

Being hush-hush, not much was recorded during the experiment but it followed the same daily itinerary, interspersed with different subjects each day. Baden-Powell had planned a full program of activities, including campfire stories, as fun ways to impart abstract concepts such as chivalry and loyalty, and games and contests honed practical skills like tracking, signalling, pioneering, and first aid. Campfire time was also the perfect vehicle for introducing the following day's theme in a light-hearted way.

The basic routine involved Baden-Powell leaving his tent, identifiable by the Union flag he'd flown over Mafeking attached to a cavalry lance, and sounding his African koodoo horn as the wake-up call at 6.00 am; the boys had cocoa, biscuits, physical drill and a practical lesson on the day's subject, followed by breakfast at 8.00 am. From then, it would be a series of exercises on the subject of the day until lunch at 12.30 pm, with the now wonderfully archaic sounding 'Rest. No talking allowed', from to 1.00 pm to 2.15 pm.

Fully recharged, it was time for scouting activities on the day's theme until tea at 5.00 pm then games and whichever patrol was selected for the 'Night Piquet' (a unit 'defending' the camp overnight) setting out to bivouac (make an improvised camp) with basic rations while the others had supper at 8.00 pm, listened to camp fire stories and said prayers before 'turning in' at 9.00 pm sharp.

As well as having his nephew Donald as his Orderly, Scoutmaster Baden-Powell appointed two Boys' Brigade officers, harpoon locator extraordinaire, George Green and his fellow 1st Bournemouth member, Henry Robson, to act as Quartermasters.

Recreating the India dream team, he got his 'best friend in the world', Major Kenneth McLaren, to act as Assistant Scoutmaster. The long-term plan was for McLaren to work with Baden-Powell in delivering the scouting scheme on a larger scale, should the experiment be a success. McLaren, Baden-Powell and the two other officers would be the overall leaders of a meticulously planned itinerary which read like a military operation, but also like the most fun a boy could possibly have. Baden-Powell was prepared and once all the boys had arrived, the scouting began in earnest.

Day one was 'Preliminaries', with all the recruits helping to set up camp before being grouped into four 'patrols' of five or six, with the eldest as leader. Each patrol was named after birds and beasts, then the boys were taught how to emulate the calls of their chosen creatures. As they settled in, practicing their roars and bird calls, the leaders had a course of instruction in the 'field', which they'd then pass on to their patrols. And so, Scouting's enduring patrol system was established.

What started off as a gaggle of excited boys became the Wolves, Bulls, Curlews and Ravens patrols, with different coloured shoulder ribbons indicating their group and all wearing khaki scarves and brass fleur-de-lis badges, supplied by B-P. Each patrol leader carried a staff with a flag depicting his patrol animal. After passing a series of basic scouting tests – knots, tracking and knowing the right way up for the national flag – they all received another brass badge, this time in the form of a scroll bearing the now-legendary edict 'Be prepared'.

'Campaigning' on day two involved 'resourcefulness', with hut and mat-making, knots, fire-lighting and cooking. Health and sanitation (always an obsession) featured large, as did traversing unknown terrain and boat management.

On the third day 'Observation' focused on memory skills, noticing landmarks, tracking and reading signs, and in 'Woodcraft' on day four they'd study wildlife, the stars and how to note details of people and use them for deduction, à la Baden-Powell's hero, Sherlock Holmes.

Day five covered 'Chivalry', or the 'code of knights', while day six was 'Saving Life' – from fire, drowning and street accidents to Edwardian era-defining scenarios, such as sewer gas leaks and runaway horses.

It wasn't until day seven that 'Patriotism' appeared, with activities relating to world geography, history, empire, helping the police and civil duties. The final day was called simply 'Games'.

Considering the lack of any press coverage or any in-depth reporting on the Brownsea experiment, the best insight by far into the minutiae of camp life comes from the boys themselves. For example, while the mixing of the social classes turned out to be a resounding success, working-class 1st Poole Boys' Brigadier, Arthur Primmer's quote on the initial impression is priceless:

> Here's something that will give you an idea of the atmosphere there. One of the upper-class boys in my patrol put up his hand one day and said, 'Please, sir, can I leave the room?' and one of the town fellows said, 'Silly fool, doesn't he know he's in a tent?
>
> scoutguidehistoricalsociety.com

(Thomas) Brian Evans-Lombe, who went with his younger brother John, recalled his camping days to the *Bournemouth Evening Echo* when revisiting Brownsea for the camp's 80th anniversary celebrations in 1987:

> My father was in the Boer War with the general and my mother knew him quite well, so when he planned the camp, I and my younger brother were invited along.
>
> I was 14 at the time and at Cheltenham College, and because I was older than most, my brother and I were given the task of escorting Baden-Powell's nephew, Donald.
>
> In fact, we were the first ones on Brownsea. We arrived three days before the others and set up camp.
>
> To us it was just an exciting holiday and I thoroughly enjoyed it. It was a terrific time and we all worshipped the general.

Even just getting to the secret location was an adventure. The excited boys were ferried there, some on a bright yellow boat owned by a local ferryman known as 'Grandfather' Harvey.

Harvey's boat service began ferrying passengers to Brownsea in 1887 and although it's under new ownership these days, the distinctive yellow craft are still intrinsically linked to the founding of the Scout movement and Brownsea.

At the age of 89, Evans-Lombe fulfilled a lifelong dream when he attended the 80th celebrations on Brownsea to honour the Harvey family with a silver goblet. 'I wanted to do this in recognition of the support that "Grandfather" Harvey gave to us and to say thank you,' he said.

Terry Bonfield, a Boys' Brigade camper, described his journey to the *Bournemouth Evening Echo* in 1989:

> I was one of seven boys picked from the Winton Boys' Brigade. There were also three from the Poole Brigade and 10 boys who were the sons of Baden-Powell's friends.
>
> The Bournemouth boys were taken to Sandbanks [in Poole] on an open lorry. We went to the island on a boat belonging to Harvey's which I think was called the *Hyacinth*.

Bonfield also touched on the ethos of the camp, which was outlined to the boys on arrival:

> The boys were deliberately chosen from different backgrounds because Baden-Powell wanted to see how they would mix.
>
> We didn't know where we were going or what it was all about. It was all very secret because Baden-Powell didn't know whether it would be a success.
>
> His idea was to bring youngsters of different nationalities together so that they would learn one another's customs and ways and then there would be no wars. Unfortunately, it hasn't gone that far.

He added: 'Equipment ... included six bell tents, a marquee and the flag, which had flown over Mafeking.'

Activities included first aid, life-saving, knot-tying, tracking, and observation skills. In the evening, Baden-Powell told the boys Boer War stories around the camp fire. After that they would turn in, happy and exhausted from the daytime's adventures.

Bonfield, 13 at the time, recalled: 'It was very exciting to a young boy, all very wonderful. We were given a ground sheet and two blankets and were told to use the kit-bag as a pillow. We scooped out a little hole for our hips. I slept like a log.'

And when B-P said 'make your bed', he meant literally. The boys stuffed their own mattresses with ferns. They also made their own bread, cooked their evening meals, camouflaged the camp and used a compass to negotiate the island unaided.

Humphrey Noble, one of the Eton boys was enthralled by the campfire yarns:

In the evening we gathered round the camp fire. There was no summertime then or daylight saving so it was dark at a reasonable hour.

He was a wonderful storyteller of tales and had the most exciting adventures and escapes during his army life, culminating naturally in the famous defence of Mafeking.

He had a very clear, resonant voice which arrested attention from the very first. So you can imagine us sitting there in the darkness round the fire listening spell-bound to some thrilling story.

Scout Island! Steven Harris

Primmer, too was spellbound by his hero's camp-fire yarns:

Baden-Powell used to tell us about his adventures in Africa and India... and on a nice summer night, with him standing in the centre of the ring and telling these tales ... that was the highlight of the camp.

Wearing a trilby hat, drooper-drawer shorts, and knee-high golf stockings, Baden-Powell was in the middle of everything.

Primmer also fondly remembered how he missed the camp-fire the time his patrol was the Night Piquet and was sent out to another part of the island with a ration of tea, flour and other basics to make a camp and cook their own supper.

It brought out the adventurer's spirit in the boys and we quite imagined ourselves on a desert island.

The adventure was heightened as we knew that B-P would try to track us down and raid our little camp in the night – which, of course, he succeeded in doing.

The only drawback ... was we missed the main camp-fire. Even after 60 years I can vividly recall the scene. One of B-P's greatest gifts was his art of storytelling and we enjoyed to the full the personality which later was to enrich the lives of so many Scouts. It gives me an understanding why even today the camp-fire is one of the most attractive parts of Scouting.

Why Brownsea? Centenary Edition
Brian Woolgar and Sheila La Riviere,

In an interview in *The Scout* 1927, pals Bertie Watts and Bonfield, both members of the 1st Bournemouth BB, gave an endearing account of the complexities of cooking bread rolls, nicknamed 'dough-boys', on piquet:

we reached the other shore and then set to work to cook our meal. After a few arguments, we decided whose coat we should use to mix the flour for dough-boys, we were glad it was not one of our coats, as it was an unholy mess and utterly spoilt.

We tried very hard, but what with sand hoppers and so on the dough-boys were not very successful, but they were eaten!

In the same interview, both men said they looked back with pleasure on their time there, but added:

Our greatest regret is that our other three pals from Winton who answered the Roll Call on Brownsea Island have since answered the Final Call, for Mr H [Herbert] Collingbourne died after the effects of gas poising, Bert Blandford was killed in Flanders and Bert Tarrant died soon after the camp. [Following a medical procedure]

Evans-Lombe, who was appointed the Bull's Patrol leader in camp and kept his staff flag for many years, never did join the Boy Scouts. Instead he followed in his hero's footsteps and joined the cavalry; his regiment was the 8th Hussars and he fought on the frontline in France and Germany. At one point he was stationed in B-P's old stomping ground of Lucknow.

He was presented with an OBE and lived to be 100. Along with the aforementioned deaths of Albert Blandford and Herbert Collingbourne, another five of his fellow Brownsea adventurers, William and James Rodney, Robert Wroughton, Marc Noble, and his own brother, John Evans-Lombe were killed in action in the First World War.

Along with the other members of the Brownsea twenty, these brave men made history and will be forever remembered, not just for giving their lives in service but for being among the lads who founded what is now the worldwide organisation for peace that is the Boys Scouts.

Pearson and his editor-in-chief, Percy Everett, had anticipated the scouting for boys experiment would be a success and visited the camp towards the end of its run; Baden-Powell had earmarked the last day of the camp as sports day and the 'proof of the pudding' for his publisher.

Always the showman, he invited the boys' parents, the van Raaltes, their illustrious guests and their children (who'd already met most of the boys and the enormously fun Hero of Mafeking, through 'accidental' encounters around the island), and all the islanders to watch a display of the scouting skills acquired by his troops. The entire performance was devised, planned and performed by the boys. It was a triumph. Parents were astonished at the change in their sons and everyone was impressed by what had been achieved in such a short time.

At the last camp-fire that night, the boys heartily sang their last rendition of the Zulu *Eengonyama* chant that B-P had taught them and sat in bitter-sweet wonder as he told them his last yarn.

With his scheme fully endorsed, the very happy Brownsea scoutmaster then bade farewell to his trusty – and no doubt very emotional – scouts the next morning and armed with what he had learnt, spent the next few months writing the full version of *Scouting for Boys*, still with the aim that it be used as a training programme by other organisations.

Initially published in January 1908 as a series of six booklets and a pamphlet of guidance for group leaders, *Scouting for Boys* was backed by a tour where Baden-Powell explained his scheme and the results of his Brownsea experiment. By the end of the month, the response to the book and lectures was so overwhelming that Baden-Powell believed that a separate organisation, dedicated to delivering the programme, might be needed.

An announcement was made to that effect at the YMCA's HQ in his army patch at Birkenhead, England, and on 24 January 1908, the Boy Scouts were born. Within two years there would be more than 100,000 Scouts in the UK alone.

Before even dreaming of writing this book, I often visited Brownsea and admired its little church but somehow never found it open.

St Mary's, built in 1853, four years before Baden-Powell was born, is still used for services and Janet Mellors, the Poole and Brownsea Scouting historian, whose mother was the church warden there until 1996 (her ashes are buried in the churchyard), offered to show me inside.

As I'd hoped, a large and age-rusted key, which Janet produced from somewhere in her Scout shirt, was required to unlock the weathered door.

Inside, it is hushed, musty and full of scouting paraphernalia. The place is dedicated as much to Baden-Powell, the god of Scouting as it is to God himself. Scouts' and Guides' marching flags flank the alter below snoozing bats and all of the cushions, kneelers and decorative banners are embroidered with Scouting symbols and milestones. Sacred ecclesiastical miscellanea shares the vestry with Janet's equally sacred Scouts files, leaflets and woven badges.

Perhaps the most striking item, though, lies in a small ante-room at the back of the church. It is a tomb, topped with a full-sized alabaster memorial carving of a man laid to rest. Bar the effigy, the room is completely empty, the leaded lights of its arched window bathing the figure in coppery, dust-specked sunlight.

The man is Charles van Raalte and the sculpture was commissioned by Florence when he died from pneumonia in India in December 1907, just four months after the first Scout camp.

'Charles only spent six years on Brownsea before his death,' says Debbie Moore. 'Florence stayed on the island for another seventeen years after Charles died. She started a successful daffodil business and provided Sunday afternoon tea parties for the islanders but the heart must surely have gone out of it for her.'

Chapter 10

Scouting for Boys

'B.P. for me has a hidden meaning. Would that everyone had such a reminder before them, applicable as it is to all circumstances, whether of peace or war, of life or death: BE PREPARED.'
From a letter from B-P to the publisher, A.M.S. Methuen

After Brownsea, Baden-Powell was a victim of his own success. With his twenty boys prepared, his scouting 'scheme' proven to work beyond expectations, and Pearson's approval for the handbook, he had much to do. He needed to finish the book, write a proposal for the scheme, plan a lecture tour based on the Brownsea findings and come to an amicable, though more official, agreement with C. Arthur Pearson Publishing.

There was also the Boy Scouts' movement itself to organise and, bearing in mind that he was Lieutenant General Baden-Powell, working for the British Army (albeit in a reduced role and on half-pay), he had to get their consent to do all of the above.

The triumph of the Brownsea island adventure, in particular the easy manner with which all the boys, regardless of background, embraced the project and, more importantly for B-P, had enormous fun while doing so, also meant that Pearson's were now champing at the bit for the handbook. He'd been hankering after having children of his own, but this new 'baby' was turning out to be a lot of work.

As the ultimate scout, whose own advice was to smile and whistle in the face of adversity and to always be prepared, he practised what he preached and prioritised his tasks, with obtaining permission from the army at the top of the list. Next was the book and the accompanying publicity tour, then last, 'selling the idea' of the Boy Scouts to the sort of people who could get involved and further the scheme.

He wrote to the Secretary of State for War, Richard Burton Haldane, asking him whether there'd be any objection to him working on his scouting scheme and 'if there was any likelihood of the army wanting my service shortly and so interrupting me in the starting of the Scouts'. In reply, Haldane invited him to Cloan, his home in Perthshire, Scotland. to discuss it. At Cloan, a fairy-tale castle in a vast estate with views over the Grampian and Cairngorm mountains, Baden-Powell discovered that Haldane had a project of his own.

In response to the abiding concern about a shortage in the country's arsenal of capable fighters, the war secretary's aim was to create a 'Territorial Army' of 300,000 volunteers, closely linked to the existing army. Haldane had no idea whether his plan would get the go-ahead, since Lord Kitchener disapproved of it and Lord Roberts still favoured conscription as the solution. Nevertheless, if it did fly, he wanted B-P to manage the training of 40,000 men who could then impart the TA system on to others.

In a nutshell, the decision was a fair way off, so he had Haldane's blessing to carry on with the Boy Scouts, provided he remained available should the TA be approved. Two months later, Parliament passed the Territorial Army and Reserve Forces Act and Haldane offered B-P command of the Northumbrian Division, with effect from 1 April 1908. He had at least six months to launch the Scouts and, joy of joys, the new army role put him back on full pay.

Next, the handbook. As it was to be serialised to build anticipation, October 1907 saw B-P fine-tuning *Aids to Scouting* to suit 'peace scouting' as well as frantically penning a new introductory chapter for leaders that explained both the philosophy of the scheme and instruction methods.

Baden-Powell assumed this would be the first section to be published, but Pearson felt that while the leaders' advance information was essential, it was far less exciting than the sections aimed at boys and, therefore, would be an anti-climactic launch option; he suggested they release it as a separate pamphlet, just ahead of the first instalment of the book, now being referred to as *Scouting for Boys*.

B-P agreed; Pearson was the king of publicity after all, and the thirty-two-page pamphlet was scheduled to appear on bookshelves with the simple title, *Boy Scouts Scheme*. It would conclude with an invitation from Baden-Powell to the readers to take up his scheme and to write to his office at Henrietta Street, London (pure coincidence but, mother's presence, it seemed, was never far away), for more information. The office was a 'bijou' space, courtesy of Pearson, in which to handle anticipated letters and manage the tour. Baden-Powell asked 'The Boy' McLaren to manage his new HQ, to which he agreed.

Come Christmas, a final thrust was needed to get the book finished, so to speed up the process Percy Everett, Pearson's editor-in-chief who'd been so impressed on his visit to Brownsea that he stayed in camp for four days, went to work with B-P.

Meanwhile, final book negotiations were proving tricky, since Pearson himself had his eye on a bigger fish, acquiring *The Times* newspaper, which was experiencing a fallow spell. However, as a purveyor of populist media, he was well aware that he'd be deemed unworthy of owning such a revered institution, so was constantly embroiled in clandestine meetings in a bid to secure the title anonymously. Too busy to manage his usual business, he appointed Peter Keary, one of his mangers, to seal the deal with Baden-Powell.

It didn't work. Keary was a corporate man, with none of his boss's enthusiasm or empathy with children. B-P was unhappy and told the uncompromising news tycoon as much in a letter that demonstrates the true grit of the rough-edged field survivor that lay beneath Baden-Powell's debonair and courteous surface. He wrote to Pearson on 19 November 1907:

In coming to a formal agreement with you as regards the Boy Scouts scheme the form now proposed seems to me to put us on a different footing than that originally planned, ...

It tends to form your staff and myself into a committee of management .... Well – I'm afraid I could never work with a committee. Could you?

I, on my part, undertake to:

Plan and organise the Boy Scouts ... and be responsible for its development under a manager of my own selection.

Explain it in the chief towns of England before the end of March.

Write and publish a handbook in January and February.

Devote the proceeds of such book to the furtherance of the scheme.

Give my name to an article in each number of *The Scout* newspaper [devised in the process of the Brownsea experiment] as long as our agreement lasts.

Be consulted about the proper expenditure of your contribution of £1,000.

You on your part, undertake to:

Find £1,000 for the first twelve months – renewal of such contribution being optional.

Run a newspaper (*The Scout*) in connection with the scheme, in which I can publish orders or information for the Boy Scouts. All the profits go to you.

This agreement to stand for one year … it may be cancelled at one month's notice on either side.

This also shows that money was never a consideration for him. Pearson realised he'd pushed his potential cash cow too far and by 1 January 1908, Baden-Powell's proposals were accepted, give or take a tweak or two.

The instruction pamphlet was published and had already sold well when the first two completed parts of the handbook were sent to the printers and on Wednesday 15 January 1908, *Scouting for Boys* was on the bookshelves priced at 4d (fourpence) a copy.

In truth it was a rushed job, printed on cheap paper to keep the cover price down and roundly sniffed at in literary circles due to its erratic, amateurish and, at times, infantile style.

People also scoffed at Baden-Powell's belief that Britain's boys would really wander the streets in short trousers, forcing 'good turns' on strangers, while wielding broom handles.

Still, it was hoped that Part 1's eye-catching white and blue cover with the fabled Hero of Mafeking's new nickname, 'B-P (LIEUT. GEN. BADEN POWELL C.B.)' writ large across the front in bold letters next to John Hassall's evocative illustration of a boy in shorts (still not remotely commonplace in everyday life) and high socks, with his staff and bush-hat lying nearby and hiding behind a rock observing people – pirates? Enemy soldiers? – coming off a boat, would greatly appeal to the youngsters of the day. And it did.

Humble-pie would, no doubt, have been eaten in certain quarters as copies of *Scouting for Boys* flew off the shelves at an astounding rate as boys – and girls – scrambled to read what B-P had to say. An intense advertising campaign by C. Arthur Pearson's publicity man, Henry Shaw, combined with Baden-Powell's punishing lecture tour – forty dates in seven weeks, at the age of 51 – had paid off.

The book's chummy tone, haphazard content, doable activities and funny sketches had the children of Great Britain hooked and by the time the entire book, cloth-bound and priced at 2s (two shillings), was published by Horace Cox in May 1908, it was less snowball effect, more avalanche.

Almost immediately, Scouting was a thing in Australia and New Zealand and the book was so popular that it had to be reprinted four times in its first year (though no precise sales figures exist) and after twenty years, excluding the British colonies, it was in print in twenty-six countries. It's believed that *Scouting for Boys* sold more copies in the twentieth century than any other English-language book, apart from *The Bible.*

Suddenly, B-P's small office was deluged with responses from his invitation to write in and, despite sterling efforts, he, McLaren and their new secretary, Miss Margaret MacDonald, were overwhelmed.

Although things were moving faster than expected, there was a way to alleviate the crisis. If they could get *The Scout* newspaper, designed to be Baden-Powell's mouthpiece, out ahead of schedule, then the Chief Scout himself could answer questions via its pages.

Pearson gave his staff a deadline of two weeks. All the stops were pulled out: Henry Shaw, whose fruitful marketing campaign had helped create the happy dilemma, was made editor; writers and illustrators were rallied and with stories and images chosen, the deadline was met.

A new weekly was born and the first edition of *The Scout*, dated 18 April 1908, was on sale by 14 April.

It was well received, thanks to it having decent content, including articles by popular boys' writers, motivational pieces, such as: 'Why All Scouts Must Keep Fit', and, in pure, unadulterated populist press style, a competition to win: 'A Fortnight in General Baden's Camp – The Most Fascinating Holiday Ever Offered – Thirty Boys Invited.'

All of these child-friendly headlines paled into insignificance, though, next to 'How I Started Scouting' by Baden-Powell, his first promised contribution.

The Scout was just as popular as *Scouting for Boys*, with early issues selling out in two days. By the end of its first year, in just eight months, its circulation was an incredible 110,000 copies a week. The Scouting movement was here to stay and Pearson's £1,000 suddenly looked like a sound investment. On the other hand, as stated in his no-frills missive, B-P gave all the profits from his book to the Boy Scouts.

By May, he was carrying out his Territorial Army duty, but he combined it with Boy Scouts inspections, mainly while traversing his army patch of Northumberland, Durham and Yorkshire. Barely had Baden-Powell taken command when, on 2 May 1908, he was in hot water over controversial remarks he made during a speech to officers and NCOs in Durham entitled 'The Territorials as a Fighting Force'.

Stressing that men needed to be prepared to resist an invasion that could occur at any moment, he was asked 'by whom?' Citing Germany as a likely candidate, he told them: 'Germany wants to develop her trade and commerce, and must, therefore, get rid of England, which blocks the way.' And on being asked where such a strike could happen, he told them London was unlikely, since although the capital, their target would be key industrial areas of the North and their strategy would be to land on the open beaches of the east coast. To illustrate this, he showed views of German battleships, explaining how they could 'embark 120,000 men on to British shores' and warned that they could lay enough mines to destroy a navy.

And when asked about *when*, he predicted a time when British people and communications channels would be least prepared, an August bank holiday, for example. This was on Saturday 2 May. On the following Monday, Baden-Powell's speech was reported in detail by the *Newcastle Daily Chronicle*, despite no reporters having been present – apparently.

Realising the panic that the article would cause, Baden-Powell rushed to London to see Haldane and explain. Predictably, there was a great furore over what was essentially a war speech and questions were raised in Parliament as to whether his alarmist and inflammatory comments were acceptable. In a chillingly prophetic question direct to Haldane, the MP for Northumberland, one J.M. Robertson asked: 'Was he [B-P] justified in speaking of Germany as a natural enemy of this country ... predicting a desperate and bloody war between the two countries?' Haldane skirted around the question, with a vague reply about not being told about aspects of the speech and stated that a 'laborious investigation' wasn't worthwhile.

The storm blew over.

A year after Brownsea, the culmination of *The Scout's* wildly popular competition to 'holiday' with B-P was a second successful camp at Humshaugh in Northumbria, this time with the thirty newly fledged real Scouts lucky enough to win places. Their uniforms, though rudimentary, included more of the trademark hat, shorts and neckerchief combo than those of the Brownsea pioneers.

Although Scouting came to be defined by its uniform at that time, so as not to deter poorer boys from joining it was kept minimal; parents could simply cut off trouser legs and turn shirts or even knickers into neckerchiefs and the boys just turned down their traditional long stockings to reveal their knobbly knees.

Shops sold out of mops and brooms as they were snapped up to make Scout staves from the handles and wide-brimmed hats became as rare as hen's teeth, all thanks to B-P's illustration of what a Scout should wear.

Other indispensable items listed were a rope on one's belt, in case of the need to drag someone from a lake or to recapture an escaped horse; an emergency tin containing matches, coins and plasters; and an axe. No Scout was truly prepared without the means of chopping down trees.

The *Scouting for Boys* juggernaut was unstoppable. People used it as their bible, setting up patrols under their own initiative and, in spite of the naysayers, children *did* wear the uniform, carry the staff and abide by the Scout Law, as listed in the book:

1. A Scout's honour is to be trusted
2. A Scout is loyal to the King, his country, his officers, his parents, his employers, and those under him
3. A Scout's duty is to be useful and help others
4. A Scout is a friend to all, and a brother to every other Scout, no matter to what social class he belongs
5. A Scout is courteous
6. A Scout is a friend to animals
7. A Scout obeys orders of his parents, patrol leader, or scoutmaster without question
8. A Scout smiles and whistles under all difficulties
9. A Scout is thrifty
10. A Scout is clean in thought, word and deed

It's no wonder Baden-Powell always said that Scouting invented itself.

His initial assumption that the scheme would be adopted by existing organisations was wrong. Trials with the Church Lads' Brigade and the Boys' Brigade weren't that successful because what he hadn't bargained for was that boys who loved scouting didn't want to be in other groups; they wanted B-P's leadership and they wanted to be Boy Scouts, nothing more, nothing less. Things were getting out of hand though, with self-appointed groups roaming the countryside and any old Tom, Dick or Harry able to declare themselves a scoutmaster and set up a Boy Scout group.

Calling on his friends and all the stout-minded, good chaps he knew, he asked them to consider volunteering, mainly as leaders to oversee either groups or regions. Many took up the baton and he was able to get on with his 'other' job, the TA.

With no breaks in two years, aside from the odd weekend away and that fortuitous Irish fishing trip, at the end of what had been eventful but exhausting year – even for B-P – he turned maverick. On a whim, which he put down to being stuck in Southampton in the rain waiting to welcome his old 5th Hussars home from India and getting a sudden waft of delicious-smelling coffee, he booked a voyage to Brazil. 'I made my mind up there and then to take a ticket for Brazil, whether I could afford it or not.'

Henrietta Grace would have confirmed that he most certainly couldn't afford it, however, since she was part of the reason for his escape, he headed to the Royal Mail Steam Packet Company and, with the promise of a travel feature for their advertising pamphlet, left with a free ticket to Buenos Aires, stopping at Rio de Janeiro. Baden-Powell was back on form and ready for adventure.

On 19 February 1909 he sailed on the *SS Argon* in 'a very nice cabin and in good company'.

A delay gave him little time in Rio, but it was Buenos Aires that was to be unforgettable anyway. The 'Hero of Mafeking' was welcomed like a god, not just by British colonials but by the Argentinian Government, too. He was entertained and given free passes, transport and military escorts wherever he went, which was just about everywhere.

In Chile it was the same; he travelled to the Andes by train, then by narrow-gauge track to a tunnel where he was taken over the pass at 12,000ft. When he left, the Chilean people crowded the station to see him off and military bands played the British national anthem.

Back home, he renewed his arrangement with C. Arthur Pearson, got a new office in Victoria Street and a new managing secretary, as McLaren had resigned due to illness – a much-questioned reason, since he was still playing polo. It is widely thought to have been an excuse to leave as he didn't get on with the staff, and this seems to be the point where 'Bloater' and 'The Boy' drifted apart.

The Scout ran a third camp competition, this time for 100 boys for two weeks at Buckler's Hard, an ancient Hampshire shipbuilding village, with a slipway that once launched some of Admiral Nelson's ships. Having heard about the Scouts, the England cricketer C.B. Fry, who ran a training school for boys, offered B-P his training ship the *Mercury* for the duration. It accommodated fifty people, so the camp was split in two, with one half of the boys under canvas, the other half on board ship. On the second week, they swapped over.

Scoutmasters included Percy Everett, now a committed Scout. The Buckler's Hard camp was plagued by rain and Baden-Powell could only visit twice due to his TA schedule. Still, it was another success and B-P left with plans to make sea scouting part of the Boy Scouts.

From this moment, mountains – nay, a mountain range – of words have been written about the incredible history and enduring appeal of the Scouts, so there is little new to add that which hasn't been gone over time and again.

Some are worth remembering, however, such as the famous Crystal Palace Rally – the first of its kind and born of a wish to bring Boy Scouts from all over the country together. Among the many things it stands out for – bringing Scouting to the attention of the world, allowing children to see their hero and cementing the movement's place in Britain and around the world – there is one important aspect of it that stands out above even these.

For it was there, on 4 September 1909, that, in the midst of a sea of boys and those who'd flocked to the event, that a chance meeting changed the lives of girls, too.

When Baden-Powell climbed onto the platform in the 'palace' in his general's uniform, he saw only boys. The atmosphere was super-charged and the crowd let out a deafening roar on seeing him, then waved their hats, raised their staves and grinned from ear-to-ear at seeing their *Scouting for Boys* idol, B-P.

At a signal, silence fell into which Baden-Powell read a telegram from King Edward, telling them all how wonderful he thought they were; B-P then delivered a rousing speech in his quirky, some might say odd, style; at the end, another ground-shaking roar went up and a programme of games began.

Off the platform and walking among his boys, relishing the adulation but at the same time gratified to see so many youngsters transformed from brow-beaten to bursting with pride and joy, Baden-Powell stumbled across a little group of seven girls and stopped in his tracks.

All were dressed in a uniform of white shirts, dark skirts and stockings and were sporting Scouts hats and scarves and holding staves. Sybil Canadine, one of the group, recalled what happened:

Suddenly, we saw a figure coming towards us and, of course, we knew at once that it was Baden-Powell, so, we scrambled down the bank and he came up and said to the patrol leader: 'And what the dickens do you think you're doing here?' and the patrol leader said: 'We want to be Girl Scouts,' to which he replied, 'Oh no, it's only for the boys.'

'Well then,' says Canadine, who had formed the group from friends and factory girls and afterwards dedicated her life to Girl Guides, 'we broke our line, we gathered round him and we said: 'Oh, please, please, something for the girls. We are the Girl Scouts.'

Impressed, he left thinking that direction, as he knew from his knowledge of society and the fact that thousands of girls had registered to be Scouts, was something that girls could do with, too. He'd have been even more impressed had he known that the girls had walked six miles, in the rain, as they hadn't enough money between them to take a bus.

A letter to *The Scout*, offers insight into girlhood at the time and poignantly highlights the lot of many of them. It reads:

> Dear Sir,
> If a girl is not allowed to run, or even to hurry, to swim, ride a bike, or raise her arms above her head, can she become a Scout?
> Hoping that you will reply,
> Yours sincerely, A WOULD-BE SCOUT

Thought-provoking, it was another motivation for an already busy Baden-Powell to consider a group for girls. But he was torn. His social conscience said 'yes' – but it was the Edwardian era; Emeline Pankhurst had only just got going with her Suffragette movement to win votes for women, so girls were still expected to be modest, calm and helpful around the house.

And it would have to be a separate beast, since if Boy Scouts didn't want to share with other boys' organisations, they'd hardly want to Scout with girls!

He consulted the two women he knew best, Henrietta Grace and Agnes; both liked the idea and Agnes, desperate to escape the house and her mother's clutches, offered to run the group for him. Satisfied, Baden-Powell called it the Girl Guides, in homage to an Indian corps called the Guides that could turn their hands to anything. Mother and sister approved of the chaperone-like tone of the name and so, a second Baden-Powell movement was born.

For obvious reasons, Agnes found plenty of willing women to form a committee to help manage the Guides and she quickly rewrote *Scouting for Boys* to suit girls, giving it the somewhat patronising title, *How Girls Can Help Build the Empire*.

Now all she had to do was convince the mothers of Britain that the Girl Guides wouldn't turn their daughters into deranged tomboys. And to let them out of the house, of course. If anyone could do it, Agnes could. According to a friend: 'Anyone who had come in touch with her gentle influence, her interest in all womanly arts, and her love of birds, insects and flowers, would scoff at the idea of her being the president of a sort of Amazon cadet corps.'

The Girl Guides was a hit and could be considered just as important as the Boy Scouts in terms of improving children's wellbeing. For while boys were suppressed and under-stimulated in many ways, at least some went to school, trained for jobs and played outside, giving them a degree of freedom and social interaction. For most girls, life was home-bound and uneventful with little, if any, formal education and overwhelming pressure to be seen and not heard. Household duties and caring for younger siblings were the lot of the lower-class girl, while learning piano, painting and bagging a suitable husband was that of their 'betters'.

Crystal Palace, while a triumph, also put Baden-Powell back in the spotlight and while success breeds success, it can also breed discontent and jealousy. And so, for a while, in a situation bearing an uncanny resemblance to the 2020 Poole Quay statue stand-off, while the majority of British people were singing his praises, some factions were criticising him.

Pacifists called the Boy Scouts a thinly veiled warmongering movement and, in extreme cases, a propaganda machine for indoctrinating Britain's boys with militaristic zeal to ease the way to conscription.

Ultra-militarists, on the other hand, accused Baden-Powell of encouraging boys to lose their sense of duty by turning life into a game and encouraging them to run wild, to be distracted and generally far too jolly to become effective soldiers.

Baden-Powell attempted to reassure both sides but failed; separatist factions, including the Empire Scouts and the National Peace Scouts, attempted to lure boys away from him, but they soon sunk without a trace; however, he was distressed and baffled by the animosity. He reminded them that it had not been his intention to start a movement, just to offer his scheme of activities to other organisations, but it made no difference. Other politically motivated camps railed at him. Socialists called him an anti-socialist, Conservatives called him a rabid socialist and others put up posters warning boys of the dangers – mainly a lack of solemnity and piety – lurking in the Boy Scouts, which purely served to pique their interests and many more joined.

The major outcry, though, came from religious groups, angry at the lack of religious content in *Scouting for Boys*. Being uncomfortable with organised religion, Baden-Powell's book had just two out of its 300 pages devoted to the subject, whereas the protesters were used to boys' groups being church-based. He couldn't win and, to add to his woes, his own money was no longer enough to fund the Boy Scouts. Pearson's £1,000 was long gone and proceeds from his book were swallowed up by the expense of managing the thing.

Welcome distraction came in the form of an invitation to Balmoral from the king, from Saturday 2 until Monday, 4 October 1909. He managed to defer his arrival by a day as he wanted to fulfil a promise to attend a gathering of 5,000 Glasgow Scouts, and arrived at Balmoral just before dinner. He was greeted by a room full of guests, including Haldane, then was whisked away to dress for the meal. What happened next is extraordinary and best told in Baden-Powell's own words, written as a postscript in a letter to his mother scribbled on Balmoral-headed notepaper at midnight after the dinner:

> P.S. Just before dinner the King sent for me. The equerry took me to his [the king's] room and while outside the door … pinned two safety pins on my coat … it was very like preparation for an execution.
>
> Then he [the king] walked in … in Highland costume and shook my hand and … told me that for all my past services and especially my present one of raising Boy Scouts … he proposed to make me Knight Commander of the Victorian Order.
>
> Then he sat down and I knelt in front of him. The equerry handed him a sword and he tapped me on each shoulder; then hung the cross round my neck and hooked the star of the Order on my coat … and off I went!
>
> So that's alright, and I hope satisfactory to you my dear Ma.

Back in the dining room, fellow-VO recipients had formed a guard of honour. 'It was all very embarrassing – and very jolly,' he said.

The explanation for the hasty knighthood was that, forgetting B-P was arriving a day late, someone had printed his dining place cards with 'Sir Robert', assuming he'd already have been knighted the day before (when in fact he was with the Glasgow Scouts), so they'd had act to quickly before he took his place at the table. Still, a pleasant interlude and a knighthood, to boot.

Scouting had now spread to India and in December 1909 there was some good news on the fiscal front. His recently formed council of stalwarts, now the Executive Committee, with Sir Edmond Elles as chief commissioner and Herbert Plumer and Francis Pixley, a barrister, in other strategic roles, had been busy. Several committee members were astute businessmen and, on seeing B-P's deal with Pearson, had brokered a new one, with the publisher signing a five-year contract in which Baden-Powell would be entitled to £500 cash up-front for *The Scout* and his weekly articles, plus 10 per cent of its profits. Regarding *Scouting for Boys*, he'd receive royalties at 20 per cent.

With the nitty-gritty now in safe hands and Agnes running the Guides, Baden-Powell could finally concentrate on leading the Boy Scouts. The Chief Scout was prepared, but realised that if he were to do it properly, he'd have to resign from the army. After thirty-four years, and done with climbing the military ladder, he did just that. Unsubstantiated rumours suggest that he was tactfully advised to resign by Haldane and the king because he had become too controversial and too busy for the army.

Whatever the truth, Baden-Powell was definitely requested to visit King Edward on 5 May 1910; he said it was for the king to bid him farewell as a retiring general. However, on arrival at Buckingham palace, he was told that the His Majesty was sorry but he was feeling unwell and couldn't see him. A new date was arranged and Baden-Powell left. King Edward VII died the following day.

Freed from his TA work, from 1910 to '11 he lived and breathed the Boy Scouts. That it had taken the British Isles by storm was surprise enough – there were now 107,000 Scouts in the UK – but considering the scheme had been written for British boys, B-P was amazed that it had also spread around the world. Canada, America and Russia had now joined the ranks, as had many European countries; global invitations poured in asking him to visit. He accepted one to Canada and one to America.

Lord Grey, an old acquaintance from Matabeleland and now Governor General and Chief Scout of Canada, paid for Baden-Powell's visit. Around the same time, *The Scout* ran a competition for sixteen boys to win a trip to Canada with Eric Walker, from Boy Scouts HQ, so Baden-Powell travelled with them. They stopped at Quebec and Montreal and went on to the Rockies, where the boys camped for two weeks, learning ranching and backwoodsmen skills. Baden-Powell camped in Quebec and, at 53, white-water rafted for the first time in his life.

New York came next on 23 September. He met Edgar Robinson, Senior Secretary of the YMCA, and his old chum and sometime sparring partner, Ernest Seton, he of the woodcraft skills and now Chief Scout of the Boy Scouts of America. He also met the former US president, Theodore

Roosevelt, who was by then Honorary Vice-President of the Boy Scouts of America.

At a dignitary-laden dinner at the Waldorf Astoria hotel, Chief Scout Baden-Powell laid to rest the old ghosts of woodcraft bickering by publicly thanking Seton and other scout leaders for their inspiration. He returned home to an invitation to visit Russia, and met Czar Nicholas II in January 1911; the Czar had read *Scouting for Boys* and ordered its translation, and asked B-P to inspect the boys from Russia's first ever Scout group.

This globe-trotting was a means of escapism as well as a means to grow the movement. Along with Crystal Palace, King George V and Queen Mary's coronation day celebration on 22 June 1911 was another scouting milestone. Constitution Hill was reserved for Baden-Powell and 200 British and Canadian Scouts. As they waited, three horses preceded the royal party; their riders were Lord Wolseley, his advocate, Lord Roberts, leader of the final column that relieved Mafeking and Lord Kitchener. All three of the country's most significant military men came to a halt to shake their old friend's hand and chat, underpinning Baden-Powell's military and scouting importance to the crowds.

This was quickly followed by the historic Windsor Great Park incident of July 1911. Baden-Powell led the largest gathering of boys the country had ever seen for inspection by the new king; Scouts from every region of the British Isles as well contingents from Malta, Canada and Gibraltar totalled an estimated 30,000. When he lined them up Zulu fashion in horseshoe formation, it was an impressive spectacle. More was to come. With the inspection over and the king and queen gathered with various dignitaries, including two Indian maharajas in magnificently opulent outfits, it was showtime.

Baden-Powell, on a black horse, moved forward and gave the signal for the 'Grand Rush'.

A sudden roar filled the air, and the whole mighty horseshoe of boys with one impulse leapt forward from either side, rushing as only boys can rush, gathering speed and force as they came, screaming out the rallying cries of their patrols as they swept, a kaleidoscope of colour, with flags fluttering, hats waving, knees glinting, in the great charge towards the King.

B-P

The crowd gasped and just when it looked as though the royal party would be bulldozed, the Scouts stopped as suddenly as they'd started and stood, completely silent. Their Chief Scout called for 'three cheers for His Majesty' and at that, up went the hats and staves as they belted them out. B-P admitted to crying at this and said: 'That was one of the most thrilling moments of my life!'

Scouting continued to spread, as did his touring schedule: Norway, Copenhagen, Amsterdam, Belgium, Sweden and Denmark, the list went on and everywhere he went, he was worshipped.

At the opening of the new year in 1912, the feather in Baden-Powell's wide-brimmed hat was the Boy Scouts receiving a royal charter in January. After that, more touring was scheduled, although this time there would be no need to blag tickets as it was an all-expenses-paid tour of America, comprising twenty dates, organised by an American called Lee Keedick, in association with the Boy Scouts of America, who specialised in staging famous-name lectures and already had the likes of Sir Arthur Conan Doyle, G.K. Chesterton and H.G. Wells on his books.

At Southampton docks on 3 January, he boarded the luxury cruiser, SS *Arcadian* bound for New York, waved off by his late brother George's children, Donald and Maud. Strolling along the promenade deck on his first morning at sea, he spotted a friend, Miss Hildabert Rodewald, walking ahead of him with another young woman, who seemed familiar. He wasn't sure who she was, but his scouting instincts recognised her distinctive 'quick determined gait' and he suddenly remembered where he'd seen her.

When the two women passed him, he removed his sailing cap and took Miss Rodewald's proffered hand as she said, 'General, I want you to meet a friend of mine, Miss Olave Soames.'

Looking directly at the smiling Olave, he was struck by her 'wise, dark brown eyes' and bowed, trilling: 'Delighted!' He told her that he knew she lived in London. She told him that she did not, she lived in Dorset, which baffled Baden-Powell as he was so certain of that gait. So he asked: 'But you have a brown and white spaniel?' It was her turn to be baffled as she replied in the affirmative. 'And you *have* been in London? Near Knightsbridge barracks?' he continued. She told him she had, but that it was two years ago.

She was the same girl! He explained that he remembered her interesting walk, which at the time, using his Holmes-esque powers of deduction, told him that she had an 'honesty of purpose and common-sense as well as a spirit of adventure'. While Baden-Powell mainly avoided the opposite sex, they were almost universally drawn to him, and Olave was no exception. More friends arrived and whisked Miss Rodewald away, leaving Baden-Powell alone with her, which surprisingly, didn't concern him in the slightest.

They lingered on the deck and chatted for hours; he talked about his tour, and she told him that she and her father were on their annual search for sunshine. Of course, Olave knew that he was the Hero of Mafeking since, like almost everyone else, she'd followed his Boer War antics; she even had a pin badge with his face on it, so she would have been at least a little star-struck. The more they talked, however, the more they found they had in common.

They both loved art, nature, dogs and horses, and even shared the same birthday of 22 February – although while Olave would be turning 23 on hers, B-P would be turning 55 on his.

They only left the deck on realising it was time for dinner, where Olave introduced him to her father, Harold Soames. Soames had inherited a profitable brewery business from his father and after managing it well for some years, sold it and was now using the considerable proceeds to fund a hedonistic life of leisure, mainly travelling, painting and gardening. He was also destined to become the great-grandfather (and therefore, Olave the great aunt) of the then yet-to-be-born, Sir Nicholas Soames, the Conservative MP and Buckingham Palace courtier who caused a media storm by interfering in Prince Charles and Princess Diana's marriage, demanding that she divorce the prince and publicly accusing her of being in the 'advanced stages of paranoia'. Harold Soames was not much older than B-P and knew the general by reputation and had heard of his artistic talents, so they had a long and easy conversation about art.

Olave's diary entry that night reads:

supremely happy sitting loafing lazily on the deck all day. Made friends with … Lieut.-General Sir Robert Baden-Powell 'The Boy Scout' who is so nice. He talks so nicely about Mafeking … and is so modest and sweet … Ripping day.

Interestingly, on the first day of the voyage, Olave had sent a message to her mother saying that among the passengers she'd encountered so far on the *Arcadian*, the 'Boy Scout man' was the only interesting one.

As the days passed, they met whenever possible, although they kept things low-key with, according to Olave, 'stolen kisses before dawn' and 'little secret notes posted in a cleat in one of the lifeboats', as they were conscious of how notorious shipboard affairs were perceived to be. According to both their accounts, they laughed and teased one another endlessly and were happy when the weather was bad, for they'd take advantage of having the promenade deck to themselves.

Some days they joined friends to gather for deck activities, such as egg and spoon races and various other distractions devised by the 'man-boy', B-P and his 'sports committee'; to his delight, Olave proved to be very fit, hugely competitive, and usually the winner. He was comfortable in her company and increasingly found himself talking about his innermost thoughts and emotions, something he'd never done in any depth with anyone other than 'The Boy'.

Olave was equally at ease with the 'Boy Scout man', and when asked to organise a show, she immediately enlisted his help. His fabled theatrical acumen was one reason, the other appears in her diary: 'Have B-P to myself all day – till 11 p.m. – much intelligent conversation – sitting aft watching the phosphorous balls of light while other people dance …

'Up before dawn again just to see him and kiss him.'

She was no over-protected, love-struck girl, though. She was as smart as a whip, confident and could be quite waspish; she'd been courted and proposed to by several suitors closer to her in age, all of whom were drawn to her aloof attractiveness and all of whom bored her to tears and were turned down. So, however much B-P insisted on describing her in unromantic terms such as 'wise', 'strong', 'adventurous', 'cheerful', 'honest', 'sporty', 'determined', etc., (his interest was based not on her looks, which weren't important to him when it came to women, but on her robust character and sporting nature) she was actually beautiful as well as strong willed.

As they neared their destination, they were despondent but resigned to the fact that Robin (which she felt suited him better than Robert) had to fulfil his touring commitment, which ran until August, and that she had a father to accompany to Jamaica. Since her parents had as good as separated, it had fallen to Olave to act as Soames' travel companion. She didn't mind, she had a prickly relationship with her mother, Katherine, and enjoyed travelling as much as he did – especially now.

Baden-Powell liked giving her gifts and sketches and being around her, even when it needed to be in the background; '…the beloved scout is always there,' she wrote, 'I *adore* him!'

Their talk turned to marriage, which Baden-Powell surprisingly mentioned first in a moment when they were alone and upset at the prospect of a long separation. He half-jokingly suggested they get the ship's captain to marry them. While they laughed at the idea, it got them talking about the possibility. He pointed out the great age gap and the fact that he was poor, while she wasn't, and warned her that her father may not be happy about it.

No fool, Olave agreed that these were valid points; she also told him that she didn't care and that somehow, they would be together. The pair made a secret pact to marry as soon as possible after he got back from America – once they'd worked out a way of selling the idea to Soames.

Baden-Powell could lavish her with drawings and romantic prose, but he couldn't offer her a ring while aboard ship and there could be no announcement of the covert 'engagement', so he gave her the only thing he had in the way of jewellery. In her somewhat self-aggrandising and rose-tinted 1973 autobiography (as told to Mary Drewery) *Window on My Heart*, she writes:

> He gave me a Scout 'Thanks' badge in the form of a swastika with the Scout fleur-de-lys superimposed. The right-handed broken cross or swastika (so called from the Sanskrit word for 'well-being') was an ancient sign of good fortune that had appeared in many civilisations as far back as the Bronze Age.
>
> Later, when the Nazis adopted the … broken cross as their symbol and it became synonymous with evil and oppression, the Scout Movement abandoned the use of [it].

Given that this was written 1973, the last part of this comment appears to be Olave's way of explaining the choice of the symbol due to accusations that her husband was a Nazi sympathiser.

In 1937, two years before the Second World War, Baden-Powell met the German Ambassador to Great Britain, Joachim von Ribbentrop, in London to discuss the possibility of the Hitler Youth being part of the world Boy Scouts movement, rather than a separate entity.

The year before, with Anglo-German relations deteriorating, Hitler had forbidden boys from being in the Scouts, or any other youth group other than the Hitler Youth, which by then was compulsory for 14- to 18-year-old German boys. The talks came to nothing since, in reality, there was never going to be any room for negotiation with Hitler and once Baden-Powell finally grasped the darkness of the Führer's agenda, he backed-off.

And so, Robin and 'b.e.' ('bulgy eyes', his nickname for Olave, as he liked how her eyes bulged when she laughed) parted company as she and Soames left for Jamaica; unable to even steal a last kiss, since they were surrounded by friends, they had to make do with an unromantic handshake. Olave wore Robin's 'Thanks' badge on a chain, hidden under her clothes for the rest of the trip.

Months of longing and emotional as well as humorous correspondence followed, with Robin writing wonderful descriptions of his travels through the United States. If the letters were upbeat, he'd sign off with a sketch of a happy little robin, tail up, beak smiling; should they be lovelorn, he'd sketch the little bird with a turned-down beak; when he wrote of coming home, his 'signature' was the robin leaping in the air, wings stretched out and grinning.

The minute Olave got home from the Caribbean, she told her mother, Katherine, that she was in love with Baden-Powell and wanted to marry him. She said nothing to her father until she knew that her beloved Robin was back in England and ready to meet with him. Unfortunately, when he did return, he rushed not to Olave's house in Lilliput, Dorset, but to his mother's house to collect his nephew, Donald, whom he'd promised to take on a fishing trip to Norway as soon as he got home.

He explained this to Olave who understood that his sense of honour compelled him to keep his promise to the boy who idolised him. Well, sort of. In fact she was understandably upset and annoyed. Her diary entry reading: 'Jolly way for a lover?!? – to treat his loved one?!? Of course … he must take his nephew as he promised to – but, oh dear!'

Worse, her family, now including her father, knew that she'd been counting the days till his return and saw how distressed she was at him not rushing straight to Grey Rigg, their home, immediately. Harold Soames was incandescent. 'It made my father very angry indeed,' she wrote. 'He wrote to Robin.' Who was already fishing in Norway.

Knowing how many years that Baden-Powell had spent frantically resisting marriage, surely this awkwardly timed trip – as well as ensuring he kept a promise to his nephew – was an elaborate, possibly subconscious, and certainly regrettable metaphorical deep breath before finally plunging into matrimony?

The content of Harold Soames' letter to Baden-Powell is unknown, but whatever he wrote, it worked. The fishing trip was cut short and he telegraphed that he would be coming straight to Dorset forthwith. Robin was genuinely relieved to see Olave still waiting for him at Poole railway station, after he'd missed the earlier train and had forgotten to shave. He was sick with nerves as she drove him to Grey Rigg, which, quite coincidentally, offered views of Brownsea Island. Olave scrounged the butler's razor for him, which resulted in a bad shaving cut that required a plaster.

And this was how, already terrified about presenting himself as a suitor to a furious Soames, but determined to resolve the situation, he endured an uncomfortable dinner before a long and exceedingly tense time in a closed room with him. Somehow, he got Soames' blessing to marry Olave and would soon be calling him his father-in-law – if he dared! He immediately wrote to Henrietta Grace.

> I have been wondering what to give you as a birthday present, but I think I've got one now that will please you – and that is a daughter-in-law!
>
> Olave Soames whom I met on board the Arcadian … .promises to be a very good one.
>
> She has only one fault … she is young, but she has an old head on her shoulders and is clever and wise and very bright and cheery.
>
> I hope you will like her half as much as I do.

Henrietta Grace did like her, as did his three brothers, Frank, Warington and Baden. Agnes reserved her judgement. When the happy couple's engagement was announced the world exploded. The media went into a frenzy, running speculative stories and hounding them for quotes and photographs.

A young Scout wrote to Baden-Powell telling him off for getting married saying: 'Of course, you won't be able to keep in with the Scouts the same as before, because your wife will want you, and everything will fall through.' Baden-Powell reassured the boy and any other worried Scouts' in his weekly article for *The Scout*.

'My future wife is as keen about Scouting as I am. She will help me in the work, so that my marriage instead of taking me away from the movement will bring in another assistant.'

The anti-marriagers were in the minority and everyone else decided it was a cause for celebration.

Without telling B-P, old army pals and scouting colleagues began planning a huge ceremonial event, aspects of which (including a rumour that each of the now 200,000 British Scouts were contributing a penny towards a wedding gift for the Chief Scout) leaked out and appeared in the press. Rumours were taken as truth: the wedding would be in December in Lilliput with a mass congregation of army and navy men; Scouts would participate in the wedding ceremony; and even that they'd perform a guard of honour around the bride's house. None of these were factual.

Things were getting out of hand. Olave suggested they elope, an idea vetoed by both families and Plan B was initiated. On 30 October 1912, Lieutenant General Sir Robert Stephenson Smyth Baden-Powell, KCB, married Olave St Claire Soames in a secret ceremony at St Peter's Church, Parkstone. 'I wore a simple blue costume and was attended only by 'Azzie' – Robin's sister, Agnes,' wrote Olave in *Window on my Heart*. She described the service as 'brief and simple, with no music at all,' and adds that aside from a couple of old friends and her brother-in-law (her sister was ill), 'we had only my father and mother and Robin's brother, Major Baden-Powell as best man.' Major McLaren was not invited. In fact the two friends, who'd shared so many incredible experiences and were once very happy together, would never meet again. The happy couple did, at least, have a peal of church bells, although not until they were safely aboard the train to London.

They rented a house in Sussex and, after a spell in Algiers to help Baden-Powell rid himself of the headaches mentioned in Chapter 3, triggered (it's thought) by his mental anguish over having sex with a woman, Olave was pregnant. Baden-Powell was ecstatic and, having recently taken his wife to see Peter Pan, suggested that if the baby were a boy, they should name him Peter.

A boy it was; baby Peter, rather considerately, arrived on 30 October 1913, their first wedding anniversary and was christened in St Peter's where they'd married. Afterwards, they took Peter to London to meet his grandmother, Henrietta, who was now 90 and in failing health. She managed to hold him, cradling him in her arms, as she had done with her own ten babies.

Henrietta died the following month and was buried beside Baden, the husband she'd missed for fifty years. His mother's death hit Baden-Powell hard. Despite the flaws in their relationship and her often harsh treatment of him, she'd been a huge influence in his life and he had remained devoted to her regardless of her challenging nature. He constantly told people that he owed everything to her, a point that's hard to argue. His bittersweet eulogy (quoted in Chapter 2) on the importance of making one's mother proud, which he delivered to his Boy Scouts, summed up their enduring but complicated relationship.

Baden-Powell now had his own family: his 'girl Peter Pan', baby Peter and hundreds of thousands of Scouts to help alleviate his grief. Life went on in a whirl of Scouting duties, rallies and tours, with Olave by his side most of the time. Exhausted but happy, the couple decided to take a break fishing in Norway – oh, the irony. But it wasn't as odd as it sounds, since their earlier 'headaches' trip to Algiers was anything but luxurious. Robin's idea of a wellbeing break had been camping in the most primitive conditions, out in the wilds, in searing heat, with just themselves and basic rations; he fished and hunted their food and everything was cooked in their only pan, which was also used to make coffee. Olave loved it and was a natural camper. After Norway, they were about to head for Cape Town where they'd visit some of Baden-Powell's special places and inspect the burgeoning South African Scouts movement.

Suddenly, on 28 June 1914 their plans – and the world – changed, when Austrian Archduke Franz Ferdinand was shot by a Serbian nationalist. Austria declared war on Serbia and things escalated fast with Germany declaring war on Russia and France and on 4 August 1914, Britain went to war with Germany for violating Belgian neutrality and to try to stave off a French defeat, which would give Germany control of much of Western Europe. Exactly as Baden-Powell had predicted, the watershed moment came during the August Bank holiday …

Born ready, Baden-Powell leapt into action, firing off telegrams to all his Boy Scouts' commissioners requesting that they prepare their Scouts for action and offer their services to the authorities. He also telegrammed Kitchener at the War Office:

Just as the boys of Mafeking were utilised to take the lighter work of men in order that these might be released to the more arduous duties, so can Scouts now give valuable assistance to the State at home – and for this their training and organisation have already to a great extent fitted them.

Kitchener, who was president of the North London Boy Scouts, knew of the extraordinary influence Baden-Powell had on his Scouts. He summoned him to his office, where he greeted him warmly and told him that the time had come for the Chief Scout to show his Boy Scouts the meaning and value of their training and to lead and inspire them in their duties. Baden-Powell proudly assured Kitchener that at least a thousand, likely more, boys were already prepared, in each and every county in the land.

Now fully on a war footing, he was juggling requests from national and local government for help from the Scouts with trying to find older, replacement men to assist him in the organisation, all the while maintaining morale among the Scouts as increasing numbers of able-bodied men were called-up, leaving a deficit of leaders. Touring the country endlessly, encouraging boys to carry on, Baden-Powell was happy to see that many of the men who couldn't fight were getting involved; he was particularly moved by how many women, although coping alone, took up the baton on behalf of the absent menfolk. The patrol system really showed its worth, as boys selected leaders from within their groups and just got on with whatever was required.

Baden-Powell became distraught about the senseless deaths of so many fine young men; when the 13th Hussars were sent to the front in France and he was invited to inspect them, he went immediately and returned regularly to boost their spirits and help out. Olave couldn't accompany her husband on his early trips to France as she'd just had their second baby, Heather Grace, on 1 June; however, as soon she was able to leave Peter and Heather in the care of their grandmother, Katherine, she did join him. She volunteered as a 'barmaid' for three months in the Mercers' Arms, a much-needed recreation hut for beleaguered soldiers on breaks from the front.

Witnessing the carnage and the scale of human slaughter of the Great War shook Baden-Powell to the core and turned him off war forever. He swore to himself that from then on, the Scouts would be a movement for peace throughout the world, its driving purpose to create a brotherhood of tolerance and inclusion that would put an end to wars once and for all.

B-P's voyages to and from France attracted the attention of German Intelligence, who were convinced that he was spying, no doubt partly based on his book *My Adventures as a Spy*, published at the start of 1915 and his booklet *Quick Training for War* hastily put out in 1914 and instantly notching up 65,000 sales. Rumours were rife, including one that he was working as a super-spy *within* the Fatherland and there were countless alleged sightings of him; the German's became deadly serious about hunting him down but never managed it. It's believed that the tales were false, but the War Office made a point of never denying them.

Scouting, instead of fizzling out in the face of war, as some had predicted, flourished with more boys and helpers than ever joining and throughout the long years of the war, they were modestly heroic, patrolling railway lines and roads; running and cycling messages around for vital organisations; helping to harvest everything from flax to turnips; and sounding the all-clear after raids.

But it was the Sea Scouts who really came into their own when it came to helping the war effort. Watching the British coastline for signs of German invasion was of great importance and their contribution to the defence of the shores was of major significance. Supporting the Coastguard by signalling to vessels, watching for enemy boats or activity and raising alarms made the Sea Scouts invaluable. They processed messages, signalling along the coast and to ships at sea, and even questioned people as to why they were on the coast. Once they found out about the work the Sea Scouts were doing, other Scout groups came forward to volunteer. Inspired by older siblings, younger children wanted to become Scouts, too, but previous trials adding smaller boys into the mix had been unsuccessful as the older boys found them annoying.

Baden-Powell had heard a theory that delinquency starts around the age of 8 and with the disruption and distraction of war, there was enough evidence of unruly behaviour to attest to the theory. What was needed was a completely different group, not a diluted version of scouting but one tailor-made to appeal to boys under 11. Numerous names went through his head such as 'Young Scouts', 'Colts' and 'Cubs'.

Eventually he settled on 'Wolf Cubs', but he needed a hook to hang it all on, a theme that would engage little boys. And then it struck him. Rudyard Kipling's *Jungle Books,* where young Mowgli, the 'man-child' lives with wolves, learning the ways of the jungle by obeying Akela, the old wolf, would be perfect. He wrote to Kipling, asking for permission to use the story as a basis for his new scheme and, being an old friend, with a son who was a Scout, Kipling readily agreed.

The Wolf Cub's Handbook came out on 2 December 1916 and, despite it being wartime, within two weeks the first Wolf Cubs were appearing at events; within a year there were 30,000 of them in Britain.

The 'boy who never grew up' had another toy to play with. And one to fix. The Girl Guides was the only one of the now three schemes that wasn't proving that successful. Baden-Powell had left it to Agnes to run and assumed it would follow the same meteoric rise as the Boy Scouts.

Looking at her handbook he thought it quite dated, considering how much things had moved on, and so he reworked it and renamed it *Girl Guiding*; he also made the Guides more visibly allied to the Boy Scouts by getting them a Charter of Incorporation. In a meeting with Agnes and the existing committee it was agreed that Olave, despite her previous offer of help being turned down, after giving her all to the Scouts was a natural choice to assist with the 'rebranding'. At 27 she had the energy for the challenge and travelled the country, finding new commissioners and committees to manage every county. After eighteen months of promoting and refining, with a brief pause to have her third child, Betty, born on 16 April 1917, she became Chief Guide.

Following an anxious period in the spring of 1918, when a German offensive had advanced at speed forcing the Allied forces increasingly to fall back, combined British, French and American forces suddenly pushed Germany back into retreat almost everywhere. Finally, in the autumn months of 1918, the war's end in was sight

With their family now expanded from two to five, and, hopefully an end to the conflict, the Baden-Powells gave up renting and bought a home of their own. They found Blackacre, a beautiful house with lovely views near the village of Bentley in Surrey, during the same week that the Armistice was finally signed (on 11 November). It stood on a rise with tree-fringed grounds and gardens that would be perfect for the children – and their parents – to play in. They moved there in 1919 and changed the name to Pax Hill. Pax for the peace that the Armistice had brought and Hill, for its elevated position.

As touched upon briefly in Chapter 4, having fathered three children, Baden-Powell eventually took his leave of the marital bed to set up a micro camp on an outside balcony of the house.

Revisiting Pax Hill for a 1995 Channel 4 documentary, *Secret Lives*, and standing on what had been her father's balcony bedroom, his daughter Betty, then aged 78, said:

> The balcony wasn't glassed-in, it was just open and this was my father's bedroom.
>
> He slept out here. He had quite a small bed … and because he slept here summer and winter, he had a canvas blind on a roller which he could put down and hook on to the balustrade if the weather was really bad.

Asked how long he slept there, she looks surprised and says: 'Well, all the years that I know of, right up until 1938 when he left.'

A comment made by her father is probably how he explained the unconventional situation:

> Living indoors without fresh air quickly poisons the blood and makes people feel tired and seedy when they don't know why.

For myself, I sleep out of doors in winter as well as summer. I only feel tired or seedy when I have been indoors a lot.

I only catch cold when I sleep in a room.

Using Pax Hill as their base, Baden-Powell and Olave, with missionary zeal, proceeded to promote the Boys Scouts, Wolf Cubs, Girl Guides and the newly formed Brownies for younger girls, with tours and rallies throughout the country and, later, all over the world. As well as the new house, Baden-Powell acquired another property, this one a gift to the Scouts.

The benefactor was William deBois Maclaren (no relation to 'The Boy'), a Scottish district Scout commissioner, who had heard through the grapevine that East London Scouts had nowhere to camp and so he offered Baden-Powell funds to buy them some land in London near their base.

B-P's HQ staff were delighted and went searching for the perfect spot. They quickly found it in Gilwell Park, Chingford, Essex, an abandoned fifty-seven-acre estate complete with crumbling mansion and bordering Epping Forest that was within deBois' price range due to its derelict state.

Most potential buyers would have considered Gilwell a costly white elephant, but these buyers were Scouts and what they saw was endless adventure, a wonderful and natural campsite, space for marching and games and campfires. As leaders, they saw opportunities for teaching, making, mending and inventing. Better still, the house would accommodate a scoutmasters' training centre – after an extensive makeover, of course.

Being Scouts, they did all the work themselves, clearing the overgrown grounds and bringing the abandoned house back to life and on 26 July 1919, Baden-Powell proudly cut the ribbon and officially declared Gilwell the property of the Boy Scouts Association.

He chose Francis Gidney, one of his most experienced and imaginative Scout leaders, as the first Camp Chief, and by 8 September that year, they hosted the first scoutmasters' training camp, basing the course on the old patrol system and the tried-and-tested Brownsea method of a subject a day, with campfire instructions, followed by associated activities. Even the Matabele koodoo horn got a good airing as the Chief Scout used it every day for signalling.

His overarching message to the scoutmasters, the one thing that would make them successful leaders, was that to understand the boys, they had to become boys themselves.

Baden-Powell knew the 1919 camp was another Scouting milestone and wanted to mark it in some way that would be personal to those taking part.

Certificates were boring so, like a child with a toybox, he delved through his hoard of army trophies and came across his 'memento' of the Zulu war of 1888, Chief Dinizulu's long, wooden-bead necklace. He presented a single bead – or 'Wood Badge' – from it to each of the men as a token of their having completed the newly christened Wood Badge Course.

As we learned previously, controversy surrounding the provenance of Dindzulu's beads has made it a Scouting hot potato, but back then, the Wood Badge quickly became one of the most sought-after accolades in Scouting and when, despite being plentiful since Dinizulu's necklace was four metres long, when the beads ran out, Gilwell staff simply whittled some more.

War had put paid, in more ways than one, to large gatherings and now was the time to put that right. Next on the agenda was a long-overdue mass meeting, à la Crystal Palace, and Baden-Powell already had plans for an eight-day extravaganza on 30 July 1920. He even had a name for it: 'Jamboree', he told his baffled staff, who told *him* he couldn't possibly call it that, explaining that it meant a rowdy, drinking spree but the Chief, a fan of humorous-sounding words, was not for turning, and 'jamboree' it stayed.

London's glass-roofed Olympia would be their stage, with him as director of the whole shebang and the thoroughly dependable Major A.G. Wade, with B-P at Mafeking and now in his Scouting inner circle, as Organising Secretary. And, boy, could he organise.

Invitations were sent out to all Scouts both UK and worldwide and thousands accepted. So many, that 1,500 who would be performing were accommodated overnight in the arena while the Old Deer Park at Richmond had to be commandeered to sleep the remaining 5,000 who would be coming. Baden-Powell wanted an immense curtain to span the entire arena, Wade provided one; B-P wanted a river, Wade arranged one; he wanted leather diplomas, Wade obliged – though he drew the line at a Shakespearean theatre.

To drive this beast of a show, Wade worked closely with B-P's new secretary, the marvellously unflappable Miss Eileen Nugent, to make everything run smoothly. So closely, in fact, that he asked her to marry him afterwards as he escorted her in a taxi across London from Olympia. She agreed and became Eileen Wade, the writer to whom Olave told her life story in *Window on My Heart*.

The British public was bombarded with flyers, posters and circulars about the event delivered by a never-ending supply of Boys Scout 'posties'. For a war-weary nation, starved of cheer and unable to go out without trepidation, it proved irresistible. Thousands came; 10,000 to be precise, and they filled the stadium not just physically but with a heady atmosphere of dizzy expectation at what might lie behind the curious green curtain.

At 2.30, with the Baden-Powells, including Peter and Heather, ensconced in the royal box with the Duke of Connaught and Princess Mary in her Girl Guide uniform, the Scout Band played the National Anthem. A bugle sounded but was drowned out by a collective gasp as the curtain rose to reveal a dioramic dreamscape of Baden-Powell's life.

On one side was Neverland, with a full-sized pirate ship; on the other, the Jungle Books with tropical plants and huts; and between them, a mountain reminiscent of Matabele's Matopos Hills, over which hundreds of Scouts poured down into the arena, holding their national flags to thunderous applause.

What followed were eight days of spectacular performances, activities and demonstrations of the wonders of Scouting, which B-P declared were the most exciting and exhausting in his life. By closing night it was streamlined to perfection and unbeknown to the Chief Scout, a plan was hatching behind the scenes. The night before, one of the Boy Scouts of America popped his feathered headdress on B-P's head and named him 'Chief Lone-pine-on-the-skyline' and the place erupted.

Now the Scouts wanted to thank their hero properly for all he'd done for them and after a quick discussion, Major Wade and the American Chief Scout Executive, James West, agreed on what was to be done. At the close of the Jamboree, with the arena obscured by Scouts, Baden-Powell stood on a dais and prepared to bid them all a fond goodbye.

He was interrupted by a boy's clear voice announcing: 'We, the Scouts of the World, salute you, Sir Robert Baden-Powell – Chief Scout of the World!' Completely dumbstruck for once, B-P could only stand and take it all in: the flags dipped in his honour; the applause mixed with the cheers and roars of his young Scouts.

All his life he had been working towards a moment of acceptance and approval like this and he felt happier than he'd ever done, for the Jamboree's international success meant that it would now be easier for him to speak directly to this new generation, to these fine Scouts and ask them to change the world. Baden-Powell was nothing, if not ambitious. Slowly, he raised his hand in the Scout salute, representing their fleur-de-lys badge, and all sound ceased until his unmistakable voice rang out, reaching every part of Olympia:

Brother Scouts, I ask you to make a solemn choice. Differences exist between the peoples of the world in thought and sentiment, just as they do in language and physique. The war has taught us that if one nation tries to impose its particular will on others, cruel recreation is bound to follow. The jamboree has taught us that if we exercise mutual forbearance and give-and-take, then there is sympathy and harmony.

If it be your will, let us go forth from here determined that we will develop among ourselves and our boys that comradeship, through the world-wide spirit of the Scout brotherhood, so that we may help to develop peace and happiness in the world and goodwill among men.

Brother Scouts, answer me – will you join me in this endeavour?

An ear-splitting 'Yes!' gave him their answer.

There was no going back now.

Chapter 11

The Final Act

'I think it was a slightly schizophrenic thing; the one side of him being the eternal child that never grew up and the other of being the adult. The experience of life and the genius of the man was the fact that he could blend the two together and then feed it back to the young people.'

Robert Crause Baden-Powell, 3rd Baron of
Gilwell and B-P's grandson

'Don't let your patriotism be so narrow as to count your own country as the only pebble on the beach. Recognise that there are other nations too, all with their good points, and with their interests and ambitions. Aim to be good friends with them and to co-operate rather than hinder their wishes. What we want in the world is peace, happiness and prosperity for all. And we can get it if all men become friends instead of rivals.'

Baden-Powell (the 1937 Jamboree)

Unlike the story of Peter Pan, life didn't deliver a fairy-tale ending for Baden-Powell's hopes for an end to human conflict.

In the wake of the needless slaughter in the trenches of the Great War, where millions of volunteers died and millions more were conscripted to take their places, it seemed that lessons had been learned and there was an almost universal determination that it would be the 'war to end all wars'.

As countries regrouped, considered the futility of fighting and began to appreciate their hard-won freedom, people dared to hope that young men would never again be called to take up arms. It was wishful thinking. Beneath the surface of optimism and despite noises to the contrary, unrest and resentment still simmered and the dark shadow of totalitarianism was leading the world inexorably towards a second conflict.

It was the stuff of Baden-Powell's worst nightmares. After more than four years, the First World War had ended as pointlessly as it had begun. Of the millions killed, 8,000 had been in the Scouting movement, many of them, like the Brownsea boys and his Scouting staff who died, were personally known to Baden-Powell.

After the Armistice, throughout the 1920s and '30s, right up until Adolf Hitler's offensive on Britain on 13 August 1940, Baden-Powell and Olave were on a mission to make Scouting and Girl Guiding movements for universal peace.

They preached that countries should unite, not fight to resolve differences, and urged leaders to reach agreement, or at least agree to differ, on one another's views through a common desire to prevent war. Driving this was how well the boys of different nationalities lived and worked in harmony during the First International Jamboree at Olympia in 1920. Spurred on by this, Baden-Powell had a plan. He'd create an International Bureau that could stage conferences for countries to discuss common problems, with a view to making Scouting more inclusive.

He consulted Hubert Martin, the Scout's British International Commissioner, about ways it might be funded and, as if by magic, he found a benefactor in the shape of Mrs Kathleen Peabody. As a young girl during the war, Peabody (née Bates) was such an effective fundraiser for British and American charities that she was nicknamed the 'Million Dollar Girl'. After the war, now married to a wealthy American called J. Peabody and, aware that the Scouts was voluntarily funded, she visited Gilwell HQ to offer her services to thank Hubert Martin who, in his other role as Chief Passport Officer of Great Britain, had previously arranged an American trip for her.

Martin mentioned B-P's hopes for a global bureau to Kathleen and, having been at the Olympia Jamboree with her husband who was captivated by the global nature of the celebration – and no doubt grateful to the Scouts for sending him a wife – the couple pledged £2,500 a year to fund Baden-Powell's International Bureau.

Now the Chief Scout of the World could really live up to his name. A small, dedicated team was set up in the Scouting Association's new London office on Buckingham Palace Road with Hubert Martin as its Honorary Director.

Robert, the 3rd Baron of Gilwell who died in December 2019, explained his grandfather's thinking:

I think he really did feel that Scouting could expand throughout the world because what he was saying to people was 'it doesn't matter whether you're Chilean, Mexican, Indonesian, Australian, British, there was no reason why a moral code couldn't extend across frontiers' ... because he'd lived in that sort of environment all his life.

He really did believe that if he could get enough people to be Scouts in other countries, following the same mores as each other, that there must eventually be world peace. Forever.

For Baden-Powell, one of the busiest men in the world, the 1920s were among the busiest years of his life, or at least his 'second life'. Olympia over, there was to be no rest.

In 1921 he was invited to India to help resolve a tricky situation. The country was ringing with calls for self-governance and British influence (or interference) was not appreciated, but its Scouting organisation had only British or 'mixed parentage' boys, since Indian boys were forbidden from joining for fears they'd 'become revolutionaries'. Only their idol, Baden-Powell, would be accepted as an adviser in this volatile situation. How could he refuse?

He and Olave disembarked at Apollo Bunder, Bombay (Mumbai), the very spot where, as a reluctant 19-year-old sub-lieutenant, Baden-Powell first set foot on Indian soil, bound for Lucknow and the start of a life of adventure.

Despite adulation on a scale that surpassed any welcome he'd experienced before, B-P was saddened that so many of the country's boys couldn't enjoy the benefits of scouting. Saying that, the Indian boys, just as determined as their Mafeking hero when it came to getting one's way, had set up their own groups in every region.

Baden-Powell purposely asked to meet with the dissenting Indian leaders and through his genuine interest in their issues and a willingness to compromise, he left with an agreement of tentative steps being taken towards merging British and Indian Scouts. It wasn't perfect, but it was a start. He left saying: 'We who had sat down to the table as a meeting of representative heads rose at the end of it a united band of brother Scouts.'

A week after returning from India, Baden-Powell's older brother, Warington, died aged 73, leaving the original siblings reduced to Stephe, Baden and Agnes.

After the funeral, it was back to a whirlwind of events. In 1922, and now in his 60s, he wrote *Rovering to Success*, a book on a new scheme for senior Scouts to address older boys wanting to leave; he organised a rally at Alexandra Palace to welcome the Prince of Wales back from his own world tour with a piercing Grand Wolf Howl from 19,000 green-capped Wolf Cubs; and staged a repeat of King George V's Grand Rush, this time with 32,000 roaring Boy Scouts.

In 1924, B-P was up to his bare knees in the two-week Imperial Jamboree in Wembley, where 10,000 British Scouts joined 2,000 from British dominions and colonies. He introduced the overseas Scouts to the king, invited the Prince of Wales (future King Edward VIII) to join them for a camp-fire singalong and joined the Duke of York, the future King George VI, and Rudyard Kipling, to watch the *Jungle Book* brought to life by 6,000 Wolf Cubs.

That same year, he and Olave attended the first World Camp of Girl Guides at their new training ground, Foxlease Park, a New Forest property donated by an American, Anne Archbold Sanderson, to mark the marriage of Princess Mary, who was then President of the Girl Guides.

As appreciated as this generous gift was, the Guides had been concerned about the upkeep of such a place at the time. However, while a fairy-tale ending would elude B-P's peace efforts, it wasn't the case in the Foxlease story. Two years prior to the first Guides camp, Buckingham Palace called the Baden-Powells with good news: Princess Mary wished to donate £6,000 of her wedding gift money to the Girl Guides to cover the cost of running Foxlease.

Come autumn, the B-Ps were off again, this time to Denmark for the Second International Jamboree in Ermelunden Forest. Unlike Olympia, where boys were accommodated indoors or in tents at the Deerpark campsite, the Danish leaders had organised what amounted to their Chief's idea of real Scouting. Boys of every nationality, in troops and patrols, brought their own equipment and built the camp themselves; they laughed and sang through rain and shine, cooked their own food and were constantly engaged in woodcraft and pioneering activities. As one would imagine, B-P loved it and declared that the camp of twenty-four nations of 5,000 Scouting friends would be the blueprint for all future jamborees.

Among the excitement and frenetic activity of forging a new world movement, another momentous event occurred in 1924 which would have been highly significant to Baden-Powell and, in earlier times, devastated him. And yet, it was barely noted.

After spending six years suffering from bouts of depression at Camberwell House, a private asylum in Herefordshire, Kenneth 'The Boy' Maclaren died of 'softness of the brain'. Baden-Powell, his beloved 'Bloater', did not attend his funeral. It seems incredibly sad, whatever their true relationship, that such a wonderful and, at the time it was formed, one could say life-saving friendship of mutual understanding, admiration and passions should end with such utter indifference.

But The Boy was from Baden-Powell's first life. Pax Hill was now his second and, in between tours, it was where B-P and Olave could be part of Peter, Heather and Betty's world, an idyllic place of ponies and pets, kindly governesses and playhouses. Wanting to make their childhood last as long as possible, the Baden-Powells took their family camping, hiking, foraging, riding and sailing whenever possible, making very good Scouts out of them in the process.

According to Betty, their youngest child, 'He [her father] developed every talent we had in the same way as he was encouraging other people's children to do the same.' House rules at Pax were strict but there was plenty of jollity and a constant flow of interesting visitors, since it was the main hub for Scouting outside of London.

Like his father before him, Baden-Powell truly enjoyed being with his children; gentle and good fun, he taught them through play and shared his practical skills by creating adventures for them. Betty remembers him as a doting father who always listened to them and never criticised their mistakes. 'I remember him as a most marvellous dad,' she says. 'I can't imagine anyone being a better father than ours was…. He was always interested in what we did. He was always encouraging. I think that's the thing I remember most about him. He was an encourager.'

Gillian Clay, Betty's daughter and B-P's granddaughter:

My father told me that he put me on my Grandfather's lap when I was probably two or three years old and told me 'You must remember this man' – but I didn't.

We lived in Zambia and my Grandparents lived in Kenya [they retired to Nyeri in 1938, disillusioned at how their hopes for world peace were crumbling around them,] where we visited them several times, but sadly he died when I was three and a half.

My cousin, Robert, named after him, [Baden-Powell], was six months older … he remembered him as a grown-up who played with him, unlike other grown-ups, like another child.

Cousin Robert and his parents also visited B-P and Olave in Africa and, although very young, he never forgot the experience of meeting his grandfather. In the 1995 Channel 4 *Secret Lives* documentary he recalls:

> As a child, I'd always wanted to know answers to my questions and nobody would ever give them, but for the first time in my life, I met somebody who would not only answer the questions but expand on it, so that it really gave me an overall picture
>
> And of course, that was the old man, and because of that, I absolutely adored him.

Robert's comment underpins the fact that, although photos of Baden-Powell, even in the early days of Scouting, show an elderly-looking man, a crinkled, diminished version of the wiry soldier he once was, his extraordinary appeal to children never seemed to grow old.

Gill Clay adds:

> My mother also told how her father never seemed old although he was sixty when she was born! She also talked about him playing with her and her siblings and their cousins who lived with them after their mother [Olave's sister Auriol] had died.
>
> She told how she and her littlest cousin were always being left behind by the older children, but one day her father [B-P] came to their rescue and showed them a short-cut, 'Just squeeze through this hedge here and you'll catch them up,' he said.
>
> Her parents used to go on 'walk-rides' with the children and her father used to give them tasks to do, for example to count the telegraph poles between here and the church and report back (when they would have to salute smartly before giving their report), so he cleverly made a game of keeping the family together on the walk!

A happy childhood certainly, however as Peter, the son and heir, got older and became an official Scout, things shifted and he came under increasing pressure to emulate his father. Encouragement morphed into expectation.

In *Secret Lives*, the aforementioned Robert, Peter Baden-Powell's son, reveals the depth of his father's distress at trying and failing to live up to his legendary father.

I'm afraid the expectations were more than he could bear. My grandparents really did wish to have a mirror image of my grandfather. This was plainly impossible.

My father was a very sickly child; he actually had a very happy childhood, but he had pressures applied to him, particularly by his mother, which were beyond his capabilities.

Looking visibly upset, Robert, who became the 3rd Lord Baden-Powell of Gilwell, then goes on to describe a disturbing scenario which paints Olave less as a benevolent, and more as a malevolent mother – a sort of reincarnation of Henrietta Grace but with added menace.

My father was so terrified of her that, as an adult, he loathed going to see her and it was very much a duty visit.

And I do remember him on occasion actually wetting his pants. This is a mature man, wetting his pants, going to see his mother.

That is the fear that she put into her son because, as far as she was concerned, he was a failure.

By 1926, a no-doubt relieved Peter and his sisters had left the home schoolroom and were attending boarding schools, with Peter eventually going to Charterhouse.

This allowed their parents to accept an invitation to the United States from the Boy Scouts of America. They were entertained at the White House by President Coolidge and his wife and met a raft of interested parties who could help further the movement. Olave, an engaging speaker and an instant hit, was delighted to learn that the (American) Girl Scouts, founded as a single company in 1912 by a friend of B-P's called Juliette Low, who didn't want to call them 'Guides', had blossomed to 150,000 members.

Of all their trips, though, the one to South Africa was their most memorable, especially for Baden-Powell and not only because they took Peter, Heather and Betty with them this time. The 40-year-old, entitled Victorian colonel who'd landed in Cape-Town in 1896, oozing entrenched Imperial opinions and prejudices, ready to suppress native rebels and who, in 1899, returned to protect a British colony at all costs from an uprising of white Boer farmers, in a battle that resulted in the deaths of many indigenous Africans, was far removed from the 70-year-old man who arrived back there in the winter of 1926–7.

This time he wasn't there to fight, he was there to promote peace and brotherhood; his uniform was not that of a bombastic colonial officer, but that of the Chief Scout of the World, who carried a stave in place of a gun. However, although he preached only peace and harmony and the non-sectarian, non-military, non-political aspects of Scouting, Baden-Powell left Africa knowing that he'd not managed to dispel the Dutch settlers' suspicions and racial issues around scouting.

Back in England, the focus turned to organising the Third International Jamboree that would be held on 29 July 1929 at Arrowe Park, Birkenhead, his old Territorial Army stomping ground. This time, 15,000 Scouts from the Home Counties camped alongside 15,000 from forty-two different countries. Other British Scouts outside the allotted quota were accommodated in auxiliary camps nearby. Prior to the event, a penny each (as previously mooted at the time of B-P and Olave's wedding) from Scouts around the world was collected in secret to buy a gift for the Chief Scout.

Olave was tasked with surreptitiously finding out what her husband would like as a present. When asked however, all Baden-Powell would say was that he had everything he wanted. When pushed harder, he piped up: 'Oh, yes, I do need some new braces.'

By this time, Baden-Powell was 72 years old and finally feeling his age. He often travelled with John Skinner Wilson, formerly the Scout Commissioner for Calcutta who had so impressed B-P during his India visit that he asked him to join him as his Aide de Camp-cum-advisor-cum-companion.

On the opening day of the Jamboree, with almost every country of the world represented, there was a sudden silence as Baden-Powell produced the koodoo horn he'd used to wake the boys on Brownsea Island and prepared to blow. Over-excited, dry of mouth or out of puff, who knows, but when the Chief Scout of the World raised the fabled horn from his Matabele days to his lips and blew, all that came out was a less-than rousing 'pfft'.

It was the perfect metaphor for how much his formerly immense levels of energy and verve were, much against his will, slowly diminishing. Within seconds, the Scouts, en masse, acted as though the horn had blasted out its loudest order ever and began the Jamboree with a march. For an hour, boys of every race, colour and creed passed before their beloved B-P, most in the uniform he'd invented for them twenty-one years before: shorts, wide-brimmed hats and neckerchiefs, but some in their dazzling native costumes. From the delight on Baden-Powell's face, none would have suspected that something was troubling him.

The day before, Eileen Wade, formerly Miss Nugent, had arrived Arrowe Park telling her boss that she had marvellous news and, grinning, handed him a letter. On reading it Baden-Powell, who loathed swearing, said one word: 'Damn!'

After folding the letter, he then said, 'Well, I suppose I can refuse it.' The 'good' news was that he was to receive a peerage, a barony, that would be conferred on him at the Jamboree. It was not at all good news to Baden-Powell; he was against hereditary titles, he didn't want to be a Lord, he disliked most politicians and he felt that a title could be a burden on his children.

After a heated and emotional meeting between himself, Olave, the Wades (Eileen and Major Wade, he of the taxi proposal after Olympia), his A.D.C. Wilson et al, Olave moved to support his decision to refuse; Eileen and others in his close circle had other ideas and tried everything to get him to accept it. They failed.

The Duke of Connaught, his good friend who'd opened the Jamboree, then stepped in; he was having none of this nonsense and told Baden-Powell that whether he liked it or not, he had to accept the title for the sake of the Scouts. The others agreed, telling him it would boost the movement and give inspiration to its future leaders, etc. etc., until, in tears, he relented, saying: 'This is for Scouting, not for me.'

They tried to cheer him up by suggesting all sorts ridiculous ideas for the place name that would follow his title. He knew that many people would have liked Lord Baden-Powell of Mafeking, however, he didn't want a military connection. Scouting was his life now and so, he settled on Lord Baden-Powell of Gilwell.

The Prince of Wales arrived at Arrowe Park and read the letter from the palace aloud to a hushed crowd. The peerage was to honour their Chief for his services to Scouting and to mark the occasion of the third Jamboree taking place on the 21st anniversary of the official start of the Scouting movement.

'Ever since its inception,' it read among other things, 'he has been the mainspring of this great adventure, from its small and … humble beginning until today, when you number nearly two million in your ranks.' At the end, as was always the way, the Scouts went into a frenzy of cheering and everyone could finally breathe a sigh of relief – until the next surprise!

Towards the close of the event, straight after a spectacular arena show that drew and audience of 60,000, Baden-Powell and his family took to the podium. Once they were settled, a Rolls Royce car trailing a caravan glided past them on the ground below, then suddenly, the President of the Danish Boy Scouts joined them on the platform to announce to B-P and the crowd that the Boy Scouts of the world had had a collection to thank him for everything and that he was there to present their gifts of a cheque for £2,800 and a portrait of B-P by the artist, David Jagger. Oh, and the Rolls Royce and the trailer.

Baden-Powell was full of gratitude at the wonderful gifts his Scouts had given him; ironically, his trusty old car, 'Jimmy', had broken down shortly before he went to the Jamboree, and he was rendered speechless at its considerably grander replacement.

There was one more gift to come – from the Irish Boy Scouts. It was an intriguing parcel presented with ceremonial aplomb and when Baden-Powell opened it, he was highly amused to see a pair of wonderfully bright green braces, strong enough to pull his new car and the trailer. It's a sign of the man he was that he laughed, slung them over his shoulders and declared, 'Now I have everything I want in this world!'

B-P's drive for peace reached a crescendo in 1933 with the 4th World Jamboree at Gödöllő in Hungary.

Where the 1920s had been full of hope and prosperity, by the 1930s many nations were in the grip of the Great Depression or under totalitarian rule, or both; it seemed a good time for the Scouts to celebrate their festival of youth. In March, prior to the 4th Jamboree, and now aged 76, Baden-Powell visited Italy to meet Pope Pius XI in a (failed) attempt to convince the pontiff to help him prevent Catholic Canadian Scouts from forming a separate group to the Boy Scouts.

As B-P was in Rome, the director of the Scouts International Bureau organised a meeting between him and Benito Mussolini, who'd absorbed Italy's Boy Scouts into the Balilla, his new youth movement, partially based on Scouting.

At that time, Baden-Powell believed that Mussolini had saved Italy from communism and 'Il Duce' was admired by many global leaders; Winston Churchill said: 'If I were an Italian … I would have been with you from the beginning to the end of your struggle against the bestial appetites of Leninism'; the Archbishop of Canterbury and Gandhi respectively described him as a 'giant figure in Europe' and a 'superman'.

When B-P met him, he was understandably taken aback by his stature describing him as 'short, rather stout … but genial and human.' While he saw merit in Mussolini's Balilla being linked to the education system and he envied its state funding, he eventually realised that the Balilla was really all about drill and fascist indoctrination; there'd be no woodcraft or citizenship lessons for these boys.

The pair argued, Il Duce telling Baden-Powell that while his organisation was like the Scouts, it was far superior. B-P reminded him that boys volunteered to join the Scouts, unlike the Balilla, where boys were forced to join. When no Italian Scouts attended the Hungarian Jamboree a few months later, B-P wasn't surprised.

He *was* surprised, though, and saddened, when the 1,000 German Scouts who'd registered to come, never left home. Previously, in 1929, the German and Italian boys happily camped with boys from the rest of the world at Arrowe Park; to Baden-Powell their absences in 1933 were a disquieting sign of where his dreams of world peace might be heading.

Italy's Scouts had always been a sort of separate entity, due to the early 1900s trend for splinter groups so, much as he hated to admit it, they seemed a lost cause. On the other hand, he still believed that since the German boys loved Scouting, fitness and outdoor living, it was a cause worth persevering with. But, of course, this was the year that Adolf Hitler came to power and as soon as he became Chancellor of Germany, he set about banning the Scout movement, decreeing it to be a hotbed of spies and making joining his *Hitlerjugend*, or Hitler Youth, compulsory.

Baden-Powell had a mountain to climb; but then again, that was one of his fortes.

The Hitler Youth model also copied the Scouting one, but with a fundamentally different and far more sinister purpose – to indoctrinate teenagers with his Nazi ideology. Unlike the Scouts, it was not designed to set boys free, but to control them.

Where the Scout's Promise was:

> On my honour I promise that I will do my best –
> To do my duty to God and the King.
> To help other people at all times.
> To obey the Scout Law.

The promise of the once carefree campers who now found themselves in the Hitler Youth movement was something far darker and uglier:

In the presence of this blood banner which represents our Führer,
I swear to devote all my energies and my strength to the saviour of our
    country, Adolf Hitler.
I am willing and ready to give up my life for him,
so help me God

Yes, much had changed in the four years between Arrowe Park and Gödöllő; there were now millions of boys in the Hitler Youth movement; by 1936 there would be more than 5 million – more than double the number of Scouts in the rest of the world. Nevertheless, as Hitler's true intentions during the early part of the Nazi party's victory were not yet widely known, Baden-Powell still thought there was a chance that he could bring Germany's boys back into the fold.

A number of B-P's Scouts leaders, including his A.D.C. Wilson and Lord Somers, both ardently anti-Nazi, still believed that appeasement could be a reality and wanted to encourage Hitler Youth groups to visit British Scouting events to see what 'normal' looked like. They advocated a 'friendship and contact' policy; other association members advised caution and called for 'rebuffs and isolation', fearing that the Chief Scout's motive could be misconstrued.

Michael Rosenthal, author of the *Character Factory* and critical of Baden-Powell's political objective, especially in connection with Hitler, said of him:

Long after Scout commissioners and advisors were trying to break connections, he was trying to keep them. He was moved by the fact that the Hitler Youth was in some ways based on his own principles.

He saw [it] as attempting to do what he was attempting to do. That was, to train boys to be obedient and accept the authorities from above.

I think he was reluctant to break relationships with an organisation which he felt shared the same values as he did, in terms of obedience and an ordered existence in support of government.

The fact that B-P went on to have a meeting with the German Ambassador, Joachim von Ribbentrop, in London as late as 1937, two years before the Second World War, to further discuss the possibility of the Hitler Youth being part of the Boy Scouts movement was either done through monumental misjudgement or monumental stupidity, and has helped fuel the fire of controversy.

Hitler, convinced that British institutions such as the Masons, the Church of England, public schools and the Boy Scouts – all of which Baden-Powell was associated with – were riddled with spies, naturally encouraged such meetings. The talks with Ribbentrop came to nothing (as an official report in the public domain confirms); likewise, an invitation to visit Hitler was immediately declined, as Baden-Powell was both appalled by and critical of the dictator's insidious creed of racial purity. Still, as he should have known, the earlier meeting has tarred him as a Nazi-sympathiser ever since and likely always will.

As well as refusing the Führer's hospitality, Baden-Powell also criticised the Hitler Youth movement in 1935, saying that its aim was to 'harness the spirit and repress individuality'.

In 1937, after the Von Ribbentrop talks and presumably with his eyes now finally open, he also condemned the 'unity being promoted (in Germany and Italy) by the enforcement and repression of ideas', calling it 'a surface unity, not coming from the heart of the people'.

And when he talked of Hitler 'using huge pageants for hypnotising his people', it was the last straw.

Suddenly, Sir Robert Baden-Powell (now a recipient of the Order of Merit, OM, awarded in 1937) was one of the names on Hitler's infamous 'death list', the *Sonderfahndungsliste G.B. (Special Search List Great Britain) or Black Book*, compiled by the SS, a secret dossier of prominent British residents to be rounded-up, arrested and given 'special treatment' upon the successful German invasion.

He was in the company of many notables, including Winston Churchill; Alexander Korda the Hungarian film-maker, Robert Smallbones, a British diplomat who granted 48,000 visas to Jews and was, in 2010, named British hero of the holocaust; J.B. Priestley; Sylvia Pankhurst; H.G. Wells and Virginia Woolf.

When Baden-Powell started the Boy Scouts in Dorset in 1907, it would be another thirteen years until the Nazi Party came into being. He created the distinctive Boy Scout uniform, the award badges and the logos between 1907 and 1908; they were, and still are, the very essence of his Scouting scheme. Adolf Hitler would have been 18, turning 19 at the time. To suggest, therefore, that the Scout uniform, the swastika 'Thank You' badge (presented in place of an engagement ring to Olave in 1912), and other aspects of Scouting had their roots in the Nazi Party, and so prove Baden-Powell's fascism or anti-Semitism, seems at odds chronologically.

His interest in world leaders, be they fascist, honourable, monstrous or otherwise, appears to only ever have been driven by one thing and one thing only: Scouting – his entire raison d'être. In an odd a way, he was like them; for he, too, craved power and to change the world, but there is no doubt that his purpose was to force peace upon it, not war.

That's not to say that Baden-Powell didn't demonstrate ridiculous levels of … what? Naivety, insensitivity, disrespect, vanity, even arrogance in communicating with obvious despots in his relentless quest. And he did have some highly questionable, ingrained ideas, on race and class, mainly developed in his formative colonial days.

In a JewishPress.com article on whether Baden-Powell was a Nazi sympathiser, Saul Jay Singer cites a disparaging and cruel caricature B-P drew of what is widely agreed to be a purposefully 'Jewish-looking woman' that certainly smacks of stereotyping of the worst kind, under the guise of lampooning the 'nouveaux-riche.' According to Singer:

> Notwithstanding the various tortured apologist theories proposed by his defenders, there is little doubt that Baden-Powell was an anti-Semite. … For example, in *Life's Snags and How to Meet Them*, his sketches are classic anti-Semitic caricatures entirely consistent with Nazi depictions of Jews in *Der Stürmer.*
>
> When criticised for his odious drawings, he responded that he would never 'deliberately' draw racial caricatures of Jews or any other race; in other words, his vile drawings were somehow inadvertent.
>
> However, the undeniable fact remains that he thought specifically of Jews when imagining people flaunting their wealth in a crude and pretentious manner.

Many of his drawings and descriptions of people from all walks of life, even sketches as far back as the late 1800s, were very unflattering and executed in the popular fin de siècle style, but this particular slur has clearly stuck.

Other uncomplimentary sketches include an overweight Scout leader bursting out of his uniform, entitled 'Scouting is developing steadily', another depicts a scrawny schoolboy being compared unfavourably to a muscular footballing lad. As we've seen earlier, his letters home to Henrietta were filled with ridicule, in one he described an English guest at a dinner party as 'a great porpoise of a woman'.

Tim Jeal, author of *Baden-Powell*, on the other hand, told the BBC in 2020 that his subject 'hated totalitarianism, twice hoped that he would be able to marry Jewish women and he chose a Jewish doctor.'

However, there's still his much-cited, if frequently edited, 1939 diary entry about *Mein Kampf* to consider. Aged 82 and retired in Africa, he was feeling shattered that war had broken out again:

> Lay up all day. Read *Mein Kampf*, a wonderful book, with good ideas on education, health, propaganda, organisation etc. – and ideals which Hitler does not practise himself.

Often, that final line is omitted when his words are quoted, and the fact that he was referring to the aspects embracing the principals close to his own heart of outdoors life and discipline.

Regardless, his baffling choice of the word 'wonderful' negates all of the above, and people now see it as him supporting Hitler – even as he's waging war over his beloved England and even more beloved Scouts …

As always with Baden-Powell, not only were there two sides to the man, there were two sides to every story, too. His entire life was one of troubled contradiction, largely due to his desperate need to be accepted, to fit in and to be loved. His split-personality, dichotomy, duality, call it what you like, was so imbedded, that he was forever at odds with himself and with others.

Vying for his mother's affection with tantrums and tears, despite being a naturally-happy little boy. Avoiding hated academia, by escaping into fantasy worlds or into the woods, despite being very intelligent. Literally acting his way through his Charterhouse school years to conceal the self-doubts and insecurities wrought by Henrietta Grace's rejections. Flamboyantly performing centre-stage, when forced into the army as a woefully ill-equipped young officer, in order to mask his crushing sense of imposter syndrome.

Attracting women through an inability to curb his natural charm and chivalry, while preferring the company of The Boy. Preaching homophobia, while repressing his own sexual feelings; and hoping to marry a Jewish girl, while being accused of being an anti-Semite.

Bloater. Baden-Powell. The Wolf that Never Sleeps. The Man Who Shoots Lying Down. The Hero of Mafeking. B-P. Robin.
The Boy-Man

Myriad names for the myriad roles that he played over the years in the Theatre of Life:

Warrior in drag; animal-lover with a pig-stick; macho-man with a boy crush; artist and killer; snob in a flat cap; fearless pioneer and mummy's boy; showboating introvert; racist who came to love other cultures more than his own – the list is endless.

Even in 2020, as the would-be statue topplers of Poole Quay accused him of homophobia, racism, anti-Semitism and a string of other offences, there was the troop of Baden-Powell's loyal Scouts, who'd set up camp around his likeness, insisting with equal fervour that he be honoured for the goodness and happiness he has brought to millions of people around the world.

The statue still stands – as do the accusations, as do the Scouts – in defence of the Chief Scout of the World

Writing in *The Spectator* about the brouhaha around the statue in June 2020, Ross Clarke said:

> For an organisation supposedly run by a Nazi sympathiser, the Scouts went on to help resettle Jewish children saved in the Kindertransport during the Second World War.
>
> Those involved were sent a card drawn and signed by Baden-Powell himself, with the words: 'I want to thank you for helping to give friendly shelter and assistance to our distressed refugee brother.'
>
> But that was not enough, evidently, to save Lord Baden-Powell's reputation …

Meanwhile, back in 1937, while the world spun on around him, the 80-year-old Baden-Powell invited its nations to attend the Fifth World Jamboree at Vogelenzang in Holland on 31 July of that year. He was looking old and acutely aware that the sands of his time were running short.

Still, he stood the entire afternoon for the opening programme as 26,000 Scouts from around the world, from America and Armenia to Sweden and Switzerland, marched by. It left him exhausted and drained, but he checked off every country and was deeply satisfied at not having missed visiting a single one of them.

To conclude what would be his last Jamboree, Baden-Powell addressed the Scouts:

The time has come for me to say goodbye.

You know that many of us will never meet again in this world. I am in my eighty-first year and am nearing the end of my life. Most of you are at the beginning, and I want your lives to be happy and successful.

You can make them so by doing your best to carry out the Scout Law all your days, whatever your station and wherever you are.

I want you all to preserve the badge of the Jamboree on your uniform … it will be a reminder of the happy times you have had here in camp; it will remind you to take the ten points of the Scout Law as your guide in life; and it will remind you of the many friends to whom you have held out the hand of friendship and so helped through good will to bring about God's reign of peace among men.

Now goodbye. God Bless you all!

He faltered and stopped, but he wasn't done. Tugging off his bush hat, he waved it overhead in an exuberant farewell and called out, ' God bless you!'

Not long after the Jamboree, Baden, the 'precious babe', the annoying little brother whom he now loved, died aged 77. He had been ill for some time so big brother Stephe had driven from Pax Hill to Kent every few days to see him.

Now at Pax and celebrating their silver wedding anniversary, B-P was still feeling down when two timely telegrams arrived. The first was from Peter, now married and living in Rhodesia, informing them of the birth of their first grandchild, Robert, named after his grandfather; the second was from Betty, now married to the love of her life, Gervase Clay, they met on a boat just like her parents had, and who'd had a daughter, Gillian.

Baden-Powell and Olave took a holiday in Nyeri in Kenya at their friends' hotel, The Outspan, a beautiful retreat in 500 acres with views of Mount Kenya and fell in love with the place. The Walkers, the hotel's owners, suggested the Baden-Powells retire there in a house built on the grounds. They were so calm and happy there they agreed and planned to have a small bungalow built, using the money they'd received as anniversary gifts. It was settled. Eric Walker would arrange everything and they would return to live there when it was ready.

On 3 September 1939, Baden-Powell's dream of a war-free world turned into the nightmare that he had been dreading. Britain was at war.

The news was broken by Prime Minister, Neville Chamberlain at 11.15 am. In a five-minute broadcast on the Home Service, he announced that as Hitler had failed to respond to British demands to leave Poland, 'This country is at war with Germany'. Chamberlain went on to say that the failure to avert war was a bitter personal blow, and that he didn't think he could have done any more.

'Oh, he was shattered,' says Robert Baden-Powell of his grandfather. 'He was very disillusioned and very upset, but by then he was a very old man and he realised that this was beyond him. All he'd worked for was falling into decay and ruin,' he added. 'He must have been very broken . . because it appeared that he was.'

A desolate Baden-Powell appointed Lord Somers to be Deputy Chief Scout of the World and asked him to take over from him. He and Olave then set about clearing Pax Hill. 'So much waste paper goes in our furnace for heating the wing,' he wrote '… there is always hot water!' It is thought that among the mountains of papers destroyed would have been any compromising letters between Baden-Powell and Major McLaren.

A month after Chamberlain's announcement, Eric Walker called B-P and Olave to tell them that their new Nyeri house was ready and on 25 October 1939, they bade an emotional goodbye to Pax Hill and left England for good.

Unbeknown to him, Baden-Powell had been nominated for the Nobel Peace Prize, however, due to the break-out of war, the prize was never presented to anyone. In a newsreel interview, just as they were about to board the ship bound for South Africa, he had these farewell words for his Scouts: 'I wish you were coming with me. Not only to see the place, but to settle there in that happy place. So come along in your thoughts if you can't come of yourselves. And remember, there are crowds of your brother Scouts ready to welcome you.'

Their new home was even lovelier than they could have imagined and they christened it 'Paxtu', a wordplay on it being their second Pax but also the Swahili word for 'complete'.

Baden-Powell was now in increasingly frail health; however, the warmth suited him and they lived in a cocoon of calm, where the busiest he got was keeping *that* diary and tending his roses.

On 8 January 1941, at 5.45 am, around his usual early rising time, Baden-Powell did not stir but instead died peacefully in his bed at Paxtu.

Little Robert, the grandson whose questions B-P had so patiently answered, when others ignored him, was heartbroken when told the news that his grandfather had died, saying later, 'I felt as though I had lost my best friend.'

Part of the Chief Scout of the World's final letter to the Scouts read:

Dear Scouts

If you have ever seen the play Peter Pan you will remember how the pirate chief was always making his dying speech because he was afraid that possibly when the time came for him to die he might not have time to get it off his chest.

It is much the same with me, and so, although I am not at this moment dying, I shall be doing so one of these days and I want to send you a parting word of goodbye.

Remember, it is the last you will ever hear from me, so think it over.

I have had a most happy life and I want each one of you to have as happy a life too.

Look on the bright side of things instead of the gloomy one.

But the real way to get happiness is by giving out happiness to other people. Try and leave this world a little better than you found it and when your turn comes to die, you can die happy in feeling that at any rate you have not wasted your time but have done your best.

'Be Prepared' in this way, to live happy and to die happy – stick to your Scout promise always – even after you have ceased to be a boy.

Your friend,
Baden-Powell

In the Africa he so loved, Baden-Powell's great life adventure came to an end. His coffin was borne with full honours, and his grave was festooned with floral tributes.

His grave in the Nyeri churchyard is marked by a simple white headstone, bearing a round blue circle with a dot in its centre, the Scouts trail sign for, 'I have gone home.'

Epilogue

The Legacy

'Try and leave this world a little better than you found it.'
Robert Baden-Powell

When twenty excited boys landed on Dorset's Brownsea Island in August 1907 to take part in Baden-Powell's experimental scouting scheme, little did they know that they were pioneers of what would become the world's largest non-religious, non-political youth movement.

Today, with more than 50 million Scouts members in 223 countries across the globe, thriving in wildly-diverse locations and with myriad interests, issues and priorities, Baden-Powell's astonishing legacy speaks for itself.

And despite its scale, the movement still marches to the Founder's original tune of preparing young people for the future, encouraging them to embrace nature and to build stronger communities.

Since that first island camp, with its revolutionary mixing of upper- and lower-class boys, B-P's aim was always to welcome all, regardless of race, belief, background, ability and even gender (thanks to those gutsy Crystal Palace girls of 1909 who convinced him to create the Girl Guides). Today the Guides number 10 million worldwide.

So globally widespread is Scouting, that as far as the World Organisation of the Scout Movement (WOSM) can ascertain, there are only five countries where Scouting doesn't exist; they are: Andorra, People's Republic of China, Cuba, Democratic People's Republic of Korea and Lao People's Democratic Republic.

Badges are its mainstay; the likes of Backwoods Cooking, Pioneer, and Camper still reward traditional aptitudes. However, Digital Citizen, Geocaching and – in a classic example of the Scouts tenet to 'be prepared' – the Great Indoors badge, designed off-the-cuff to keep Scouts motivated through the Covid pandemic, are unmistakably twenty-first-century.

To fully understand the enduring popularity of Scouting and to envisage its place in the future, one needs only to look to the past. Robert Baden-Powell's original concept was simple: to take the extraordinary compendium of skills he'd amassed and refined throughout his childhood and, more especially in his army career, and use them to improve the lives of deprived Victorian boys who could then be of service to their communities and the country.

Driven by a sub-conscious desire to be a boy himself again after an adulthood of challenging, even life-threatening situations (albeit often self-inflicted) in battle-ridden pockets of the British Empire, and a later Damascene awakening to the futility of war, he formulated a scheme that enabled him to relive his childhood.

A specialist in transforming even the most reluctant recruits into capable soldiers, Baden-Powell felt that he could also 'train' Britannia's rudderless boys to live happier and healthier lives by learning to be useful, inventive, self-efficient and fit.

The reasons that his vision was so clear were threefold:

One: the crucial role of the boy 'regiment' in Mafeking's defence against a Boer army far outnumbering the British one. Recalling how the lads relished taking on the adult responsibilities which allowed the troops to get on with the business of war, informed much of his Scouting scheme.

Two: writing *Aids to Scouting* in the grip of a siege. This galvanised his thoughts on training, convincing him that his method of teaching practical skills, good discipline, independence and a sense of purpose was as important to achieving a purposeful life as any academic knowledge.

Three: returning from years in the colonies and seeing the plight of Britain's lower-class children, most of whom were uneducated, neglected and impoverished, he felt compelled to act.

Add Baden-Powell's underlying anxiety about the poor physical state of the young men who might be expected to defend the Empire, and one can see how he became obsessed with preparing them for whatever life they may face.

A survivor in every sense of the word, he could be self-sufficient in the harshest conditions and his ingenuity knew no bounds; his ambition was to impart these qualities to boys, via a sort of 'rescue package', and shape them into the sort of chaps who could, if not run the country, at least help it.

He did it and it worked; in both war and in peacetime.

Baden-Powell lived to see his Boy Scouts' superb efforts in the Great War and he would have been gratified by how invaluable they were in the Second World War, channelling the Mafeking scouts by stepping into the shoes of absent fighting men and, often literally, keeping the home fires burning.

Eventually, though, his mission changed from preparing them for war to preparing them for peace. It wasn't to happen in his lifetime, but it's the norm today for many of his young ambassadors.

And the legacy of the Brownsea boys, around half of whom were from the 1st Poole and 1st Bournemouth Boys' Brigades, lives on in modern Scouting in the towns where it began.

Jack's story:

In 2020, when Baden-Powell's statue was under siege, 26-year-old Bournemouth Scout leader, Jack Saunders had to find ingenious ways to keep his Cubs scouting in the middle of the Covid pandemic with its consequent lockdowns.

Meetings took place live online; gardens were transformed into campsites linked via the internet, and rooms in houses became badge-earning opportunities wherever possible.

Jack was born into a Scouting dynasty, moving from young Cub to leader, or Akela, of his own Cubs' group at the age of 23; he also carries out the role of District Administrator.

In a nutshell, he's the modern-day epitome of Baden-Powell's dream Scout.

His parents met at Scouts when they were 17, his mum was a leader for years, his dad still is and he and his wife met at Scouts.

When I became Akela, I did it jointly with a couple of friends for a year, one happens to be my brother's fiancée and I was the best man at the other one's wedding.

We have pictures of me at Scout camps as a baby, with mum and dad in their uniforms, it's in my blood.'

Like so many in the movement, it's not a hobby, it is a way of life.

He's disarmingly honest, as all good Scouts are, about his decision to remain in Scouts and become a leader, saying that while it was so that he could pass on his skills and knowledge to younger members, there was another reason.

> I just didn't want to leave. I've had such an amazing life as a Scout and I've got so many happy memories; my earliest is of my moving ceremony when I went from Cubs to Beavers.
>
> For the ceremony, we Cubs all lined up on one side of the room with the Beavers facing us on the opposite side. There was a long, blue ribbon that ran along the floor between us. It represented a river and during the ceremony the Beavers beckoned us over and helped us across the 'water' to show their support.
>
> It was such a lovely experience. We still do it today. I do it with my Cubs now.

In an unpredictable, ever-changing and sometimes downright scary world, it is admirable that Scouts still observe these simple, and for younger children, quite magical traditions, many based on B-P's love of nature and the great outdoors.

Moving from this micro snapshot of a life lived through the lens of the Brownsea legacy, to looking at the bigger picture. If there's anyone who is the ethos of today's Scouts made flesh, it is Ann Limb, the first ever woman to be Chair of the Board.

When asked how it felt to hold the historic title, she replied:

> I was appointed in 2015 and was the first woman to hold the role in the movement's 114-year history. This was quite a statement at the time, underlining the fact that Scouts is open to all, regardless of gender, sexuality, faith, or no faith.
>
> As someone committed to diversity in all its forms, it felt important to show that we're reaching out to everyone. I believe all young people, not just the privileged few, have a right to informal education; to develop the skills they need to succeed in life.
>
> Of course, it felt a little daunting taking on the role, but exciting too. I wanted us to be brave, to think and dream big and that's exactly what we've done, with a new strategy, brand and taking Scouts to areas it's needed most, communities and families who've fallen behind. Since I joined, we've opened over 1,250 new [Scouts] units in the UK's one hundred most deprived areas.'

As well as improving children's lives, Baden-Powell's main aim as Chief Scout was world peace.

So in what way does Ann carry that torch on his behalf?

Working towards world peace never goes out of fashion. One of the key ways we do this is by encouraging our young people to attend international jamborees. The year I became Chair, Scouts were heading out to Japan and in 2019, they attended the jamboree in Virginia....

These are huge festivals of peace and friendship, where Scouts from over 200 countries cook, eat, play and work together. That's an incredible way to understand different customs, thoughts and perspectives.

It's also such a powerful way to forge bonds and increase understanding between nations.

We promote international understanding in our programme from our youngest age range; it's a core part of what we do.'

Asked how this is maintained in today's world, she explains:

We're a movement and not an organisation. That means we're not afraid to change with the times to stay relevant. If we don't change, then we become an anachronism. The key thing is listening closely to our young people. We're proud to be shaped by [them] ... and of asking them what issues they want to act on as part of our social action project, A Million Hands.

On the sort of things they suggest, she says:

everything from supporting refugees to promoting kindness in communities and across generations.

I'm especially proud that our Scouts are taking a stand against climate change with our Promise to the Planet. Each Scouts is making one simple promise to safeguard our future – and challenging world leaders to do the same.

No doubt Baden-Powell would have been impressed. 'It's a green mobilisation on a massive scale. But while we change, we never forget our core values of cooperation, care, respect, integrity, and belief in the power of what we do.'

I remind Ann of the little group of Edwardian girls who had to push through real and metaphorical barriers at Crystal Palace to beg B-P to let them join his movement and ask how things have changed.

She says: 'I'm so proud of those gutsy girls … we've had girls in the older age ranges of Scouts since 1976, and across all age ranges since 1991, but that wasn't widely known when I first joined.

> Today, three quarters of the public know we have girls in Scouts, which is a significant improvement, but there's still more work to do. I think our diversity is a strength. The fact that fewer people are surprised to see female Scouts speaking on the news, says everything about how far we've come. A third of our movement is now female, including inspirational role models like Helen Glover and Ellie Simmonds, who are both proud Scout Ambassadors.

Is there true diversity and inclusivity, though? *Can everyone join the Scouts?* Ann is unequivocal here:

> The simple answer is – yes – anyone who lives and upholds our values can be a Scout. We're so proud to be open to all.
>
> We have over 10,000 Muslim members of UK Scouts for example. You'll see us at Pride marches and championing inclusion in every walk of life.

On racism, again, she's gratifyingly clear: 'We're working hard to be actively anti-racist as a movement. It's not enough simply to declare that we're against racism. We need to prove it in our work, our programme and the way we educate our young people.'

I put hypothetical question to her: 'I'm a girl, I'm Jewish/LGBT/disabled or any other perceived barrier that still exists and I don't know much about the Scouts, why should I join?'

> We're a family that celebrates difference and have plenty of stories where young people have been supported by other Scouts while they were discovering their identity.
>
> There's a great sense of acceptance and belonging in Scouts that says everything about our culture. We have over 7,000 Scout Groups across the UK, and you're rarely more than a mile from your [nearest] meeting place.

All you have to do to join is visit www.scouts.org.uk and type in your postcode to find your nearest group and contact number. We do have a waiting list in some areas but it's well worth the wait.

Ann's term is coming to its six-year end, and in 2023 the board will appoint a successor to Chief Scout, Bear Grylls, so, of course, anything is possible.

However, Ann is confident that Baden-Powell's legacy will be in good hands:

> One thing's for sure, we'll never forget our promise to do our best and help other people. We've learnt some amazing things during this pandemic, not least about the power of working together.
>
> For example, we raised more than £1,000,000 for groups and communities in need, with a virtual hike to the moon and a race round the world – big, inspiring moments like that remind us what we can do together. It's about kindness, solidarity and believing in ourselves.
>
> Without a doubt, the next big thing for us is the launch of Squirrels (in September 2021).
>
> This will be the first time we've officially welcomed four to five year olds into the movement, so a real milestone.

She explains the reason for this historic move. 'It's in these critical early years that so much of our character and outlook on life is formed. Get it right then, and we can shape better futures.

> What's even more significant is that we're prioritising opening 'Squirrel Dreys' in communities that have fallen behind.
>
> It's about delivering skills for life when and where it matters most. So, the future looks bright for Scouts – and I couldn't be prouder to play a small part in inspiring a new generation.

In 2011, Ann Limb was awarded the OBE for work in education and in 2015 'upgraded' to CBE for public and political services. She is Deputy Lieutenant of Buckinghamshire, where she has lived since 1986; in March 2016 she received a lifetime achievement award by Milton Keynes Business Leaders and in 2019, was named #1 LGBTQ+ public sector role model in the *OUTstanding List* and one of the fifty most influential women born in the North of England in the *Northern Power Women Power List.*

Flying Baden-Powell's legacy flag of helping young people to achieve fulfilment in another way is his great-grandson, Adam-Baden Clay, Betty's grandson. Adam's work on youth education projects, including supporting indigenous people, in places such as East Africa, Australia and Canada, where he now lives with his wife, Nicole and two children, would have impressed his great-grandfather. As would his voluntary activities to help the planet in this time of momentous climate crisis.

I ask Adam whether there is a specific way in which Baden-Powell's objective to help future generations and instil a love of the natural world is relevant to him today;

> I think he was in significant part interested in service – service to one's community and country. He was very keen for people to appreciate the importance of attempting to 'leave the world a little better than you found it', and I think that was a principal focus for him in founding Scouts and Guides.
>
> And of course, that is absolutely a driving force of my own in my work, whether my paid employment, working in youth leadership for social change, or in my volunteer activities, working towards climate justice, and I'm a volunteer firefighter.'

So far, so Baden-Powell.

Does he occasionally stop to consider how his work reflects Baden-Powell's social consciousness and his ethos of inclusivity, diversity and tolerance?

> Absolutely. I think it's wonderful, and probably not at all a coincidence, that my work is focused on youth leadership for social change, and is based upon a solid foundation of justice, peace, inclusion, and love.

And his own children? Do they fly the community-spirited flag?

> Our son, Cameron, who's now 9 years old was in Beavers, but our local Scout group hasn't yet reopened since the pandemic began and our 11-year-old daughter, Emma, is very actively involved in the community, primarily through dance.

We talk about when Adam first realised that his great-grandad was famous.

The family always talked about him so I can't recall a specific moment, I just gradually became aware of it and started reading his books and thought, wow, what an interesting man.

Adam is aware of the controversy surrounding some of Baden-Powell's actions and opinions, and while he feels that some are exaggerated or misinformed, he accepts that he wasn't perfect – and a stereotypical man of his time. While from today's enlightened point of view generational differences are no excuse, Adam believes that the happiness and life-enhancing skills that his great-grandfather has given to so many of the world's young people through the Scouts, is a reason to be extremely proud of him.

We go on to talk of Baden-Powell's ingenuity and his maverick antics in school:

I really admire how ingenious he was and all the survival things that he could do as a young boy. I like the story of how he would hide high up in the branches of a tree and watch his teachers below knowing that they had no idea he was there.

Adam and Nicole visited the place in Africa where his grandparents lived in their retirement. I asked him how that felt:

We were in Nyeri in February 2009. It was an incredibly inspiring experience. We had just climbed Mount Kenya, and returned in time to participate in the Founder's Day activities there.

There were tens of thousands of Scouts and Guides there, mostly from Kenya, but also from around the world. They were so excited and full of energy and life, and that feeling was certainly shared!

Some of our conversations were via Zoom and at one point, our chat was interrupted by noises drifting in through the Baden-Clay's open kitchen window. Adam looks outside and then explains, 'It's just the children playing.' When I ask what they're doing, he says: 'Oh, they're outside tapping the maple tree for syrup.'

The legacy continues.

Bibliography

Baden-Powell, R., *Adventures and Accidents, RBP, Methuen & Co*, London, 1934
—— *African Adventures*, Pearson, London, 1937
—— *Indian Memories*, Herbert Jenkins Ltd., London, 1915
—— *Cavalry Instruction*, Harrison & Sons, London, 1884
—— *Lessons From the Varsity of Life*, Pearson, London, 1933
—— *My Adventures as a Spy*, Pearson, London, 1915
—— *Pig-Sticking or Hog-Hunting: a Complete Account for Sportsmen and Others*, Harrison & Sons, London, 1889
—— *Playing the Game: A Baden-Powell Compendium for Scouts Old and Young*, Pan Macmillan, London, 2008
—— *Scouting for Boys*, Pearson London, 1936 edition
—— *Reconnaissance and Scouting*, William Clowes and Sons, Ltd, London, 1891
—— *Rovering to Success*, Herbert Jenkins Ltd., London, 1922
—— *The Downfall of Prempeh, Methuen & Co*, London, 1896
Baden-Powell, O., as told to Drewery, M., *Window on My Heart*, Hodder and Stoughton Ltd., London, 1973
Bakowski, J., *Rose Hill 1832–2008: The history of one of England's oldest prep schools*, Rose Hill School, Tunbridge Wells, 2008
Blyton, E., *Five on a Treasure island*, Hodder & Stoughton, 1942
—— *Five on Kirrin Island Again*, Hodder & Stoughton, 1947
Brown, H.E. Haig, *William Haig Brown of Charterhouse*, Macmillan & Co., London, 1908
Charterhouse Football Annual, Charterhouse, Godalming, 1876
Chicago Tribune, 1990
De Beaumont, M., *The Wolf That Never Sleeps*, Girl Guides Association, London, 1959
Greyfriar Magazine, Charterhouse, Godalming, 1880
Harris, Steven, *Scout Island*, Lewarne Publishing, 2007
Hartley, L.P., *The Go-Between* Hamish Hamilton, London, 1953
Hillcourt, W. and Baden-Powell, O., *Baden-Powell: The Two Lives of a Hero*, Heineman, London 1964
Jeal, T., *Baden-Powell*, Pimlico, London, 1989
Pakenahm, T, *The Boer War*, Little Brown, London 1991
Selous, F, *Sunshine & Storm in Rhodesia: Being a Narrative of Events in Matabeleland Both Before and During the Recent Native Insurrection up to the*

Date of the Disbandment of the Bulawayo Field Force, Rowland Ward & co., 1896

Rosenthal, M., *The Character Factory,* Harper-Collins, August, 1986

Schreiner, O, *Trooper Peter Halket of Mashonaland,* Roberts Brothers, Boston, 1897

Woolgar, B. and La Riviere, S., *Why Brownsea? The Beginnings of Scouting. Centenary Edition,* Minster Press, Wimborne, 2005

Yorke, E. and Flower-Smith, M., *Mafeking: The Story of a Siege,* Covos-Day Books, S.A., 2020

Sources
News
Bournemouth Daily Echo
Charterhouse School's Football Annual, (Charterhouse, Godalming, 1876)
Daily Mail
Dominic Winter Auctioneers, Cirencester
JewishPress.com
Newcastle Daily Chronicle
Poole History Centre, via Katie Heaton MCLIP, Local History Librarian, Poole Museums
Scouts Heritage
Secret Lives C4 documentary 1995
The British South Africa Company
The Independent
The Spectator
The Sunday Times
The Times
The Scouter (magazine)
The Scouts newspaper (mother's eulogy, Chapter 2, *The Scouts Newspaper,* October 1914) Scouts Heritage archives
Wikicomms
Wikimedia
Wikipedia
www.britishbattles.com
www.scoutguidehistoricalsociety.com

Author Biography

Lorraine Gibson is an award-winning journalist of twenty years, who cut her writing teeth on her local paper in Bournemouth.

Inspired by her beautiful Dorset surroundings, she is widely published in regional and national titles and is now a freelance writer, with a passion for local history.

Living close to Brownsea Island, she became intrigued by its role in the birth of the Scouting movement while writing a feature about it. After delving deeper into the world of the Boy Scouts and their famous founder, the extraordinary and astoundingly eccentric Robert Baden-Powell, she was hooked.

When, in the summer of 2020, she covered a fight between Scouts and protesters, hell-bent on throwing Baden-Powell's statue off Poole Quay, directly opposite Brownsea, there was no going back.

Robert Baden-Powell: A Biography is her first book and it is, like its subject, thought provoking, contrary and full of ripping yarns.

Lorraine lives in Bournemouth with her husband and two teenage daughters.

Index